# AUTOMATING GLOBAL FINANCIAL MANAGEMENT

# AUTOMATING GLOBAL FINANCIAL MANAGEMENT

By
**Business International**

Sponsored by

**Financial Executives Research Foundation**

WILEY
**John Wiley & Sons**
New York · Chichester · Brisbane · Toronto · Singapore

ISBN 0-471-61284-7

Printed in the United States of America

10 9 8 7 6 5 4 3 2 1

# Preface

To explore the latest applications of computer and telecommunications technology to the full range of finance department activities—from accounting and control to financial planning and treasury management—Business International (BI), in conjunction with the Financial Executives Research Foundation (FERF), conducted a pioneering study entitled *Automating the Global Financial Function.* This book presents important findings identified by the study and is set in a worldwide context.

To begin the study, FERF organized a steering committee composed of senior financial managers of leading corporations, banks, and accounting firms to formulate objectives, scope, and research methodology. In conjunction with steering committee members, BI put together a project team who constructed a four-part direct mail questionnaire and targeted personal interviews. To ensure the effectiveness of the surveys, the BI project team pretested the questionnaire with a select group of corporate financial executives, computer software companies, and systems consultants.

This highly targeted direct mail questionnaire was then sent to 1200 companies in North America, Europe, and Asia to determine their current and future use of automation to upgrade the finance function. In all, 326 firms participated in the survey, yielding a response rate of 27%—extremely high in light of the length and complexity of the questionnaire. Data collected from the questionnaires were coded, keypunched, and sorted according to key market segments.

Following the completion of the surveys, the BI project team conducted extensive personal interviews to provide the vital qualitative component of the study. The BI project team interviewed 123 companies in 15 countries: Argentina, Australia, Belgium, Brazil, Canada, France, Germany, Hong Kong, Italy, Japan, Mexico, the Netherlands, Switzerland, the United Kingdom, and the United States. The companies interviewed represented a cross section of firms as measured by indicators such as size, industry, organizational approach, and degree of automation. Interviewees at these companies included senior executives from the treasury, financial planning, accounting, and MIS functions. To ensure that these executives provided high quality and substantive information, anonymity was guaranteed.

At the end of the project, the BI team produced an interpretive analysis of the survey results, supplemented by material drawn from the personal interviews. That material serves as a foundation of the comprehensive evaluation of automating global financial management that is presented in the chapters that follow.

The Financial Executives Research Foundation representatives were Roland L. Laing, Director of Research, and Frederick H. Ober, Senior Research Associate. The BI project team included Louis J. Celi, Jr., Project Director; Cathy A. Lazere, Research Manager; Jeffrey E. Kealing, Senior Research Associate; Bradley Asher, Research Associate; and Barry Rutizer, Project Editor.

The BI research team thanks the FERF project coordinators, steering committee members, and Stephen G. Racioppo of Arthur Andersen & Co., who served as project advisor. Without their kind support, this project would have been impossible.

# Steering Committee Members

---

## CHAIRMAN

Edwin H. Eaton
Treasurer
The Procter & Gamble Co.

## COMMITTEE MEMBERS

Clayt Daley
Director, Financial Systems
The Procter & Gamble Co.

Talmage Fish
Manager, Corporate Systems
Burlington Industries

Robert Harris
Director of Financial Reporting
IBM Credit Corp.

Richard Matteis
Senior Vice President
Chemical Bank

Frank L. Minter
Vice President and CFO
AT&T International

Robert E. Northam
Senior Vice President
J.C. Penney

Richard Scurry
Senior Vice President
Chemical Bank

Adrian M.S. White, F.C.A.
Vice President
Bank of Montreal

Donald Wood
Partner, Administration
Touche Ross

# Contents

## PART 2: AUTOMATING TREASURY MANAGEMENT

# AUTOMATING GLOBAL FINANCIAL MANAGEMENT

# Introduction

## AN OVERVIEW

An electronic revolution has now touched virtually every aspect of international finance. Computer and telecommunications networks link the world's currency and money centers into a truly global financial marketplace with 24-hour-a-day trading and exchange of information. Leading international banks arrange complex financings, transfer funds, trade currencies, and deliver vital data to corporate customers at the push of a button. But the degree to which these developments impact on the inner workings of corporate finance departments is yet to be discovered. Tangentially, a question remains as to how far firms have gone in automating the global finance function.

The Financial Executives Research Foundation (FERF) survey of 326 firms provides answers to these questions. To start, it shows that multinational corporations are deeply committed to financial automation. The majority of respondents—65%—consider computer and telecommunications technology important to improving overall global financial management practices. When asked to predict action over the next few years, the numbers are dramatic: An overwhelming 83% of respondents believe that automation will be important to their firms in the future.

Even more telling, companies are acting upon their beliefs. As shown in Table 1, 84% of respondents have automated at least some

**TABLE 1**

**Level of Corporate Automation
(Percentage of respondents)**

|  | At time of survey | Three years after survey |
|---|---|---|
| Largely automated | 31 | 59 |
| Partly automated | 53 | 29 |
| Not automated | 15 | 6 |
| No answer | 1 | 6 |

aspects of their finance function. Over the next few years, that percentage should rise to 88%, while the percentage of companies that are largely automated will nearly double from 31 to 59%. In the near future, only a scant 6% of companies will still be conducting financial activities manually.

Personal interviews support these quantitative trends. Consider the following examples:

- Through automation, a giant United States conglomerate has overcome the inefficiencies in redundant accounting systems for its 40 strategic business units. It centralized key accounting procedures in several centers that administered general ledgers, accounts payable, fixed assets, payroll, taxes, and insurance. As a result, the firm decreased its accounting and payroll staff by 25 to 30%, standardized its accounting systems, and freed up local managers' time so that they could concentrate on operations analysis.

- A multinational retailer responded to the failure of one of its major divisions by investing in state-of-the-art decision-support software for efficient financial planning. Previously, the firm operated as a loose affiliation of companies, with each major unit submitting financial forecasts on an ad hoc basis. By automating major aspects of the financial planning process—including reporting, operational budgeting, financial forecasting, and performance evaluation—and by standardizing hurdle rates corporate-wide, the company hit its ROI target last year.

- An American pharmaceutical manufacturer recently upgraded the performance evaluation system of its 100 subsidiaries, which are located in 55 countries. Monthly, 500 to 800 line items are transmitted electronically to headquarters, where analysts assess performance by region, entity, market, and product line. A special executive decision-support subsystem allows senior management to identify and evaluate the impact of changes in sales, volume, currency fluctuations, product mix, and price increases on operating results.

- Using sophisticated in-house technology, a major computer manufacturer developed a United States-based reinvoicing center that controls literally all of the company's cross-border transactions. The computer system provides daily worldwide exposure reports, facilitating centralized exposure management, aggressive leading and lagging strategies and substantial savings on hedging costs each year—an impossible chore without a computer.

These vignettes highlight the fact that companies are lavishing much time and effort on automating the finance function. Three central reasons lie behind most efforts:

1. **Automation streamlines operations.** In today's highly competitive business world, firms strive to increase productivity and slash costs. In fact, a growing number of companies are instituting austerity programs to cut layers of corporate management, especially on the international side. Computers play a critical role in this effort. By automating finance, companies can reduce headcount and dramatically improve the speed and accuracy of many routine tasks.

   For example, the controller of a leading American automobile manufacturer believes that computers are essential to producing a cost-competitive car: "Within the finance arena, handling such things as accounts payable involves lots of people. Every division has its own group of payables processors. By automating and simplifying the system, you can cut the number of these people from 200 to 40. That's what makes your car cost competitive. It's a make or break situation."

2. **Automation helps companies manage globalized businesses.** As part of their drive to be competitive, many companies now run each of their component businesses as worldwide organizations, and plan their manufacturing and sourcing strategies on a global basis. To manage their far-flung operations effectively, firms

increasingly turn to computers. As one financial executive at a large multinational noted, "We receive data from over 50 markets. Without computers we couldn't possibly coordinate that volume of data quickly and efficiently."

The controller of a giant American chemicals firm concurs by stating that his company switched to a global orientation because "labor costs lead you to the notion of a worldwide business." For instance, the firm's battery business, which was formerly organized on a regional basis, is now considered a global enterprise. Batteries are manufactured in the cheapest locales and then shipped to other markets. All manufacturing and inventory decisions are made for this line of business as part of a worldwide strategy. According to the spokesperson, "You couldn't run a global business effectively without automation. You cannot control foreign operations if you don't have good communications."

3. **Automation helps companies take advantage of fast-changing opportunities on international capital, currency and money markets.** In response to the deregulation of financial markets and the new tools offered by the banking community, many companies are now taking a closer look at their internal treasury management systems and balance sheet structures to reduce financial costs. In the words of the treasurer of a huge electronics firm, "Part of being a worldwide business is the ability to raise capital and to manage cash according to economies of scale. To do this you need a systems orientation."

A United States high-tech company, for example, has established a fully automated in-house factoring company in Geneva. Using state-of-the-art internal and bank systems, the factoring operation manages and trades currencies, invests excess cash, and funds subsidiaries on a centralized basis. The result: nearly two million dollars in annual savings from lower borrowing costs, reduced funds transfer fees, and forex gains.

In addition to these three main reasons for automation, another critical factor that cannot be overlooked is the widespread availability of inexpensive, convenient microcomputers. The personal computer (PC) has already become a fixture in finance departments the world over, nearly as common as telephones and calculators. As one assistant treasurer put it, "People are drawn by what PCs have to offer.

**TABLE 2**

**Type of Computer Used Most Heavily for Global Financial Management (In percentage of respondents)***

|  | When surveyed | Three-year projection |
| --- | --- | --- |
| Micros | 34 | 42 |
| Minis | 30 | 34 |
| Mainframes | 61 | 51 |

* Percentages may exceed 100 due to multiple responses.

For a small investment of time and effort now, you can perform financial analysis more quickly and easily. The result—increased productivity."

As can be seen in Table 2, the FERF survey shows that about a third of respondents rely heavily on PCs for global financial management; over three years, that figure will rise to 42%. Over the same time horizon, corporate use of mainframes will drop 10 percentage points from 61 to 51% of respondents. In fact, many interviewed firms are consciously adopting a policy of downscaling. That is, for new systems for subsidiaries, they deliberately install microcomputers instead of mainframe hardware and software.

## THE IMPACT OF COMPUTERS ON ORGANIZATION

To minimize risk, cut costs, and boost profits in the face of rapidly changing global financial and economic conditions, many companies are implementing policies of strategic business decentralization. They are reducing or even eliminating corporate management staff and delegating profit and loss (P&L) responsibility to divisional, regional, or operating unit levels.

But while the business side of many firms is becoming increasingly decentralized, finance is bucking the trend. Peter Drucker explains this dichotomy: "When it comes to finance, the autonomous subsidiary becomes a menace. . . . Now that fluctuating exchange rates, subject to sudden wide swings and geared primarily to capital movements and governmental decisions, have come to be the norm, localized financial management has become a prescription for disaster for anyone operating in the international economy."

**TABLE 3**

**Impact of Computers on Key Financial Functions
(In percentage of respondents)**

|  | More centralized | More regionalized | More decentralized | No impact/ No answer |
|---|---|---|---|---|
| Treasury management | 45 | 3 | 9 | 42 |
| Accounting control | 29 | 8 | 25 | 37 |
| Financial planning | 33 | 5 | 18 | 44 |

Many respondents to the FERF survey agree. Fifty-nine percent of the companies have centralized the finance function at parent or regional headquarters; 32% plan to become more centralized over a three-year period. As the finance director of a major French multinational company (MNC) stated, "We're centralized for finance because money is the only completely fungible item that you have in a company."

In this drive to centralize global finance, companies find automation to be an effective ally. Table 3 shows the impact of computers on the organization of three major financial functions.

As shown in the table, in companies where automation has had an effect, the trend is toward increased centralization. This is especially true for treasury management and financial planning. The trend for accounting control is less pronounced because companies still need some decentralization to fulfill differing local legal requirements (for a further discussion of accounting organization, see p. 29).

**Finance's New Relationship with MIS**

During the adverse economic conditions and sagging profitability of the late 1970s and early 1980s, the finance function was elevated to a high position in the corporate hierarchy. The CFO of an Italian MNC summed up the trend: "Until just a few years ago, the administration department was much more important than finance. But with the recession . . . finance has become most important. The company knows how important money is now."

To improve internal controls and contain costs, senior management now encourages finance staffs to work more closely with other departments. As a result, financial directors are seeing their roles expand into such operational areas as marketing, credit and collection, and production. Noted the CFO of one American consumer goods firm, "You can't be an effective CFO unless you get involved in every aspect of the business. As CFO, I have to look beyond accounting and finance to strategic planning, marketing, and production. They are all related to finance's prime objective—to ensure that the company is profitable and remains profitable in today's uncertain business environment."

The finance function's more prominent role in the corporation is also reflected in its growing control over corporate MIS departments. When computers were first introduced, many MIS departments reported either to operations managers or controllers. But as can be seen in Table 4, FERF's survey shows that today over half of MIS or EDP departments report directly to senior financial management.

A driving force behind this trend is the shift within companies from mainframe/minis to PCs. Microcomputers have freed finance staff from complete dependence on MIS departments, and have provided them with more control over software development and data management. A director of financial information operations explained the change this way: "A few years ago, we would have to go to data processing for almost everything. Now we can do a lot

**TABLE 4**

**To Whom Does the Head of EDP/MIS Report?**

|  | Percent of respondents* |
|---|---|
| Senior financial management (CFO, finance director) | 52 |
| General management/operations | 16 |
| Accounting/control | 12 |
| Administration | 12 |
| Treasury | 4 |
| Planning | 4 |
| Other | 7 |

* Total exceeds 100.0% due to multiple responses.

**TABLE 5**

**Control Over Software Development
(In percentage of respondents)**

|  | MIS/EDP* | Finance |
|---|---|---|
| Micros | 41 | 54 |
| Minis | 54 | 21 |
| Mainframes | 76 | 14 |

* Percentages exceed 100% because of multiple responses.

ourselves. DP used to be so busy with mainframe requests. They'd prioritize and put our projects at the bottom of the list."

Table 5 clearly demonstrates the rising independence and authority of the finance function in this area: Over half of the respondents to the FERF survey report that finance plays a major role in developing or providing software packages for PCs, while MIS or EDP continue to work on mainframes and minis.

To avoid chaos, however, firms must ensure that finance and MIS departments collaborate to develop compatible systems that link mainframes and micros, and one brand of PC with another. At one United States telecommunications firm, for example, corporate MIS and finance studied available PCs and recommended one brand for corporate-wide usage. Then the firm set up a discount program for users interested in buying PCs. MIS also offered training, software, and maintenance. The incentive program worked so well that out of 350 PCs in use at the firm, only seven were outside of the boundaries established by the program.

The vice president of corporate systems at the firm explains the reasons for the program's great success: "We didn't put any restrictions on anyone. The subsidiaries didn't feel like we were holding them back. We encouraged development of the PC."

## Building Computer Links with Other Departments

As finance departments give greater direction to corporate MIS applications, senior financial officers are becoming what one spokesperson called "information czars." That is, when computers spread to other functions and information becomes critical to a company's success, the CFO becomes even more powerful.

The FERF survey lends support to this contention. As seen in Table 6, finance is fast becoming the heaviest user of corporate central databases. The results showed that within three years, accounting and control, financial planning, and treasury will outdistance other units in access to databases by as much as 56 percentage points.

As positive as this picture is, however, the task of constructing an integrated database can be long and arduous. For many firms, existing databases are often fragmented, and serve only limited needs. Within the finance function, treasury, financial planning, and accounting may work with different sets of numbers with little data flowing automatically from one unit to the next. Furthermore, computer links may not exist between finance and other areas such as marketing and production.

Lack of central database planning is both inefficient and annoying. For example, the director of financial information systems at a major consumer goods firm feels impeded by lack of financial database integration. He described the firm's haphazard system of collecting data this way: "Most of our reporting systems are outdated and inflexible. Often they were designed for a specific operation. Therefore, we proliferate a lot of different systems throughout the company for different functional groups. We have a system to

**TABLE 6**

**Access to Central Databases
(In percent of respondents)***

|  | At time of survey | Three-year projection |
|---|---|---|
| Accounting and control | 75 | 90 |
| Financial planning | 48 | 77 |
| Treasury | 47 | 74 |
| Marketing/sales | 45 | 58 |
| Personnel | 44 | 59 |
| Production/operations | 39 | 47 |
| Purchasing | 36 | 48 |
| Taxation | 28 | 46 |
| Strategic planning | 22 | 41 |
| Research and development | 21 | 27 |
| Investor/external relations | 10 | 20 |
| Legal | 9 | 18 |

* Percentages exceed 100% because of multiple responses.

accommodate the needs of the controller's group, the tax group, treasury, and strategic planning. While it's true that a lot of the information is cross-pollinated from one another, each group requests information directly from each subsidiary. So each month each subsidiary sends in five sets of separate numbers. You could wind up with five different sets of numbers."

To eliminate such problems, some firms are building on-line, real-time information exchanges within finance and between finance and other departments. A good example is *Company A*, a producer of electronics components with $320 million in annual sales.

The firm has a well-developed production, inventory, sales, and accounting database system that works as follows. A central computer at the firm's parent headquarters is linked to all of the company's factories and warehouses. When a manufacturing facility finishes a production run, the plant relays data on product availability to the parent computer automatically. The computer then determines the level of inventory at Company A's various facilities and notifies the plant how to package and ship its products, and in what quantities.

Sales data also feed directly into Company A's accounting database. As one financial manager noted, "We've taken an accounting module and attached it onto the side of a customer service system, and the numbers are rerouted through our accounting system programs. We've taken a warehousing and manufacturing system and changed it into an accounting system. When the information is gathered, depending on how the information is massaged, you can get a lot out of it." Besides helping in the monthly closing of accounts, Company A's database can be tapped for other finance department purposes such as sales and inventory variances.

*Company B*, an American apparel manufacturer with $500 million in annual sales has a more advanced system. The firm coordinates its seasonal sales efforts using information collected at a centralized corporate database. According to the company's controller, "The purpose of the collected data is to allow each division to look at its product line's performance to identify problems and opportunities. The security system allows certain designated people from each of our divisions to gain access to the system—someone in accounting, someone in marketing, someone in production, and a CEO at the division."

The sales information in the system is current; information is entered no later than 48 hours after an order is received. The computer automatically processes each order to the warehouse for shipment at the plant level. Financial managers have on-line access to see the latest bookings and shipments.

When deciding what to produce, marketing and production managers also tap into the system for historical sales information and general economic conditions. "Each division takes a shot at models based on what sold last year and what the trends are," noted the controller. "Most of our stuff is fashion items and future-oriented. You plan to produce it early and you want your sales force to sell what you produce. So you manage your sales force with quotas on different products at each division."

The controller believes that one centralized information system gives him a good handle on the financial performance of each division. "You can look at one division in more detail and see who's below budget on sales, what manufacturing variances exist, and what the gross profits are. The system is unique because it captures information at a low level (product-line) and presents it in a clear and concise format."

## Computers Scale the Corporate Ladder

In addition to reshaping relations between finance and other departments, computers are also having a profound impact on the management structure of the finance department itself. Many firms predict a future of leaner corporate staffs where computer knowledge will be critical to career advancement. Said one financial manager, "We look for people receptive to computers. The assistant/junior accountants are now responsible for data entry. Computer knowledge is now essential to becoming a financial manager."

In fact, the FERF survey shows that all levels of financial management are increasing their reliance on automation. This is especially true for CFOs, who will nearly double their use of computers over the next few years, as shown in Table 7.

The development of relatively simple decision-support software and the easy-to-use PC has boosted the growing computer literacy of senior financial managers. For example, one United States con-

**TABLE 7**

**Which Level of Financial Management Uses Computers?**
**(Percent of respondents)***

|  | At time of survey | Three-year projection |
|---|---|---|
| CFOs | 29 | 56 |
| Treasurers/controllers/planners | 60 | 85 |
| Assistants/treasurers/controllers/planners | 77 | 85 |
| Financial managers/analysts | 79 | 85 |

* Percentages exceed 100% because of multiple responses.

sumer goods firm has created an extremely user-friendly PC-based Executive Decision-Support System. Financial analysts feed information directly into the system for top management to use in making informed and effective treasury and planning decisions. The executives, including the firm's CFO, are receiving monthly exchange information for 35 different currencies, including actual and forecasted transaction and translation rates.

The system is so simple that senior managers have only to learn which menus will yield the desired data; no programming skills are required. As the firm's manager of financial planning described it, "There is a PC-interactive program to walk the individual through the section he wants. It is very graphic and was developed for upper management. They can use it day to day and can go through an inquiry type procedure."

Such developments are having an unanticipated consequence—what some observers call "the demise of the middle manager." As more senior financial managers rely on their own PC analysis, lower-level managers spend less time on report writing. As one concerned financial analyst put it, "By installing PCs in their offices, top managers are reducing our work." In fact, computers have made report writing so efficient that fewer analysts are needed. Thus, whole levels of finance staff are becoming unnecessary.

The corporate accounting manager of a food processing firm described what seems to be a widespread phenomenon. "As a result of the computer system, we've added a lower level of management and knocked out the middle level." The experience of a financial manager at a chemicals firm is similar. Through increased computer use, the layers of financial management at corporate headquarters have been reduced considerably. In his opinion, "Because of computers, we've already flattened out our hierarchy."

## BARRIERS TO FINANCIAL AUTOMATION

Although computerized financial systems are gaining in popularity, many companies have been stymied in their efforts to successfully select, install, and implement the hardware and software that best suits their needs. The FERF survey identified the following major stumbling blocks that firms should consider when automating the global finance function: lack of training, system development time, system incompatibilities, staff resistance, and excessive cost.

### Barrier #1: Lack of Training or Inexperienced Staff

This is the primary complaint about automation, voiced by over 65% of respondents to the FERF survey. When companies give short shrift to educating end-users—usually in a last-minute rush to meet schedules—the whole purpose of a new or upgraded system may be defeated.

Savvy companies take care to properly train both managers and support staff, adapting the method to the individual user. This process may require several days or even several weeks of preparation and include presentations and hands-on practice sessions. The schedule depends on the product. "If a new system is universally applicable, then a firm can hold centralized training sessions for supervisors at headquarters," noted one systems manager. "But if everybody needs something different, you've got to spend a lot more time and money."

Training can, however, disrupt the regular work cycle and impede internal acceptance of the system. Good systems developers are keenly aware of time constraints and try to tailor their training schedules to suit the needs of all involved parties. As one controller put it, "When the new system has been developed, there may be two systems people familiar with it and 50 people who still use the old system. Taking users away from their everyday routines can be disruptive and cause conflicts with managers. You have to steal time from managers for training."

## Barrier #2: System Development Time

An equally pressing problem, cited by slightly less than 65% of respondents to FERF's survey, is lengthy delays in development. These often stem in part from sheer naivete about the process of systems development. Too often, companies establish schedules for planning and implementation that are unrealistic and which ignore the complex technical and organizational issues that have to be resolved to get a system on stream.

For example, one firm allocated five staff members to a financial systems project that took five years to get off the ground—for a total of 25 person-years. Despite the best efforts of the team, the system never worked to management's satisfaction. Consequently, the firm then hired a consultant, who took another year to install a system. Although this might seem an extreme case, it is not at all uncommon for companies to spend two or three years developing a system that may then require a major overhaul.

A common reason for overshooting schedules is that companies fail to divide projects up into manageable components so that each segment can be completed in a reasonable time frame. "Theoretically, no project should take over 18 months," said one MIS manager. "If it does, you run the risk of the business changing so much that the system doesn't fit."

## Barrier #3: Incompatibility with Other Systems

This obstacle is especially tough to overcome in decentralized firms, where the parent, regions, divisions, and subsidiaries have developed computer hardware and software separately. In the words of one treasurer, "The biggest problem we have is standardization, because all our businesses have been run separately for years."

Attempts to standardize systems can pose horrendous technical as well as organizational difficulties. According to the marketing director of an American software vendor, "If you have an IBM mainframe running Cullinet software, with Gandalf modems and AT&T supplying the telephone lines, and maybe an IBM PC with Lotus software—you've got all these different vendors out there and then you have to start writing your specific communications code, which involves another level of complexity."

To solve such problems, corporate headquarters would be well-advised to simply make recommendations rather than try to impose software and hardware requirements on the entire group. *Company C,* which produces men's toiletries, is a good case in point. Its director of international systems explained how the firm handles the situation of dealing with a far-flung network of international operations, all of which have unique needs for automation. "We make recommendations for packages. We say 'here's our experience; here's what the best packages are.' For example, for word processing we recommend Wang if they can support it or the IBM PC with Multimate. For a spreadsheet, we suggest Lotus 1-2-3 or Sideways. For a database, we recommend Dataease. For telecommunications, Orion. For graphics, Chartmaster or Signmaster."

Company C's current goals are modest in terms of the degree of standardization desired. "We hope over the years to have a common general ledger, budget, forecast, and fixed assets system for minis," stated the spokesperson. "We started to develop the budget and forecast system overseas; it's currently being used by 10 or 11 subsidiaries. But the people in Latin America don't like it because they have different needs. I think a common system should be developed around regional locations because Europe won't like Latin America's system and vice versa."

## Barrier #4: Resistance

A total of 42% of respondents are hindered by staff resistance to new automated systems. Furthermore, BI's survey pinpointed three main hotbeds of resistance: foreign subsidiaries, senior management, and MIS.

Resistance from foreign subsidiaries was reported by 27% of surveyed firms. Foreign operating units, especially those in highly decentralized firms, are often unwilling to devote the time or money to set up a system they believe benefits the parent company more than themselves. As a case in point, the assistant controller of a consumer goods company has had difficulty selling the idea of world-wide systems development to foreign subsidiaries, which contribute about 16% of his firms's sales. "Because of our decentralized nature," he says, "I've had to fight a battle to convince subsidiaries that this is what we want to do."

Although many subsidiaries had complained about the inefficiency of traditional communication methods such as telex, facsimile, telephone, and mail, this assistant controller first had to convince them that computer-to-computer links would make their jobs easier. Then, he had to prove that the new systems would be cheaper for them in the long run. Subsidiaries often balk at the cost of purchasing hardware for a computerized financial system. Finally, he showed them that volume purchases of hardware and software by parent headquarters would save each foreign unit a considerable amount of money.

Resistance also comes from the upper echelons of many firms. Fifteen percent of BI's respondents listed top management resistance as a hindrance to automation. Though not as common a problem today as several years ago, there are still diehard senior managers who present an insurmountable barrier to systems development. As one beverage goods controller put it, "Upper-level management has not been a strong force to help us in systems development. Typically, they will say 'yes, we would like such a system if it doesn't cost too much.' I guess in this regard we're still in the stone age."

Another facet of this problem is that senior managers often have a short-term perspective and ignore the cost of maintaining older, antiquated systems that, in turn, can require large programming staffs and drain hundreds of thousands of dollars in personnel costs alone. Many firms that upgrade their financial systems or install new ones have been able to cut staff by 20 to 30%, yet senior managers often fail to recognize these potential savings.

Even though senior managers are among the main beneficiaries of smoother information flows with more advanced automated systems, they often fail to recognize this point. For example, senior financial executives at one capital goods firm were very resistant to computers. Yet many of these same managers also wanted access to information from other departments. Noted the company's controller, "I had to sell them on computerizing the central database so that they could extract summary financial data for their own reports."

Another common type of resistance comes from MIS. Fourteen percent of BI's respondents mentioned MIS unresponsiveness as a chronic problem. They accuse systems personnel of hiding behind a barrage of technical mumbo jumbo instead of giving them straight answers about system capabilities. In addition, finance managers dislike having to queue up behind other departments demanding MIS attention.

One of the other reasons for distrust between finance and MIS is the natural distance that exists between people who speak different languages. The director of MIS at one firm has addressed this issue: "Our goal is to bridge the gap between the user and the systems specialist. We're trying to train people to know both systems and finance."

### Barrier #5: System Expense

Excessive system costs disturb 32% of FERF survey respondents. And no wonder. Computerization of the finance function requires outlays for hardware, software, personnel, and telecommunications. Additionally, many companies have difficulty estimating the ultimate cost and are often shocked by the size of the bills. For instance, a $75,000 software package might actually cost five times that amount if the time spent on customization, outside consulting and training is considered.

PC purchases are another area in which costs are frequently underestimated. Often the hardware offering price is drastically below what a firm will eventually spend. Complained one high-tech company's systems director, "The cost of a PC and printer comes to around $6,000, but the real cost, including maintenance, is $20,000. If you add up PCs at $20,000 a clip, pretty soon you can justify a mainframe."

## STRUCTURE OF THIS BOOK

To help companies avoid these pitfalls while reaping the benefits of automating the finance function, this book will explore the current and projected state of treasury, accounting, and financial planning systems. The book draws on both quantitative findings of the FERF survey and qualitative dimensions revealed in personal interviews with financial executives around the world. It examines the pressing concerns of financial managers who are actively engaged in the complex process of automating financial systems.

The book is composed of two parts, each of which addresses a function of financial management. Part I, "Automating Accounting, Control, and Financial Planning Systems," consists of three chapters.

Chapter 1, "The Relationship Among Corporate Needs, Organizational Goals, and Computerized Accounting Systems," examines the rationale behind automating accounting and control systems. It goes on to discuss the impact of automation on organization, and how computers can be used in both centralizing and decentralizing accounting and control. Chapter 2, "Automating Key Accounting Procedures," evaluates the steps in the automation process. The chapter focuses on the use of computers in facilitating accounting procedures, from data transmission and preparation to database management, analysis, and external reporting. Chapter 3, "The Missing Link: Automated Financial Planning Systems," explores the latest developments in automated financial decision-support systems. It provides detailed case examples of how firms are automating each aspect of financial planning, including operating and capital budgeting, capital structure, and tax planning.

Part II of this book, "Automating Treasury Management," consists of five chapters.

Chapter 4, "An Overview," discusses the critical issues of how firms are automating the reporting and analysis of treasury data, and what hardware and software decisions they must make to do so. Chapter 5, "Improving Cash Management Through Automation," investigates how companies use computers to upgrade every aspect of the cash cycle, from reporting and forecasting to receivables and disbursement management, short-term borrowings and investments, and banking relations. Chapter 6, "Automating Foreign Exchange Management," examines the state of the art in automated forex reporting and forecasting, monitoring currency contracts, and making transaction and balance sheet hedging decisions. Chapter 7, "Automating Cross-Border Treasury Management Systems," discusses the latest computer applications for the full range of cross-border techniques and vehicles: leading and lagging, cash pooling, netting, reinvoicing, and in-house factoring. Finally, Chapter 8, "Electronic Banking: The New Frontier," details sophisticated bank-

ing services specifically designed to support the treasury function—
including automated balance reporting, electronic transaction initiation, and treasury workstations. The conclusion, "The Not-So-
Distant Future of Financial Automation," discusses four major trends
that are shaping the future of corporate finance.

# PART 1

# Automating Accounting, Control, and Financial Planning Systems

# CHAPTER 1

# The Relationship Among Corporate Needs, Organizational Goals, and Computerized Accounting Systems

## INTRODUCTION

Of all the areas of finance that firms are now automating, accounting and control is receiving the lion's share of attention. In fact, over three quarters of the respondents to the FERF survey gave top priority to automating this function. Thus, one United States controller spoke for the majority of his colleagues in summarizing why this area merited particular attention: "Automation of accounting and control is the blood and guts of any company. It's also the easiest to automate. Because accounting has set rules that are perfectly geared to computerization, the impact of automation is immediate. By automating accounting you can definitely decrease the size of staff. You can replace bodies with a machine and appreciate the increased efficiency instantaneously. By automating you can invoice quicker, dun quicker, determine your outstanding payables quicker and improve the efficiency of the operation."

Automation for accounting has also proceeded more swiftly than for treasury or financial planning because, in this spokesperson's opinion, "The canned applications such as worksheets, word processing, and databases are perfect for the accounting function so that information can be combined and disseminated faster." The controller of a high-tech firm agreed: "The applications are there. There isn't as much in treasury. The real application in treasury is at the bank—that's why there's so much electronic access. But for accounting, the software resides in the company."

Indeed, canned accounting packages are now available for all major aspects of accounting, including accounts payable and receivable, budgetary control, fixed asset accounting, forecasting and modeling, general ledger, inventory management, order processing, purchasing, payroll, and sales forecasting. And with the advent of sophisticated software, noted the controller just cited, "you can write whatever you want."

Given the great importance and ease of mechanizing the function, it is no surprise that 57% of the firms are highly automated—that is, largely dependent on computers—for accounting procedures. By comparison, only 16% of the treasury and 17% of the financial planning units have reached that level of automation. And automation of accounting will continue to take the lead in the future: As shown in Table 1–1, over the next few years, more than 80% of the

**TABLE 1–1**

**Percentage of Firms with Highly Automated Financial Functions**

|  | At time of survey | Three-year projection |
|---|---|---|
| Accounting and control | 57 | 81 |
| Treasury management | 16 | 53 |
| Financial planning | 17 | 52 |

firms surveyed expect to have highly computerized accounting systems.

## THE RATIONALE BEHIND AUTOMATING ACCOUNTING AND CONTROL SYSTEMS

Companies are automating the accounting function for the following reasons:

- **To improve decision making.** Sixty percent of the respondents identified upgraded analysis and decision making the primary benefit of automation. According to the controller of one firm with automated functions, "The effort involved in reporting and information gathering has been reduced considerably. As a result, decision making by middle managers has improved. A middle manager can now go through a number of different scenarios and present those to senior management. Once that is done, the reaction time by management is quicker. For decisions involving a large component of quantitative analysis, decision making is therefore better. We can now know things with more certainty."

- **To gain easier access to financial data.** Thanks to computerization, financial information ranging from the lowest transactional detail to the highest summary level is available instantly at the organizational level that management authorizes to access the information. This key benefit of automation, cited by 59% of the respondents, was explained clearly by a United States controller: "You have easier access to financial data. You can hook eighteen people onto the same data. Networking is easy."

- **To ease monitoring of historical data.** Fifty-eight percent of the firms surveyed believe that automated accounting has helped them to track historical data better. Through automation, accounting staffs can respond to a greater number of requests for information and perform trend analysis more easily. Records can be spun off the central database and downloaded to microcomputers. This data can be used by financial analysts to do sales and cash forecasting.

- **To ensure the receipt of timely and accurate data.** Automated financial systems ensure virtually instantaneous transmission of data and have sophisticated audit trails that reduce the human error inherent in a manual system. For this reason, 58% of the surveyed companies point to the benefit of improved delivery speed, while 47% believe they receive more accurate information. In the words of the director of MIS at an American chemicals firm, "There's a general need for timely, accurate and flexible business information. The only way that's feasible to get this information is to go electronic."

- **To save time and reduce staff.** Automated accounting systems shave days, sometimes weeks, off monthly external and internal reporting schedules. Indeed, 56% of the survey respondents reported reduced clerical time from automating accounting, while 24% reduced staff. As one controller put it, "Aging accounts receivable and payable can be done by the computer in seconds. For a clerk to do it would take hours. The preparation of dunning letters would take hours instead of days. Preparation of the management accounting system would take me days, now it takes me hours. I can run it overnight. That's real personnel saving. We had a 25-person staff and ended up with a 17-person staff."

- **To improve accounting discipline and procedures.** Automated, standardized reporting systems have enhanced overall managerial control for 53% of those surveyed. For example, the assistant controller of an intermediate goods firm has found that "standardized reports have enabled corporate headquarters to have more input into what goes on at each of the subsidiaries. We can better direct, instruct, and possibly implement corporate accounting policies and practices. We do this by getting the data faster here at corporate and having more time to analyze it."

- **To provide a central financial database.** Forty-one percent of the survey respondents found that by automating accounting and control they have also laid the foundation for a corporate database. The reason was explained by one firm's controller: "Treasury and financial planning can piggyback off our database to get what they need." In the future, "We will have an extensive database for each profit center on actuals, comparisons to budget, prior year and forecasts," predicted the controller.

- **To upgrade intracompany communication.** Automated accounting systems help improve communication between headquarters and reporting units. The survey shows that 26% of the respondents have more frequent reports, whereas 14% of the firms surveyed have reduced their need for formal reports.

Against this backdrop of survey information, let us now examine how a corporation's size, industry type, level of international business, domicile, and organizational style influences the design of its computerized accounting system. Likewise, let us consider how computers impact the organization of the accounting function and how automation is used to achieve financial and organizational objectives.

## THE IMPACT OF CORPORATE CHARACTERISTICS ON COMPUTER USE

Sharp differences exist between the levels of automation among the accounting systems of respondent companies. Some firms are clearly at the state of the art, such as one $10 billion United States multinational that installed a fully integrated network of PCs for its overseas operations, giving them a direct link to the mainframe at corporate headquarters. Others are woefully behind the times, such as a Fortune 50 company that still receives all accounting information by mail from its foreign subsidiaries and suffers from what its spokesperson calls a "first-class incompatibility problem."

The degree of automation greatly depends on each company's particular situation. One criterion to consider is location. For example, North American firms are more automated for accounting and control than their European and Asian counterparts. Indeed, 61% of firms headquartered in North America consider themselves highly automated for accounting and control, compared with 51% of European and Asian firms. This trend mimics worldwide technology flows: Many computer hardware and financial software innovations have originated in the United States. Noted a director of financial reporting at a high-tech firm, "Traditionally North America is way ahead in automation because it is more responsive to technology. For this reason, we introduce products into the United States first and later into other regions."

But the survey also reveals that this geographical gap is closing quickly. According to the survey results, 82% of North American firms will be highly automated for accounting and control over the next few years, as compared with 81% of European companies and 77% of Asian firms. This trend is at least partly the result of the many North American multinational firms that export cutting-edge systems to overseas subsidiaries.

In addition to a firm's domicile, size plays a critical role in automation. The larger the company size, the higher the degree of automation. The study shows that 65% of firms with sales over $2 billion are highly automated, as opposed to 48% of firms with sales under $200 million. Similarly, 66% of firms with over 40 foreign operating units are highly automated for accounting and control, compared with 52% of firms with under six foreign operating units.

The rationale behind this behavior is clear cut. "Large companies have more economic incentive to spend money on automation," noted one assistant controller of a multibillion-dollar firm. "In fact, for the largest multinational firms, automation is now a necessity. When you are as big as we are, you need to gather the data effectively so that you can use it. You can't rely on the mail. It would be incredible to keep track of all our activities without the aid of a computer."

The type of industry involved also has some bearing on the automation issue. Manufacturing firms are typically more highly automated for accounting than service companies. According to BI's survey, 61% of manufacturing companies are highly automated as compared to 46% of service firms (e.g., engineering and publishing). The reason is that manufacturing companies need to keep track of large inventories and sales volumes that are often spread over far-flung operations with a wide customer base. This, in return, requires good communication networks. By contrast, service firms have little, if any, inventory and generally fewer customers. As the director of MIS at a major advertising firm asked, "How do you automate the nuts and bolts of advertising? Because advertising is a low overhead business there is relatively little need for automation."

Finally, the organization of the finance function does not appear to have any measurable impact on the use of automation. Specifically, 59% of centralized firms are highly automated, compared with 62% of regionalized firms and 54% of the decentralized ones. Clearly, all forms of organization stand to benefit equally from automation. Centralized companies can use automation to collect more detailed information for corporate headquarters and to respond in a timely manner to corporate management's questions. For decentralized and regionalized firms, computers give local management the tools to assess their operations effectively and to make informed decisions.

## ORGANIZATION AND AUTOMATION

### The Impact of Automation on Organization: The Corporate Debate

Although corporate organization may not influence the degree of automation, the question remains as to what effect computers have on how companies organize accounting and control. According to the survey, there is considerable controversy among companies in this area. The largest group in this ongoing debate, 36% of respondents, believes that computerization has no impact on the structure of the accounting function. Such firms are often not yet highly automated and thus have not felt the need to revamp their organizational structures. They believe that organizational structure is primarily a function of senior management philosophy, not automation.

As an example of this mindset, consider the case of a high-tech firm with annual sales of under $200 million that, like many other small firms, initially had centralized accounting. But, as the company grew, decentralization became more attractive. "Decentralization came from growing up. You have to encourage entrepreneurs at the local level," remarked the manager of financial reporting. When the company's automated accounting system was in its beginning stage, the subsidiaries accessed the company's mainframe through time-sharing. However, the manager continued, "It was costing us too much to use time-sharing so we decided to develop a system in house. Then, when we became more decentralized we let all the foreign units have local computer systems."

Thus, in this case the changes in the computer system merely paralleled management's decision to change the organization structure. Computers followed the organizational change dictated by senior management; automation was not the driving force.

However, it is important at this point to evaluate how these companies interpret their own situations. To that end, a self-evaluation of organizational types is warranted.

*Centralized vs. Decentralized Approaches to Accounting and Control*

To understand how automation influences organization, it is first necessary to see how companies manage their accounting and control functions currently. Of the firms surveyed, more than half (51%) consider themselves decentralized for accounting and control; 27% consider themselves centralized. However, an important issue to evaluate at this point is how these companies define these labels for themselves. To that end, FERF/BI interviewed controllers and found several points of consensus. Firms that are *centralized* for accounting and control possess more than one of the following characteristics:

1. **Reporting requirements are heavy and the bulk of analysis and control is done at corporate headquarters.** For example, one highly automated firm requires operating units to submit detailed trial balances for as many as 1000 line items per unit. The company's controller explained the rationale: "It is of no interest to me to know what income is halfway through the year. That's why we get trial balances in local currency and do all the translation and analysis at headquarters."

2. **Key accounting procedures are pooled in one location to take advantage of economies of scale.** Commonly pooled procedures include payroll, general ledger, taxes, payables, fixed-asset accounting, insurance, and travel and living. As a controller at one firm that has used pooling pointed out, "Twenty years ago we had 10 credit card accounting centers. Now, because of computers, we have one."

3. **Financial reporting and computer use is highly standardized.** In highly centralized firms, corporate headquarters can often ensure the uniformity of information from subsidiaries by insisting that all units use the same hardware and software to handle the major accounting areas. For example, one American consumer goods firm has coordinated 94 computer sites worldwide by installing the same mainframe model at each location. The firm also monitors the use of nearly 1000 microcomputers. Corporate MIS insists that the computer sites purchase the same brand of

microcomputers and software, and has become actively involved in training the PC users.

Switching to the issue of decentralization, controllers agree that firms that are *decentralized* for accounting and control have a very different attitude toward data analysis, standardization of reporting, and responsibility for key accounting procedures. For such companies the following statements apply:

1.  **The bulk of analysis and control is at regional, divisional, or local level.** For instance, one Fortune 50 conglomerate is so diversified that it is not possible to centralize financial data. According to the concern's assistant controller, "Each group is different in terms of its market. Aircraft engines have an entirely different operational environment from elevators." As a result, analysis is performed at the divisional or local level.

2.  **Key accounting procedures are done at each operating unit.** Under this arrangement, subsidiaries take care of their own general ledgers, order entry, and other basic activities. For example, the director of MIS of a large advertising firm explained why his firm moved to a decentralized approach: "A few years ago [the company philosophy] was more centralized. For example, client billing for domestic divisions was done at the holding company. But it didn't work. It was decided to push it out to the field and to let the division worry about the client. It wasn't working to have central billing because you don't have close client contact. Payroll for domestic is still centralized, but the day-to-day keeping of the books is done at the agencies. In contrast, treasury is much more centralized. The money is kept in the holding company because advertising has a massive cash flow."

3.  **The degree of standardization can vary.** One company that had no choice but to let its subsidiaries develop their own systems is a large conglomerate that acquired many of its operations through unfriendly takeovers. As a result of this worldwide investment strategy, each corporate group has developed its own unique chart of accounts and accounting system. For instance, one of the more advanced corporate groups, which manufactures capital goods, has designed a sophisticated front-end pack-

age with a computer service company to translate financial data from 60 to 70 subsidiaries. Data is telexed to a central site, validated, and translated into United States dollars at a rate set monthly. Information is then accessed from the mainframe after direct computer-to-computer transmission of data. In contrast, translation systems used by sister corporate groups are less automated and, in some cases, handled manually.

## How Computers Can Centralize Accounting and Control

As seen in the previous comments, a significant minority of firms, 29% to be specific, feel that computers lead to greater centralization. The spokesperson for one Fortune 500 company made the case emphatically: "Computers will enable corporate headquarters to have more input into what goes on at each of the subsidiaries. We can better direct, instruct, and possibly implement corporate accounting policies and practices. Computer-to-computer transmission means that we get the data here faster and have more time to analyze it."

To evaluate this philosophy, consider one firm that uses automation to centralize strategic accounting decisions at corporate headquarters, and to cut down on bureaucracy at the regional and divisional levels. *Company A* is a United States chemicals firm with over 60 foreign subsidiaries. According to its manager of international reporting, "In the past, there were too many managers between the field and corporate headquarters. We wanted to eliminate intervening layers." Automation of the accounting function enabled the firm to meet this goal by cutting its worldwide accounting staff from 4500 to 3000 without sacrificing any of the detail necessary for decision making.

Every month, each of Company A's overseas units sends operations and financial accounting data via computer to headquarters. Operational departments analyze the data for approximately 4000 product lines. Included in the P&L data are sales and transfers, other operating revenues, cost of goods sold, finished product distribution expense, selling expense, administrative expense, pretax earnings, and taxes.

The highly centralized nature of the system is epitomized by the great amount of detail received by corporate headquarters. Noted the manager of international reporting, "We get a lot of detail other companies don't get—product line information. We break down sales to a very low level. For example, we could tell you how much X-ray film we sold in a particular region."

Surprisingly enough, the automated system has not changed the level of detail required by management. Even before the automated system was up and running, corporate headquarters still received hard numbers on every product line. The big difference between pre- and postautomated data is that a global roll-up of each product is now available each month. Management can therefore determine how much X-ray film was sold in one country and worldwide, and how profitable sales actually are.

Company A's centralized accounting system is paralleled by its centralized treasury function. All cash, debt, or borrowings are run on a total company basis, and all decisions about these are made at corporate level.

The company plans further centralization of the accounting system by trying to standardize the foreign subsidiaries' general ledgers. Currently, the subsidiaries keep their general ledgers in local currency and United States dollars. There has been some standardization in Europe, but in Latin America and Asia/Pacific each ledger operates independently.

Within the next three to five years the firm will move toward what it calls a gateway system, a more advanced, highly integrated general ledger that includes other accounting subsystems. The goal, according to the manager of international accounting, is to "Integrate payroll, accounts receivable, and fixed assets all the way back to the plants; and to achieve a paperless system."

According to the spokesperson, senior management is also considering centralizing translation at corporate headquarters. Like most firms, Company A now receives subsidiary dollar results reported according to United States GAAP. But having the subsidiaries do the translation, says the manager, "creates an administrative burden. We have to tell 60 subsidiaries worldwide what to do. FASB changes the rules every day. You have to train those people. And then you have to worry about whether the data are reliable." The manager believes that corporate headquarters should take on translation responsibility. Corporate staff should translate the local currency figures and send back the results to the subsidiaries. However, while the manager admits that centralizing translation can be expensive, he believes that the potential control and accuracy will justify the cost.

## How Computers Can Decentralize Accounting and Control

Twenty-seven percent of the companies surveyed believe that computers lead to decentralization and 8% believe that they lead to regionalization—almost the same number, when summed, that focused on the centralizing effects of automation. *Company B,* a major United States food producer with over $4 billion in worldwide sales is a good example of a firm that has used automation to decentralize. The firm, with operating units in 45 countries, has organized its activities into four regions: North America, Asia, Europe, and Latin America. These operations fall under two key market segments: consumer and industrial goods.

The consumer segment, with sales of $2.5 billion, has been decentralized through the use of a sophisticated computer system. The manager of financial systems reports that, "the company is decentralized because we have strong management teams that are responsible for their areas. Corporate doesn't have access to the regional accounting data until it has been analyzed and then released by regional management. There may be some adjustments before it gets to corporate headquarters." This organization style is necessary because of the diversity of Company B's product mix and consumer markets. According to the spokesperson, "We've got a complete management team at each of the regional headquarters. At each unit, you've got accounting, finance, R&D, marketing, and engineering people. That is because each business is different. So we've got completely different marketing structures in each country."

Each unit in the consumer division manages its own receivables, payables, and inventory, and does cost measurement. Every month, each unit completes and sends a standardized form to regional headquarters. For example, each of the European units reports to Brussels regional headquarters. These reports show sales, expenses, income, exchange gains and losses, interest taxes on income, fees, and royalties. Regional headquarters then has the ability to manipulate the report data on-screen for a few days before it is sent via GEISCO to corporate headquarters. If the data doesn't look correct, regional headquarters can go back to the country in question and adjust the information. Moreover, the system has a safeguard because reports cannot be released until all required data has been submitted and balanced by the system.

Regional headquarters translates the financial results based on rates prescribed by corporate headquarters. Control is maintained at regional headquarters until they press a release button to allow corporate headquarters to see the data. According to the director of international reporting, subsidiaries were hesitant to enter data online until they were given this capability: "Without the release button, the control function would be centralized. The function keeps a lot of people happy. Politically it is a good feature."

At corporate headquarters, a database contains information on all the individual units. Operating units can then tap into their own data if needed, but not that of other units. A unit can download information pertaining to its own company off the mainframe onto a PC, and then use a Lotus spreadsheet for what-if analyses of sales and forex.

The units requested that this historical database be maintained at corporate headquarters so as to make it easier for them to analyze past performance and forecast future results. According to the director of financial reporting, "Before the central database was established, each unit had to input its own data into models or spreadsheets. Now the data is stored for them at corporate headquarters and all they have to do is download."

Computers have enabled the company to successfully decentralize, relieving corporate headquarters of some of its financial analysis duties. Computers have shifted the majority of performance evaluation and control tasks to the local and regional levels. As a result, corporate staff at the consumer products division is lean. At the same time, corporate headquarters can get more information than before.

### Case Example: A Firm's Pooled Accounting System

To avoid the duplication of effort under a decentralized approach to accounting and control, some concerned firms use computers to pool fundamental accounting procedures. One firm that is using this state-of-the-art technique to save millions of dollars is *Company C,* a diversified United States corporation with over $28 billion in annual sales. As part of a corporate-wide thrust toward increased productivity and competitiveness, this innovative firm decided to centralize a number of critical accounting activities. The idea was to reduce the time spent at the local level on everyday accounting activities.

The change was part of an overall strategy to redefine *Company C's* organizational structure worldwide by removing unnecessary management layers. In the past, the company managed through an unwieldy system of international reporting. Individual operating units reported to both an international sector and a product sector. Today, there are 40 strategic business units (SBU) created along product lines, and the head of each SBU reports directly to the Corporate Executive Office. There is no longer any international or regional headquarters to delay the reporting process. Greater autonomy and business accountability for each SBU has resulted from this restructuring.

The company also restructured the accounting function to improve local decision-making capabilities. When American financial managers met two years ago to discuss their contribution to this goal, they arrived at the idea of pooling generic accounting procedures at regional accounting centers. At that time, the firm operated as many as 55 accounting centers for domestic operations, a total of 300 reporting units. By moving many time-consuming accounting and payroll tasks to four pooling centers, managers hoped to increase efficiency and decrease costs.

The first step in the scheme was to define and isolate the "generic" accounting procedures, those that were not unique to any type of business and that could be performed efficiently on a large scale and at a centralized location. Business-unique activities, such as customer billing, inventory accounting, and program cost accounting were not considered generic because they could vary from one business to another. The pooling centers, therefore, were designed to handle all of the generic functions, including the general ledger, accounts payable, fixed asset accounting, travel and living expenses, taxes and insurance, and payroll.

The next step was to locate sites for the accounting centers. The company used the following criteria to select a pooling site:

- **City size.** The firm wanted a center with a thriving metropolitan area. It looked for small to midsized cities with ample labor and potential for future growth.

- **Availability of financial professionals.** The new center would require employees trained in accounting or with considerable experience in a service environment. An area with strong financial services industries was the ideal.

- **Appropriate facilities.** The new center needed space for start-up and adequate room for expansion in the future.

- **Quality of local educational institutions.** The firm assessed the quality of the accounting and finance curriculum offered by local colleges. To ensure the best possible financial services staff, the firm wanted facilities nearby for training employees and as a potential source of new talent.

As a result of the search, with these criteria in hand, the company opened four pooling centers with a staff of 850 (several hundred less than before). One center was built from scratch; the other three were associated with major operating facilities.

*Company C's* management has recognized four key benefits from the pooling centers:

**Decreased costs.** The firm has already achieved substantial cost reductions by pooling accounting functions. Explains the manager of pooled accounting services, "When a unit enters the pool, we achieve a 25 to 30% reduction in its accounting and payroll staff. Accounting expenses have gone down dramatically because of our overall finance productivity program." Over several years, this will translate into tens of millions of dollars.

**Standardized activities.** Pooling accounting information provides common, corporate-wide accounting systems for processing generic activities at as few locations as possible. "Ultimately, there will be one payroll system rather than the 30 that existed a few years ago. Any changes for new [employee] benefits or enhancements will only have to be done once," says the manager.

**More time for operations analysis.** Before pooling, local financial managers devoted substantial amounts of time and computer resources to functions that didn't enhance competitiveness. Now, they can focus on responding to customer needs. Notes the manager of pooled accounting, "The local financial manager only needs to worry about the operations analysis and cost side of his shop, and he applies his resources accordingly."

**Upgraded accounting systems.** Pooling has allowed the firm to move away from incompatible, scattered systems toward a corporate-wide computerized financial network. According to the manager, "We're upgrading all our accounting systems in just a few locations for benefits across the entire company. Our new approach incorporates a shift towards an IBM-based software philosophy, with common systems administered by core support groups."

Pooling has also been established in several overseas locations, including the United Kingdom, Canada, the Netherlands, and Brazil. As in the United States, generic accounting functions are being pooled at centralized locations, as are certain legal services, licensing, patents, and credit and collections.

Management believes that other firms could benefit from its example of pooling and organizational restructuring. "We haven't found any other firms that have pooled to the extent that we have, although we do see some starting up. Other people are looking at what we are doing, but we may be one to two years ahead of them," notes the manager of accounting pooling. To this end, the manager of corporate pooled services offers the following advice to other companies considering pooling centers:

**Ensure that each pooling center provides the same level of service offered previously by an individual unit.** Users of the pooling center, including employees and suppliers, will expect a high level of service. They must be able to communicate easily to correct problems. "The individual businesses can blame every problem under the sun on a pooling center," notes the manager. Supervisors of pooled centers should get to know the financial managers of component units to allay their fears about inadequate service.

**Provide good documentation for the conversion process.** During the changeover period, when each business shifts from operating independently to operating as part of a pooled center, there is much room for error. To decrease the risks inherent in the conversion, clarify in writing who is responsible for what.

**Do not exceed the optimal size for pooling centers.** Pooling centers do have certain limits. For example, for payroll systems, the company discovered that a pooling center could only cover 50,000 to 60,000 employees. Beyond that number, they encountered what management called *processing window problems*. That is, the ability of the people running the system to keep up with the volume of transactions became strained.

## SUMMARY

This chapter discussed three facets of automating accounting and control. First, it provided a backdrop of issues against which automation challenges can be played out. Next, it sketched a profile of which type of company is automating this function now and who is expected to do it soon. Finally, it evaluated how the organizational structure of a company affected its automation prospects and vice versa.

The important benefits gained from automation were to aid decision making, provide easier access to financial data, help monitor historical data, improve the speed and accuracy of data transmission, save time and reduce staff, sharpen accounting processes, provide a central database, and improve intracompany communication. Although these are laudatory qualities, no matter what the object, they are especially important for accounting because of the almost totally objective nature of the business. Controlling this function means having a firm grasp on the numbers. And we shall see in the next chapter how that control is essential in areas such as inventory and control.

Firms taking advantage of automation have a distinct profile today, but the features of that generic face should blur over time. North American firms currently are more automated in this function than their European and Asian counterparts, but the percentages should be equal within a few years. Likewise, larger firms are more likely to be automated than smaller ones, and manufacturing concerns are more automated than service companies. That is, firms with high-volume, set-inventory operating systems can, and do, benefit from computerizing the systems that track the dollars associated with a fairly regulated flow of goods.

Finally, automated accounting can be accomplished by any type of firm—be it centralized, decentralized, or regionalized. Of the firms surveyed, scarcely more than half consider themselves centralized or regionalized. FERF research also showed that more firms believe that computerization leads companies toward centralization than decentralization. These are important themes and debates that echo throughout the remainder of this book and, as such, should be evaluated by every reader in light of his or her particular organizational bent.

# CHAPTER 2

# Automating Key Accounting Procedures

## INTRODUCTION

Chapter 1 evaluated some reasons why companies chose centralization or decentralization when automating accounting and control. Once this decision is reached, evaluating how the automation should proceed is next. To that end, this chapter will analyze how companies are turning to computers to facilitate the full range of accounting procedures, from data transmission and preparation to database management, analysis, and external reporting.

The chapter is divided into sections that correspond to the stages through which data flow in an accounting system of a multinational firm. It first examines automated techniques through which data are delivered to parent headquarters from overseas operating units, then analyzes how this information is consolidated and translated to ready it for financial preparation. Next, the chapter examines database management techniques used to maintain the general ledger, store historical data, and develop a central database. This is followed by a discussion of how firms manipulate data, including sales and inventory analysis, cost measurement, and productivity. Finally, the chapter concludes with an evaluation of new directions in external reporting.

## SUBSIDIARY-TO-PARENT DATA TRANSMISSION SYSTEMS

Recent discoveries in computer and telecommunication technology have revolutionized how corporate headquarters receive financial data from overseas operating units. Indeed, the survey reveals that the method of transmitting accounting information from foreign units to corporate headquarters by computer is fast replacing traditional means of information reporting. This trend is demonstrated in Table 2–1, which shows how foreign operating units report accounting information. Currently, mail is the preferred transmission method of the surveyed firms, followed by telex, facsimile, and telephone. But in the near future, the number of firms reporting by computer, tape, or electronic transmission will double, while the number using mail, telex, facsimile, and telephone will drop substantially.

Why are companies making this major switch to automated reporting? The survey shows that firms turn to computers to collect a higher quality of information in less time without additional staff. Just as important, by eliminating time-consuming clerical tasks, automation frees financial analysts to devote more time to carefully study data and track subsidiary performance. For some firms, automation has even improved corporations' external images by enabling speedier submission of information to ratings agencies and timely distribution of reports to shareholders.

**TABLE 2–1**

**How Foreign Operating Units Report Accounting Data**

|  | At time of survey | Three-year projection |
|---|---|---|
| Telephone | 22 | 15 |
| Mail | 84 | 61 |
| Telex | 59 | 35 |
| Facsimile | 33 | 24 |
| Computer tape/disk | 9 | 17 |
| Computer-to-computer | 25 | 51 |

Despite these clear benefits, overseas subsidiaries often cannot send all data electronically because of high technological costs and storage limitations. As the controller of one consumer goods producer pointed out, "It's really a question of dollars and cents. It's not as important for some information to come in on a systematic electronic basis. We can wait a little longer to get that information—we're always worrying about costs."

Consequently, when developing a worldwide automated financial reporting system, companies must choose which information would be best delivered electronically. To enable you to compare your financial reporting system with those of other companies, Table 2–2 gives a full breakdown of how the different types of accounting information are delivered among the survey respondents now and in the future.

---

## WHY SOME FIRMS DO NOT AUTOMATE REPORTING FROM FOREIGN SUBSIDIARIES

Despite its myriad attractions, automated reporting may be difficult to accomplish on an international scale. For instance, sophisticated computer technology and trained workers may be in short supply in many lesser-developed nations. Moreover, some countries, such as Brazil, impose restrictions on cross-border data flows and on the types of computer hardware that may be used. Some companies also may find that foreign subsidiaries are simply too small to justify automation, or that local systems are incompatible with those of the parent company's.

For all these reasons, firms may be forced to automate more selectively than they would choose. For example, a United States high-tech firm with 75 worldwide reporting units has taken a sensible approach to global automation. Although the firm is committed to computerized reporting and has a sophisticated automated reporting system, it only automates when it makes sense. Consequently, while computer-to-computer transmission is possible for 36 countries that account for 85- to- 90% of the firm's business, the remaining affiliates, mostly in Latin America or the Far East, use an old cable system for monthly financials because the scope of their business is so limited.

## TABLE 2–2

### How Foreign Operating Units Report Different Types of Accounting Information to Parent Headquarters*

| | At the time of survey | | | | | |
| --- | --- | --- | --- | --- | --- | --- |
| | Computer to computer | Computer disk/tape | Telephone | Mail | Telex | Facs |
| Profit and loss statements | 20 | 4 | 4 | 48 | 29 | 21 |
| Sales Information | 19 | 5 | 7 | 39 | 36 | 18 |
| Balance sheets | 19 | 4 | 4 | 50 | 28 | 19 |
| Intercompany transactions | 14 | 3 | 6 | 50 | 32 | 17 |
| Cash flow Information | 13 | 2 | 12 | 35 | 39 | 22 |
| Inventory Information | 13 | 3 | 4 | 48 | 21 | 11 |
| Budgets | 12 | 4 | 3 | 67 | 15 | 13 |
| Accounts receivable | 12 | 3 | 4 | 45 | 18 | 10 |
| Accounts payable | 10 | 3 | 4 | 43 | 17 | 9 |
| Forex positions | 7 | 2 | 12 | 31 | 34 | 16 |
| Three-/five-year plans | 7 | 2 | 2 | 68 | 12 | 12 |
| Accounting/financial regulations | 3 | 1 | 4 | 60 | 60 | 8 |

## Three-year projection

| | Computer to computer | Computer disk/tape | Tele-phone | Mail | Telex | Facs |
|---|---|---|---|---|---|---|
| Profit and loss statements | 47 | 11 | 3 | 21 | 10 | 11 |
| Balance sheets | 46 | 11 | 3 | 22 | 10 | 10 |
| Sales Information | 39 | 9 | 4 | 20 | 18 | 12 |
| Cash flow Information | 39 | 7 | 9 | 17 | 19 | 16 |
| Intercompany transactions | 37 | 10 | 4 | 25 | 13 | 10 |
| Inventory Information | 31 | 8 | 2 | 28 | 10 | 8 |
| Budgets | 31 | 9 | 2 | 41 | 7 | 8 |
| Forex positions | 29 | 5 | 9 | 17 | 18 | 12 |
| Accounts receivable | 28 | 6 | 3 | 27 | 10 | 8 |
| Accounts payable | 26 | 6 | 3 | 27 | 9 | 7 |
| Three-/five-year plans | 23 | 6 | 2 | 44 | 5 | 9 |
| Accounting/financial regulations | 15 | 3 | 3 | 44 | 8 | 6 |

Table 2–2 reveals that companies most commonly automate the following information:

- **Profit and loss statements and balance sheets.** Companies put the heaviest emphasis on automating balance sheet and P&L information because it is the backbone of internal management reports and external financial statements. At present, 24% of the respondents send P&L information by computer (either computer-to-computer or by physically sending a computer disc), and 23% of the respondents transmit balance sheets electronically. Over the next few years, the figures will more than double.

- **Sales information.** Currently 24% of firms send sales information by computer, with the number rising to 48% over the next few years. By automating sales data, companies can improve their ability to assess sales performance, forecast future trends, and track customer purchases. Furthermore, sometimes such reports can lead to higher sales, as the assistant controller of a retail chain explained: "Sales analysis is highly automated because we make a lot of high-level visits where our management will meet with the management of a major buying office. By providing our management with better information on sales, they can tell a better story, which results in more business."

- **Intercompany transactions.** These transactions include information about sales among corporate entities and remittances of dividends and profits, which is all essential data for multinational firms establishing pricing and tax policies. Respondents to the survey are currently heavily dependent on mail and telex for this data transfer (50% and 32%, respectively). However, while only 17% of firms now use computer transmission, over the next few years that figure will nearly triple.

- **Cash flow information.** As cash flow becomes a more pressing concern, especially for those firms seeing their profits squeezed, the number of companies automating the reporting of this data is growing rapidly. In fact, although computer transmission now accounts for only 15% of respondents, within the next few years this number will triple. "We need a short response time for cash flow information to correct deficiencies and make use of surpluses," reasoned one controller whose firm has recently computerized this area.

- **Inventory information.** Inventory information is still sent predominantly though the mail, with only 16% of respondents relying on computer transmissions. But that number will climb to 39% over the next few years. The reason, according to the controller of an American consumer goods producer is that, "we want to closely monitor what is just about our most valuable asset."

- **Budgets.** Budget reports are usually examined on a monthly or quarterly basis and sent through the mail (67%). Currently, just 16% of firms have automated the transmission of budget data, but 40% intend to switch to computers over the next few years. By automating budget data, management can pinpoint variances and take action with a minimum of delay. At a large United States conglomerate, summarized financial data transmitted computer-to-computer has permitted financial analysts to prepare a monthly *President's Report* that describes variances from budgeted amounts. Thanks to this computerized report, top management can now quickly identify and correct problems.

- **Accounts receivable and accounts payable information.** This type of information is not considered time sensitive by many controllers, and it is not critical for parent headquarters because receivables and payables management is usually delegated to the subsidiary level. As one controller explained, "If you're a day late, it's no big deal. For those procedures, you would not go computer-to-computer because of time sensitivity." Therefore, only 15% have computerized reports on accounts receivable and 13% on accounts payable. But in line with the overall trend toward automated reporting, these numbers will more than double over the next few years.

- **Foreign exchange positions.** Forex positions are usually reported only quarterly or annually at some firms and then mostly by mail and telex. Only 9% now automate reporting of forex positions, and the number will almost triple in the next few years. However, there is relatively little time sensitivity with them. According to one controller, "Foreign exchange positions don't warrant a monthly report. You also might look at this report two months before the end of the year to see the impact on financial statements."

- **Three- and five-year plans.** These plans are computerized by only 9% of firms, with the vast majority of respondents (68%) still depending on the mail. Over the next few years, the percentage of firms using electronic transmission will grow, but mail will continue to be the predominant delivery mechanism. As one consumer goods firm controller explained, "It's really a question of dollars and cents. It's not as important for this information to come in on a systematic basis. We can wait a little longer to get that information—we're always worrying about costs."

- **Accounting/financial regulations.** Regulations are now the least automated data with a scant 4% of respondents currently automated. However, an increase to 18% is expected in the future. One controller discussed what is behind the change: "We are moving to computerize reporting of financial regulations. We need to know how such things as tax proposals would have an impact on our intercompany transactions. Subsidiaries should understand that impact as quickly as possible."

## DATA PREPARATION

Once an effective financial reporting system is in place, companies may want to take advantage of the latest computer applications to prepare data for analysis and presentation. For multinational corporations, for example, the preparation procedures of most critical importance are the consolidation of interim and annual results and the translation of financial results. To assist in this effort, this section examines the various approaches to computerized consolidation and translation of foreign operation unit results, as well as how firms adapt systems to their own peculiar organizational styles and information needs. The information in Table 2–3 summarizes the current and projected status of companies' efforts in this field.

**TABLE 2–3**

**Percentage of Firms Highly Automated for Consolidation and Translation**

|                                    | At time of survey | Three-year projection |
| ---------------------------------- | ----------------- | --------------------- |
| *Type of Transaction*              |                   |                       |
| Consolidation of interim results   | 49                | 78                    |
| Consolidation of annual results    | 46                | 77                    |
| Translation of financials          | 31                | 63                    |

## Consolidation of Financial Results

Companies are making major strides in automating the interim and annual consolidation of financial reports from overseas operations. About half of the respondents to the survey have already automated their consolidation procedures, and about three quarters plan to do so within the next few years.

In the view of most companies, developing an effective automated consolidation system is critical for the success of a firm's reporting structure. To do so, companies need to keep three key issues in mind:

1. **How many line items of financial data are really necessary?** Management philosophy influences how much data subsidiaries should send to corporate headquarters. Without automation, consolidation of results from many operating units would be a nightmare, especially if a company were managed on a centralized basis. A decentralized advertising company is a good case in point. The corporate office receives 30 items per month on the P&L statement and 40 items on the balance sheet, but the data comes from 200 entities—which is overwhelming.

   In contrast, subsidiaries of a more centralized automobile company transmit detailed trial balances for consolidation at headquarters, which means more than 1000 line items from each operating unit. This system gives corporate management the ability to make quick, intelligent decisions, but it is very expensive from a staffing and telecommunications standpoint.

   Because automated consolidation makes it easier to manage financial data, firms are sometimes tempted to ask for unnecessary and costly data. Yet moderation can be an economic virtue. As the controller of one high-tech firm cautioned, "We're satisfied with the degree of detail. In fact, we're probably getting too much detail. We'd like to limit it to information we specifically need." His firm currently receives about 300 line items at corporate headquarters after several sub-consolidations (the major operating groups receive trial balances from foreign subsidiaries).

2. **How much control should you give to regional/divisional staff?** Some companies established computer systems that enable regional and divisional staff to consolidate and manipulate data

before it reaches corporate headquarters. One such firm, a United States food producer, created a computer system with a release button that regional headquarters must press before divisions or corporate can access the data. "When the firm first began the on-line system," noted the director of financial reporting, "subsidiaries were hesitant to enter data. But with the regional headquarters' release function, they now have a couple of days to screen data before it goes on to corporate."

3. **How many sub-consolidations do you need before the corporate consolidation?** Firms with strong regional or divisional groups might prefer several consolidations before data reaches corporate headquarters. When consolidated data is analyzed at several different corporate levels, automation can organize the data in one centralized location for easy access.

   A consumer goods firm with over 40 worldwide operating units offers a good example of how to consolidate financial data below corporate headquarters. Basically, it's a four-level process: Information flows first from the operating unit to regional headquarters, then to divisional headquarters, and finally to corporate headquarters. For example, each reporting unit in Germany has an assigned unit code. When data for a particular month must be reported, the unit inputs its code and the consolidation system sorts out where the data should be reported—in this case to European regional staff. This staff then signs on after all operating units throughout the region have reported their data, and one computer command collects the data from all units and puts it into a database. After the regional staff finishes analyzing the data, it is released to divisional headquarters in the United States. There it is summarized and sent on to corporate for final consolidation.

### Translation of Financial Results

According to the survey, only 31% of firms automate translation, but over the next few years this number will more than double. The size and global perspective of a company has a significant impact on computerization in this area: Of those respondents with over 40 foreign units, half are now largely automated because they need to keep track of so many currencies.

Companies interested in developing a translation software package should note that computer systems can be designed to allow foreign currency translation at either the subsidiary or the parent company. Most firms give subsidiary or regional managers control of translation so that they can be fully responsible for operating results in both local and parent currency terms. In the opinion of the director of technical support at one high-tech firm, "We want to keep translation at the local level because, from a corporate point of view, our business is reported in United States dollars. We feel that the local entrepreneur has to know how profitable he is in United States dollars. Particularly if the currency is going up or down, he should know whether to build or reduce inventories."

However, some firms prefer translating at the corporate level, especially those with businesses in countries with volatile currencies. The assistant controller of a diversified conglomerate explained: "Translation for Venezuela is done at the parent company. We were probably one of the few businesses who ever made a switch back to corporate for translation. We decided to do that at the time of the devaluation in 1983 because it wasn't foreseen by the local staff there. We felt that the parent headquarters staff should maintain control in this area." To ensure that both staffs maintained the same financial perspectives, however, the Venezuelan affiliate recently purchased an IBM XT and uses the same software (Lotus) as the parent company. This enables the firm to "swap disks back and forth," and makes the translation from bolivares into dollars easy for the parent company.

## DATABASE MANAGEMENT

With computerized systems, firms can now aggregate and store large quantities of data at corporate headquarters. However, the design of such a system for a multinational corporation may be affected by the firm's organizational philosophy and the information requirements of local, regional, divisional, and corporate managers.

Generally speaking, database management can be divided into three broad areas: maintaining the general ledger, storing historical

data, and developing a central database. Corporate trends in automating these functions are shown in Table 2–4 and a detailed
discussion follows.

### Maintaining the General Ledger

Maintaining the general ledger forms the core of the accounting
function, so it comes as no surprise that firms typically assign top
priority to automating the task. In fact, 76% of respondents were
highly automated at the time of the survey, and 88% planned to be
highly automated within the next few years—the highest percentage
for any accounting procedure covered in this book.

When automating the general ledger, firms must first decide who
should develop or purchase the software. Decentralized parent
companies sometimes guide local units in the selection of general
ledger computer packages, but generally give subsidiary managers a
free hand so long as summary level detail to headquarters is provided.
For instance, according to the assistant controller of one decentralized high-tech firm, "The local subsidiaries manage off of the general
ledger. Corporate provides them with advice—the format for their
software—but after that it's up to them to choose a package."

Regionalized or centralized companies usually dictate more
requirements about subsidiaries' general ledger systems and attempt
to standardize existing software or install new common packages.
One such example is a regionalized high-tech firm that decided its
European affiliates should all use the same package. Designed in the
firm's regional development center in Belgium, the new system
delivers information both for local reporting requirements and for

**TABLE 2–4**

**Percentage of Firms Highly Automated for Database Management**

|  | At time of survey | Three-year projection |
|---|---|---|
| *Function* | | |
| Maintenance of general ledger | 76 | 88 |
| Storage of historical data | 42 | 70 |
| Developing central database | 23 | 59 |

consolidation at parent headquarters. Dollar translations are done in the country of origin.

The system filled a need felt by everyone. Remarked the firm's manager of international systems, "The system fulfilled a very visible need for the subsidiaries. They have to make those submissions. Before the general ledger system was installed, translation was done manually or on accounting machines. So this system addressed most of the major problems they had for financial reporting in their own countries and satisfied our needs. Therefore, there was little or no resistance to the system."

Once the software package is in place, the next issue is to decide the degree to which ledger account numbers should be standardized. A highly diversified firm with many products and operating units must somehow overcome two problems. One is finding a common accounting language that suits the needs of different product lines. The other is overcoming resistance and inertia at the foreign subsidiaries.

The following examples show how firms have successfully overcome these obstacles.

*Case 1: Company D,* a United States consumer goods firm, is committed to standardizing general ledgers. To achieve this goal, Company D has given its highly centralized MIS department carte blanche. The director of international systems reports to the director of finance and is responsible for 92 computer sites worldwide. There are 22 computer sites in the United States, 16 in Latin America, two in Africa, 48 in Western Europe, and six in Asia/Pacific.

To meet the needs of different product lines, a committee composed of the international controller and the international systems group scrutinizes six general ledger packages for a good fit. To overcome resistance from foreign subsidiaries, the director of international systems sets two rules. First, it is important to develop a common system for each region separately. The rationale is that because the Europeans won't like a Latin American system and vice versa, the director plans to use a common system in each region, but not the same one worldwide. Second, it is paramount to decide what can be done locally and what can be done by company-wide systems. According to the director, "We have a matrix of what should be done locally and what should be done centrally, and we show it to the subsidiary controllers. No one at headquarters wants to touch order entry, invoicing, accounts receivable, accounts payable, payroll. These are local functions. But the following are candidates for common development: budget and forecast, general ledger, fixed asset, shop work order accounting, and cash management."

*Case 2: Company E* is also attempting to standardize general ledgers. The MIS director of this consumer goods firm with annual sales of over $2.8 billion admitted that the company is still operating in "the stone age."

Company E is divided into four reporting units: Europe, Australia/Asia, Latin America, and North America. Each region reports into the firm's international headquarters in New York. Yet the company still cannot transfer information electronically. Although the operating units prepare the information on computers, the link between their computers and those at headquarters is nonexistent. Operating units send in information on paper to regional as well as to corporate headquarters.

To bridge this information abyss, the MIS director has developed a general ledger package with spreadsheets that headquarters is making available to the local managers. That way operating units can standardize their software.

The MIS director also applies an 80/20 rule for standardization. The rule states that if 80% of the software used in one country's package can be used without modification in another country in the region, that software should be adapted for use throughout the region. But if less than 80% of the software can be used without modification, management should develop or use a different package. For instance, the company developed a package in Puerto Rico that was also used, with some modification, in Mexico, Venezuela, Portugal, and Spain. By adjusting the package to comply with different government regulations and reporting practices, the company successfully developed a standard general ledger system for all its Spanish- and Portugese-speaking affiliates.

## Storing Historical Data and Developing a Central Database

According to the survey, only a minority of firms are heavily automated in these areas. Under half of the respondents are highly computerized for storage of historical financial data and about one quarter have a highly automated central database. However, within the next few years, these numbers are predicted to about double their current levels.

The emphasis placed on information storage depends on how tightly corporate headquarters wants to manage the process. If a firm is decentralized, much of the financial analysis will be delegated to divisional, regional, or local headquarters, and a low priority will be given to developing a central database. An assistant controller at a highly decentralized high-tech conglomerate summed this position up best: "Our decentralized structure does not require an integrated source of information. There is no central database due to lack of interest."

However, if a firm is centralized and has a large corporate staff that performs extensive financial analysis, it makes sense to store financial data in an accessible central database. For example, a highly centralized high-tech firm stores five years of data, including 300 to 500 line items off the general ledger of 30 of its companies. The data is accessible to financial analysts and executives in several departments, including accounting, treasury, and marketing. The controller at another centralized firm claimed, "Our whole automation thrust has been an organized effort covering all systems. Financial data is stored for five years back, including forecasting data. The database can be accessed by PCs for individual analysis."

## Company F's Sophisticated Central Database System

Companies that want to set up a central database may want to consider the example of *Company F,* a high-tech firm that installed an advanced system that can be easily accessed by users at both corporate headquarters and subsidiaries. Before this central database was developed, the accounting department had to field requests pouring in from treasury, marketing, and planning departments. The staff had neither the time nor the technical capacity to handle the demands for data. Even simple accounting consolidation was done manually under the old system.

To tackle this challenge, the accounting staff first investigated whether to design the system in house or go for outside help. After some research, it decided on a system offered by a bank's consulting group because the company's own data processing group said it would take two years to develop an in-house system. In contrast, the bank's system took six months. In addition, according to the spokesperson, "It made more sense to buy a package that was top-of-the-line. The bank's system had another advantage—it was geared for financial analysts, not systems people. The system has a data manager function, report generator, graphics, simulation models, financial analysis (Net Present Value, Internal Rate of Return), and permits econometric techniques such as trend forecasting."

The central database now includes monthly P&Ls, balance sheets, quarterly funds flow, annual budget, and annual five-year strategic plans for the firm's 30 SBUs. To do competitive analyses within each industry, the database includes some external information—Compustat's, Standard & Poor's, and DRI's econometric series of historical data and forecasts. Additionally, one extremely useful feature of the system is that it can be accessed from both mainframe and PC links. Moreover, data can be downloaded to a spreadsheet or uploaded from the spreadsheet into the mainframe.

## DATA ANALYSIS

The preceding sections looked at three key stages of the internal data flow cycle, namely the collection, consolidation, and storage of worldwide accounting data. This section will examine the final internal stage—the *analysis* of the financial results of operating units, including sales, costs and productivity. Although these procedures are crucial to the control function, they tend to be less automated at corporate headquarters than most other accounting tasks. As can be seen in Table 2–5, over 40% of the firms surveyed have not automated any aspect of their productivity measurement.

There are two main reasons why firms have been slow to computerize these areas: the low level of the staff who traditionally analyze the data, and the lack of urgency generally associated with its preparation.

In respect to the first point, consider the fact that at multinational corporations, lower levels of management, not those at corporate headquarters, are often responsible for detailed analysis of accounting data. Large multinational firms with diverse product lines and

**TABLE 2-5**

**Percentage of Firms Automated for Data Analysis**

| At time of survey | | | |
|---|---|---|---|
| | **Not automated** | **Partly automated** | **Largely automated** |
| Sales analysis | 14 | 38 | 49 |
| Inventory analysis | 20 | 49 | 31 |
| Cost measurement | 24 | 45 | 31 |
| Productivity measurement | 44 | 41 | 15 |

| Three-year projection | | | |
|---|---|---|---|
| | **Not automated** | **Partly automated** | **Largely automated** |
| Sales analysis | 5 | 23 | 72 |
| Inventory analysis | 8 | 29 | 63 |
| Cost measurement | 9 | 35 | 56 |
| Productivity measurement | 19 | 44 | 37 |

extensive international operations find it difficult, if not impossible, to analyze all financial data relating to their operating units. Therefore, corporate headquarters at these firms generally rely on summary information, and leave local, regional, or divisional management to conduct thorough analyses of their day-to-day business.

As the controller of a major conglomerate expressed it, "We don't have a corporate staff of any great consequence, and it takes people to do analysis. Every once in a while we will pause and ask, 'Do we have our fingers on the important key indicators of our business?' We try to keep the analysis and decision out in the field with the people who know the market."

The slow pace to automation is also compounded by the issue that because of the expense of automated systems, firms tend to focus on computerizing the most essential data first. Sales and inventory analysis are the most highly automated analysis procedures because they have a direct impact on the day-to-day operations and overall health of a company. For most firms, daily appraisals of productivity or costs are not worth the additional expense of collecting and transmitting the information.

However, in the next few years, firms intend to devote money and energy to the full range of these tasks, adding all the bells and whistles of financial analysis. The controller of a $4 billion pharmaceuticals firm described his company's desire to have a fully automated analysis system: "When you're a big company like this, you have to have an overall vision of what you want to do. So far our systems development has been a sort of 'put out the fire' approach according to minimum needs. The result has been a lot of disjointed systems at the divisions that don't talk to one another. There is more and more pressure for information and our current mix of systems can't handle it."

### Sales Analysis

Sales analysis is currently one of the most highly automated components of a firm's accounting and control system. About half of the firms surveyed are now highly automated for sales analysis—making this critical accounting function second only to maintenance of general ledger in the level of automation. And, over the next few years, firms surveyed plan to place an even greater emphasis on automating this function.

By industry, intermediate and consumer goods firms rank far ahead of their counterparts in the service, capital goods, and high-tech sectors. For example, 66% of intermediate goods firms are now highly automated for sales analysis compared with 29% of service firms. This trend was best explained by the assistant controller of an oil company: "Sales information is the lifeblood of these [intermediate and consumer goods] companies. [They] have to keep track of a lot of small transactions. Service companies have the main job of making sure that everybody's time is fairly billable. Sales analysis is therefore not that important for service firms."

A good illustration of an automated sales analysis system is provided by *Company G*, a United States clothing producer with annual sales of over $500 million and subsidiaries in Europe, Mexico, and Canada. As is the case with many firms, the company first automated its general ledger and other basic accounting systems before computerizing its sales analysis. The assistant controller described the progression: "The general ledger was automated 13 years ago. In the 1970s, the division began automating fixed assets, payables, and receivables. Accounts receivable are on-line for good credit follow-up. We exchange information between divisions on the people who are paying slowly." To provide management with even greater details on sales, the firm developed an automated system in 1985. Careful sales analysis is crucial because of the seasonal nature of Company G's business. Said the assistant controller, "Each line has three seasons—spring, fall, and holiday. So you're committing for production four to six months before you're going to sell a piece of it. We look at historical sales and general economic conditions to decide what to produce."

Each domestic division can now report its monthly sales information on the top 200 stores electronically to parent headquarters. The data are then fed into corporate headquarter's mainframe database, along with sales data received by mail and telex from overseas subsidiaries. To facilitate analysis, sales information is summarized into several classifications—major retail stores, chain stores, military, and discounts. In addition, the software program standardizes information received from the divisions and enables each division to access its own data.

The sales analysis system is extremely user friendly; it allows management to instantly compare this year's sales with last year's results. Color coding of entries highlights sales above or below the same period last year (green for above 5%, red for below 5%, and white for no change). "The software is self-navigational," said the MIS manager. "You can find out whatever you want. Top executives just have to position the cursor and they can get the information they want. Before the system was instituted, they used to scramble around and call each division to find the information."

According to the MIS manager, the system is also very accurate: "We're only a few days behind in keeping track of the information. The longest period from the time an order is received until it's in the corporate computer is 48 hours."

The sales system includes yet another bell and whistle: tip sheets that break down the sales of major divisions into product lines. "Someone accessing the system can look at the tip sheet and see problems and opportunities," noted the assistant controller. "So you get a feel of how one of our brands is doing versus another and in one store versus another." The information is available to designated individuals in each division's accounting and marketing departments, the CEOs of each division, and senior corporate management.

Sales data may be used for what the assistant controller calls "leveraging our brands." For example, the tip sheet might reveal that a particular store in Cleveland is not selling enough of one product line. The firm can now present information that even the retail client doesn't have readily on hand. "In one case," says the assistant controller, "a couple of our products in one division weren't being bought. By using the detailed computer printout, our senior executives were able to convince the retailer to buy the other lines." The result: an extra three million dollars in sales in the one store alone.

In sum, the system gives the company's managers all they need to fully access the sales and financial performance of the company—from the division down to the product line.


### Inventory Analysis

Because most firms, especially those in seasonal businesses, have established clearly defined ratios of inventory to sales, it comes as no surprise that automation of inventory analysis parallels that of sales data. In fact, the survey shows that 31% of respondents are now highly automated for inventory analysis; this number will double in the next few years.

Once again, intermediate and consumer goods firms are the industry leaders: Although 41% of intermediate goods firms surveyed report highly automated systems, only 21% of service industries report that level of automation. The main reason for the gap between these industries is that both intermediate goods firms and consumer goods firms have to track large numbers of units while service firms do not.

The main issue confronting companies when automating inventory analysis is how to get accurate inventory counts from the manufacturing plants. To be most effective, inventory analysis has to be built from the bottom up. Thus, the more highly automated the plant level, the more facile the analysis at corporate headquarters. However, a gap often exists between corporate headquarter's desire to track inventory detail and the level of inventory automation at the plant.

The director of MIS for a major chemical firm voiced a common complaint about a lack of automation at the plant level: "The problem is motivating the plants to automate." Many plants still rely on an antiquated cardex system, and this poses a serious threat: "Because its record keeping is so cumbersome, a plant could have $3 million in inventory that it shouldn't have," noted the MIS director.

Despite these problems, some firms have established sophisticated, automated inventory measurement systems. For example, *Company H,* an electronics concern with annual sales of $350 million, is committed to extensive inventory analysis. Not only is the firm highly automated at the plant level, but its inventory analysis system is fully integrated with its sales analysis and general ledger systems at corporate headquarters. The firm has emphasized inventory analysis because of the need for quick inventory turnover in the high-tech industry.

To achieve its goal of quick and accurate inventory analysis, the company put mainframes in many of the plants and installed a software system with some of its own modifications for scheduling, capacity planning, and materials and resource management (MRP). The program is standardized in each of the company's 40 manufacturing units.

The manager of financial reporting can point proudly to the progress that has been made since the system was automated: "In the past, the plants were merely expediting orders. Now, we're planning the materials management so that components are available to manufacture the products as they are needed. Reduction of inventory is just one of the benefits that has come out of the system."

Another advantage of MRP is the link with sales analysis data or the product line distribution matrix at the plants (PLD). The company has several product lines including fiber optics, flat cable lines, and connectors. Because of the automated system, said the manager of financial reporting, "We can now analyze on a product line basis, not just a unit basis, to come up with actual, versus budget, versus prior year, versus forecast." Financial analysts at the plant level can extract information, download it, massage it, and put it into the database used for financial reporting, on-line query, and trend analysis.

The firm now plans to enhance the MRP inventory control system at the plant level with a just-in-time manufacturing system to conform to the needs of large customers who have rigid delivery schedules. Noted the spokesperson, "It's the next generation after MRP. For example, one customer demands that we give them zero defects in the products that we ship to them. If we send them 5000 parts, there better not be three which are bad. And they want it sometime between Tuesday noon and Tuesday at five o'clock; they don't want it the day before, and they don't want it the day after."

Meanwhile, at corporate headquarters the firm has an advanced, zero-balance system that tracks inventory up to the hour. The corporate inventory manager monitors the finished goods shipped from the plants from five centralized warehouses for intracompany transactions. According to that manager, "Each of the manufacturing units reports in to a regional warehouse, which reports into corporate headquarters. There are five warehouses (distribution centers) located throughout the country. They are places for packing and shipping the inventory. We get reports from them on a daily basis. The mainframe here is the central computer for all of the distribution centers." Corporate's mainframe then determines the level of inventory at the facilities throughout the country, based on orders that have been entered. At that point, the computer contacts the manufacturing facility as to how to package it, in what quantity, and where to ship it. It also prints all the labels and addresses for the products.

Explained the inventory manager, "The computer tracks all this information with a daily, zero-balancing system. There are no leftover pieces at day's end. There is a zero balance at every manufacturing facility and at every warehouse. If a product is shipped from *Point A*, it's got to reside at *Point B* or at other points where it was supposed to go. The programs are set to zero-balance themselves. They will spit out edit reports when there's not a zero balance." For example, "Suppose *Manufacturing Facility A* ships 100 units to *B* and *C* split 75/25. But what if *B* receives 75 and *C* receives 24? We cannot go to the next step until somebody gets the house in order. This means that we have to get the extra one over to *C*, unless it's found that the manufacturing facility actually didn't ship 100 units."

The system permits the inventory manager to check the production status of each of 40,000 items at any given point of the day. "What we really have is an accounting module attached onto the side of a customer service system so that all of the transactions that take place are in the customer service system, and then rerouted through our accounting programs."

Each month, the controller's office analyzes inventory data by downloading the information from the mainframe onto PCs. Such a process has pros and cons. "We've successfully written programs for downloading," stated the firm's manager of inventory analysis. "We've found other areas where it's not cost beneficial to write programs for downloading to PCs. It's easier to do it via an analyst who has experience in the area. We also have built history gathering into our system. We have the ability to do it on-line, as well as hard copy, for the last three years by part, family of parts, by specific transaction—just about any configuration you can think of. It makes it quite easy to do any analysis work that needs to be done. We can also use the information for forecasting because we have the database in place."

According to the spokesperson, an advanced inventory system has numerous benefits: "Inventory analysis is critical for this company because we have more than $90 million in inventory, $59 million of which is finished goods. You can save many hundreds of thousands of dollars in the manufacturing process with a highly automated inventory management system. We would not be able to close our books so quickly—within five days—without it. We probably wouldn't be able to approach three weeks for closing if we didn't have such a system. There's a benefit in time savings and forecasting; and it saves us tremendous amounts of money in our warehousing effort."

There are people savings as well. Before the system was fully automated, the department had six or eight times as many people as today. Now, inventory analysis is handled by the manager of inventory analysis, a financial analyst, and a clerk. "Accounting today has reached the sophistication level where it's not 'think work'—it's 'think smart'—think of things you can do on a computer more productively."

## Cost Measurement

Of the companies included in the survey, 31% are now highly automated in cost measurement, a figure that will nearly double over the next few years. As in the case of sales and inventory analysis, intermediate goods firms lead with 38%, while service companies trail behind with 21%. As the assistant controller of an oil company put it, "Intermediate goods companies like ourselves are the most advanced for cost measurement because cost of goods sold is usually a relatively high percentage of revenues for firms in the oil and chemicals industry—as much as 80%. By contrast, production costs for other firms might only be 15 to 20% of revenues."

At the corporate level, most companies focus on evaluating variance from manufacturing or purchasing budgets, delegating most detailed analyses of costs to the divisional or operating unit level. The rationale is that these tiers of management are closer to the business and will therefore understand the cost structure of different products better.

### Tracking Costs in Hyperinflationary Environments

Monitoring costs for a multinational firm is difficult enough, but for companies operating in risky environments, where inflation is rampant and sudden devaluations an ordinary occurrence, it can be a nightmare. That is why *Company I*, a divisional headquarter of a United States electronics corporation, turned to computers to simplify the task of monitoring six foreign manufacturing operations in Brazil, Mexico, Venezuela, Argentina, Turkey, and the Philippines.

Each month, five of the six operating units electronically transmit reports to divisional headquarters in Cleveland (Turkey panafaxes the information because of problems accessing computer lines). These monthly reports provide detailed cost breakdowns as well as information on return on sales, net income, days sales outstanding, inventory turnover, and other key financial measurements. Most of the data are manipulated through PCs, although the division does have access to the mainframe. "If we start to get any problems," commented the assistant controller, "we have hardwiring from our PC into the mainframe in Cleveland. So if I have a large database, I can reinput into that mainframe and unload summary data into a file for the PC."

Because sales of Company I's products are normally very stable, heavy emphasis is placed on cost control and analysis to ensure profitability. To monitor costs effectively in the difficult environment in which the firm operates, it developed its own software and performance evaluation system. The assistant controller described how it works: "For hyperinflationary countries, you have to look at local currency price and the translation to United States dollars. Typically, our variance analysis will have the current period's number, the base period's number, and a variance. We run four different columns on the variance: sales volume variance, costs, local currency, and dollar translation." The variable costs are defined as direct material, labor related specifically to the product, utilities, and supplies. Base (fixed) costs include administrative costs, corporate charges, and depreciation. The exchange variance is put into base cost; interest costs go into other income and expense.

For cost analysis, the exchange variance and interest expenses are lumped together into financial costs. According to the spokesperson, interest and exchange variances are merged because it would be unfair to hold managers in hyperinflationary countries accountable for the high cost of financing or for a major depreciation in their base currency. "It's very difficult for a general manager overseas to understand and control the differences between exchange rates. We have the foreign operating manager worry about operations costs, and understand that he's got to recover financial costs, but he doesn't have to worry about the difference between exchange and interest costs."

The automated system has also spurred positive administrative changes in the division. When the monthly reviews were done manually, the division spent a great deal of time inputting figures. Now, because the affiliates can give them numbers almost instantaneously, staffing at the division has been cut.

## Productivity Measurement

Compared with other analysis procedures, productivity measurement ranks low: Just 15% of firms are now highly automated in this area. However, in the next few years this number should double. The companies surveyed reported two levels for automated productivity analysis—corporate and local. At the corporate level, analysis often consists of measuring the company's overall productivity against other firms in the same industry. At the local level, interest centers on the productivity of plants or products.

*Company J,* a highly diversified conglomerate, is an example of a firm that does its analysis on a corporate level. It depends heavily on comparative analyses of the productivity of other companies in similar industries. In the words of an assistant controller at the firm, "There are no standardized ratios corporate-wide. You can't compare the turnovers of semiconductors with elevators. But automation has enabled us to run trend comparisons of our diverse operations with those in similar industries. We can now look at asset turnover, inventory turnover, and sales to asset ratios in different industries."

One of the prime sources of competitive productivity analysis is Standard & Poor's Compustat. The system stores up to a maximum of 20 years of detailed 10k and 10Q information and has quarterly information going back ten years. "By creative manipulation of the data, you can calculate such ratios as sales per employee, and cost of goods sold per employee," notes the assistant controller.

The automated database helps corporate headquarters expand its vision of who its true competition is and how the firm stacks up against its prime rivals. "If you ask major corporations how many competitors they have, they'll say two to five," claimed the spokesperson. "However, when you start looking at their product and service diversity by segmented business detail and line of business, you see that a company with only three segments might be competing with 330 other segments. You can also look at the impact of corporate restructuring on the company, which is especially relevant given the number of conglomerates these days."

At the local or divisional level, firms tend to concentrate on measuring the productivity of individual plants or specific product lines. Like many firms, *Company K,* a United States manufacturing conglomerate, decided to let local subsidiaries monitor their own productivity. According to the firm's assistant controller, centralized corporate control of productivity measurement didn't make sense because "you're talking about a couple of million dollars spent on corporate staff to accomplish some cost savings. It's the old accounting story, 'What is the cost of control?'" However, Company K did give the affiliates the means to conduct an automated productivity analysis—a PC software package—as well as the responsibility of analyzing and acting on the analysis. The package includes specific productivity measurements such as unit costs per 1000 units, utilization of capital equipment and inputs (e.g., metal), the percentage of scrap, power usage, and worker schedules.

The assistant controller cited an example of the savings realized since the software program was instituted. For many years, the firm's Venezuelan subsidiary manufactured a certain kind of paint can. Metal punched out at one stage of the manufacturing process was considered scrap. But the subsidiary discovered that the metal scrap could be used to make more cans. The productivity software helped them to calculate a yearly savings of seven dollars per thousand cans, or $75,000 per year on that process alone.

## THE NEW FRONTIER: EXTERNAL REPORTING TO GOVERNMENT AGENCIES

Over the last few years, companies have devoted most of their time to automating internal accounting procedures. But companies are now exploring the new frontier of accounting automation—electronic transmission of reports to government regulatory authorities. According to the survey, 5% of companies are now largely automated in generating reports to government, and 36% are partly automated. These numbers are expected to rise over the next few years to 24% and 49%, respectively.

Despite the mutual benefits of electronic reporting of external accounting data to both government authorities and corporate participants, only the United States has a full-fledged program for computerized reporting to its Securities and Exchange Commission (SEC): the Electronic Data Gathering, Analysis and Retrieval System (EDGAR). Other nations are interested in EDGAR, but are lagging behind the United States. A project official noted that, "A lot of countries don't have reporting requirements—period. Others don't require the information for public distribution. There is no comparable organization to the SEC in other countries. Our disclosure laws are much stricter; we get seven million pieces of paper each year. There is a growing realization that handling mounds and mounds of paper isn't the most productive way to manage. There is a motivation for going electronic."

However, with the increasing globalization of capital markets, and ensuing cross-border debt and equity issues, electronic financial reporting to non-United States government agencies is inevitable.

The following sections will discuss United States corporate concerns about EDGAR and examine how one foreign firm has benefited from participation in the experiment.


## The EDGAR Project

The EDGAR pilot program started with 140 companies in September, 1984. It is expected to be fully operational by the end of 1988, with most of the nation's 11,000 public firms filing required reports electronically. According to a spokesperson for EDGAR, the glitches so far have been minor: "There were some difficulties with telephone lines and blank diskettes but there have been no big systemic difficulties."

Potential participants generally have three key questions about the project:

1.  **Do the benefits outweigh the inconveniences?** The corporate reaction to EDGAR has been mixed. Some pilot participants have complained about the effort involved in getting onstream, and feel that there seem to be more benefits for the SEC than for themselves. But in the future, quicker filings should enable firms to better meet market windows and, since they will be sold through a contractor for public dissemination, evaluate their competitor's filings.

    The main complaint reaching the agency currently involves formatting requirements. According to an EDGAR official, "One of the problems is that computers are fussy, so we have a whole set of formatting requirements. But that's not unusual; we had certain type and paper requirements with paper filings, too." Still, companies complain about the nuisance.

    EDGAR officials respond by pointing out that the new system is extremely accommodating and can take diskettes from over 85 different word processors. This feature has elicited praise. As the assistant controller of a major automobile firm put it, "All we had to do was add a modem to a PC. We didn't need to retrain anybody. It was just a question of getting used to the formatting standards, which are rather rigid. In three weeks, we were filing. The whole transition cost about $1000—the cost of the modem."

2. **Is EDGAR more efficient than hard-copy reporting?** Many corporate spokespersons, especially representatives of small firms, express skepticism about whether transmitting the data electronically is more efficient than mailing the reports. In response, the SEC officials in charge of EDGAR point to the case of a major capital goods firm. A company spokesperson described what happened: "Under the old system, we had one horrendous experience trying to make an issue. The airport closed down because of snow, so we couldn't fly anyone to Washington to make the filing. By the time we could file, the terms of the deal were looking a bit shaky, so we were penalized quite a bit. With EDGAR, we don't have these worries anymore."

   Even better, EDGAR has yielded what the spokesperson called "surprise savings." Printing costs have decreased because, instead of printing out two or three drafts, the controller can just press a button on his PC and send the filing to the SEC. Furthermore, the clerical staff no longer has to spend time compiling several copies of the filing. Asked the spokesperson, "How do you quantify savings like that?"

3. **Is security adequate?** EDGAR officials admit that they had to foil one attempt by a hacker to break into the system. However, they consulted with the FBI and other agencies before the system was off the ground to ensure that the PIN (password) system was as secure as possible.

   A major oil firm participating in the project has been satisfied with the security precautions taken by EDGAR. "I didn't like the PIN at first," said the assistant controller. "We're very security conscious here. It takes four people to complete a filing. One person has access to one part of one PIN, two others have access to other parts. No single person has access to all the information."

## Reporting Across Borders: How One Canadian Firm Taps United States Markets

*Company L,* a Canadian corporation with annual sales of $108 million, produces data communications equipment and was a pioneer in the manufacture of packet switching. Its role as a leader in the high-tech industry made it a natural candidate for the EDGAR project. The director of reporting explained why: "When EDGAR was first announced, we could see that this was the way the world was going anyhow. We had a few reservations, so we didn't sign up right away. We just wrote away for the manual and had our operations people look at it. I looked at it from the administrative standpoint to make sure that we didn't have any problems in trying to comply with both Canadian and American requirements."

Company L had another good reason for joining the EDGAR project. It is listed on the Toronto Stock Exchange and on the American NASDAQ exchange. To date, the firm has issued commercial paper in the United States, and it plans to tap the American market again sometime in the future.

After an evaluation period, company officials were willing to go ahead with external electronic transmission because the firm had been reporting that way for internal corporate reports for several years. The director noted that "We have computer links with our foreign companies in the United Kingdom, the United States, and Australia. Our distributors in Hong Kong and Japan are all linked, too. Telecommunications is the lifeline of our operations."

In spite of management's optimism about the project, the firm encountered some problems in trying to transmit data cross-border. "The SEC pulled the rug out from under us on our first actual filing when they withdrew their subscription to Tymenet. We said 'Fine. We can't go via Tymenet, which is our normal means, so we'll go direct dial.' The SEC said communication would work with asynchronous transmission. However, it does not. The SEC seems to be heading toward an IBM world, which requires synchronous transmission."

So although the firm looked for an easy solution, it didn't find one. Instead, it decided to wait until EDGAR officials could clear up the problems. "We decided that EDGAR was not friendly, and that they're going to have a real problem. We're still on the program, but we're sending floppy disks until we get to the stage where we have a synchronous modem on hand and it's convenient to use."

But even this improvised and obviously less-than-optimal solution is more convenient than previous transmission methods. Before EDGAR, corporate employees had to type up the 90-page report, make seven copies, bind them, and then ship them in cartons to the SEC. Now the reporting process is much more efficient. "We input the data here, and then we send it by electronic mail to our main-frame in Ontario," said the director. "We have them put the material on the PC, using a floppy diskette that EDGAR will like. Then we just send the disk to the SEC. We put it in a special envelope so that X-ray equipment at the border won't erase it. We're comfortable with this method because there's no doubt it's going to get there."

The director of reporting believes that virtually all companies should consider electronic reporting to the SEC: "Maybe there are a lot of companies that aren't filing electronically, but I would bet that 90% of the companies have a word processor that they're doing their work on. Really, there's no reason not to file electronically. We haven't spent a cent on EDGAR except for the time it took our computer manager to sit down and take a look at their materials. We knew it was going to require a little bit of skill and know-how, but other than that, everything else was already sunk cost. We had an electronic office, so it was just a matter of using our resources effectively."

## SUMMARY

The final comment from the Director of Reporting at Company L provides an appropriate way to end this chapter. Just as his company concentrated on "using [their] resources effectively" to deal with EDGAR, so have the surveyed companies applied their resources rationally to automate their critical functions. And, for over three quarters of those companies, accounting and control is that primary critical function.

The first chapter demonstrated that the degree of automating could be correlated with location, size, and industry type. A perfect candidate for automation would be a large, North American-based, manufacturing firm. Additionally, the chapter showed that basically any type of organizational structure could benefit from automating this function. The jury is still out on how automation leads to decentralization and others insist that it leads to centralization.

In light of these operating assumptions about automating accounting and control, this chapter tracked how it could be accomplished. It demonstrated that data transmission between remote operating units and parent headquarters will occur increasingly through or on some type of computer apparatus—be it synchronous data lines or dual-density diskettes. The traditional, favorite media—mail, telex, facsimile, and telephone—will be used less frequently. The data sent through these means is also being collected, consolidated, stored, and analyzed with increasing frequency through database management software. Currently, general ledger maintenance and annual results consolidation are largely automated by 76% and 46%, respectively, of FERF respondents and those percentages should grow, respectively, to 88% and 77% within the next few years.

Increasingly, firms are focusing attention on automating more sophisticated data analysis applications. Sales and inventory analysis, in particular, have been singled out as high priority items by firms confronted with stiff competition and diminutive profit margins. Automated cost and productivity measurement, as well as the creation of central databases, are also starting to gain wide acceptance. In sum, firms are automating the most massive and manually intensive applications first, and then turning to programs from which they can get the greatest yield on their software dollars.

Finally, internal reporting mechanisms, which link intercompany databases, are slated for development in many companies, but external reporting to government agencies is now a reality. The SEC's EDGAR project, which allows companies to file financial reports electronically, will count as participants one quarter of FERF's respondents in the next few years. A higher degree of participation will probably result when the SEC resolves the same automation issues as faces its reporting base of companies.

# CHAPTER 3

# The Missing Link: Automated Financial Planning Systems

## INTRODUCTION

To minimize risk, cut costs, and boost profits in today's ever-changing world, many companies are revamping their investment/divestment strategies, reorganizing and streamlining corporate structures, re-thinking ownership patterns, and reshaping balance sheets. And behind these profound strategic shifts is a new commitment to financial planning. As one director of financial planning put it: "Lack of financial planning is like walking a tightrope blindfolded without a safety net. You can do it, but you're taking a big risk."

Survey results show that more and more firms are agreeing with this opinion and are turning to automation to assist in their financial planning. Although only 10% of respondents now give top priority to financial planning automation (compared with 77% for account-ing), over the next few years that figure will nearly quadruple. Even more important, the number of firms that are largely automated for the function will more than triple in the future.

Computerization of financial planning has received a boost from two major developments: the PC revolution and the installation of accounting databases. First, the new PC technology permits easier systems development and integration and has been a blessing for financial planners. Thanks to vastly improved software, firms can integrate user-friendly PCs with corporate mainframes, downloading data from central databases and uploading analysis from microcomputers. Noted one financial planner at a telecommunications firm, "We can move data down from our decision support system to spreadsheets with a couple of keystrokes, or have the package input the data into the mainframe."

The second development is equally as exciting for planners. Before they can automate financial planning, companies must first install sophisticated accounting databases. In the words of one financial planner, "When you implement financial systems, you're trying to answer two basic sets of questions. First, you have to answer 'what happened?'—that's your accounting database. Then you move on to 'what if?'—that's your financial planning database. Typically, a firm will take one to two years just concentrating on what happened. If you haven't automated your chart of accounts and you don't know how to relay the information so that it is consistent, then you can't automate financial planning." And, as was discussed in Chapter 1, the majority of firms have already solved this riddle; 57.3% of respondents are now largely automated for accounting, and an overwhelming 81% will be highly computerized within a few years. Thus, most companies now have a firm foundation for sophisticated financial planning.

To help companies take advantage of these new opportunities for automating financial planning, this chapter will explore the latest developments in decision-support systems. It will analyze which types of firms are the best candidates for automation and how computers impact the organization of the function. Most importantly, it will provide detailed case examples of how firms are automating the following areas of financial planning:

1. **Operating budgeting and control,** including forecasting earnings, forecasting funds requirements, and performance evaluation of operating units.

2. **Capital budgeting,** or the strategic, long-term allocation of company financial resources. Capital budgeting includes project investment analysis, forecasting financial trends, long-term port-folio planning, and political risk analysis.

3. **Capital structure,** which focuses on how companies fund their major, long-term investments. This includes long-term borrow-ing decisions, debt-equity mix, and dividend policy.

4. **Tax planning,** which evaluates the impact of existing and pend-ing tax regulations on the full range of financial decisions.

---

### WHICH FIRMS ARE AUTOMATING FINANCIAL PLANNING?

The survey reveals that the same types of companies that are automating the accounting function are in the vanguard of firms computerizing financial concerns. This trend is easy to explain because companies must first install and organize ac-counting databases before they can turn their attention to such sophisticated applications as decision support for financial planning.

Specifically, research has uncovered three key trends:

1. **North American firms lead the world in financial planning automation.** As illustrated in Table 3–1, North American corporations are much more likely to have highly computer-ized financial planning than their European and Asian counterparts.

   As in the case of automated accounting, North Ameri-can firms have achieved this advanced position because of their technological edge in software and hardware systems.

**TABLE 3–1**

**Percent of Respondents with Highly Automated Financial Planning**

| Location | At time of survey | Three-year projection |
|----------|-------------------|-----------------------|
| North America | 21 | 54 |
| Europe | 14 | 51 |
| Asia | 6 | 43 |

But the gap is rapidly narrowing: Over the next few years, European companies will be neck and neck with their North American competitors, while Asian firms will follow close behind.

2. **Large firms with extensive overseas operations are the best candidates for computerization.** Given their much greater resources, it is no surprise that companies with annual sales of over $500 million are the most highly automated. But as Table 3–2 shows, the survey found that smaller firms will register the highest percentage rates of growth in financial planning automation in the future. However, rather than develop separate financial databases, which are often prohibitively expensive, some of these firms piggyback off of inventory or sales monitoring systems.

3. **Manufacturing concerns have the greatest need for state-of-the-art, decision-support systems.** According to the director of financial systems at a consumer goods firm, "Planning is of paramount importance. [Manufacturing] companies tend to be very financially oriented—towards cost control, tracking historical results, and plotting future events." Table 3–3 illustrates the director's point:

**TABLE 3–2**

**Percent of Respondents with Highly Automated Financial Planning**

| Annual Sales | At time of survey | Three-year projection |
|---|---|---|
| Over $2 billion | 20 | 53 |
| $500 million–$2 billion | 24 | 60 |
| $200 million–$499 million | 10 | 48 |
| Under $200 million | 12 | 44 |

**TABLE 3–3**

**Percent of Respondents with Highly Automated Financial Planning**

| Industry type | At time of survey | Three-year projection |
|---|---|---|
| Intermediate goods | 21 | 58 |
| High-tech firms | 18 | 54 |
| Capital goods | 18 | 53 |
| Consumer goods | 18 | 53 |
| Services | 13 | 43 |

> Service organizations, on the other hand, have fewer customers and inventory, less tangible products, and shorter time frames than manufacturing enterprises. These features, in turn, suppress their appetite for computers.

## HOW COMPANIES ORGANIZE FOR FINANCIAL PLANNING

To meet the challenges of the late 1980s and beyond, many multinational firms are decentralizing their businesses. As part of the process, these companies have adopted austerity programs that cut layers of corporate management, and place responsibility for profit and loss squarely on the shoulders of operating units. But despite these measures for global operations, the survey shows that firms are taking a different tactic when it comes to financial planning. In fact, the majority of firms centralize financial planning decisions at corporate or regional headquarters: 50% of respondents now consider themselves centralized for financial planning, 16% regionalized, and 34% decentralized.

Why the trend toward centralized financial planning? For many firms, the new decentralization demands tough internal controls and highly coordinated financial planning, including capital budgeting, performance evaluation, and tax management. As the director of financial planning for a diversified chemicals and machine tools company explained, "Even though our operations are autonomous, our financial controls need to be centralized. Individual plans come in from the units and we consolidate them and make sure they fit our policies. We have all these different companies dealing across many states and countries so they have to be looked at from a centralized point of view. We have to look at all of our earnings, profits, and foreign tax calculations from a centralized perspective."

### BUCKING THE TREND

The high-tech industry is one notable exception to the trend toward centralized financial planning. According to the survey results, such firms are far more decentralized for financial planning than any other sector—46% versus 34% for total

**TABLE 3–4**

**Financial Planning Organization per Industry Type**

|  | Capital goods | Intermedi- ate goods | Consumer goods | Services | High-tech firms | Total |
|---|---|---|---|---|---|---|
| Centralized | 50 | 54 | 53 | 57 | 29 | 50 |
| Regionalized | 19 | 14 | 11 | 16 | 25 | 16 |
| Decentralized | 31 | 32 | 36 | 27 | 46 | 34 |

respondents, as shown in Table 3–4. The planning director of a computer manufacturer explained the phenomenon: "If you look at revenue per employee, high-tech firms are more people intensive than other types of companies, like capital or intermediate goods. Those firms need more centralization because they are more capital intensive. They drive their planning process through their capital planning. To them, their investment in capital is their lifeblood."

But high-tech concerns, this spokesperson continued, are "moving toward more decentralization of financial planning. Planning should be done by people who know the operations best. At our firm, those people are at the divisional and local levels."

## The Impact of Automation

Most companies use computers as tools to achieve their financial and organizational goals. Consequently, it should come as no surprise that respondents to the survey believe that increased automation of financial planning procedures will lead to greater centralization of the function. Thirty-eight percent of respondents expect financial planning to become more centralized at parent or regional headquarters because of automation, while 18% anticipate becoming more decentralized. To lend support to the majority, said one controller, "Automation helps us centralize substantially better and determine the immediate impact of unit activities on our income statements and balance sheets."

A United States chemicals concern with operations in more than 100 countries, and annual sales in excess of $6 billion, provides a good illustration of how firms can use computers to centralize financial planning. As part of its drive to streamline operations and cut costs, and thereby regain its competitive position, the firm's top management firmly adopted a philosophy of centralized financial planning. The director of corporate planning explained why: "If you have a local entity looking at planning from a strictly local perspective, the people there tend to lose sight of the entire corporate profit picture. At corporate headquarters, we can make financial plans with the idea of keeping us as a low-cost producer."

With this objective in mind, the firm has achieved a high degree of centralization in recent years while, at the same time, paring down its financial staff both at the corporate and subsidiary levels. For example, the corporate finance department numbers about 30 employees today as compared with the staff of 55, four years ago. And, financial managers at the company's manufacturing operations cannot hire any new financial planning staff and must pass on the lion's share of planning work to the parent.

The firm has achieved such dramatic results because of management's commitment to state-of-the-art planning hardware and software. In the words of the spokesperson, "Automation had a lot to do with it. We couldn't operate our function with as few people as we have without automation. The investment in automation is nominal. A fully loaded PC, with everything I want on it and then some, is only about $8000. That's nothing compared to hiring another person." To supplement this new hardware, management has invested in the most sophisticated financial planning software. Recently, the firm purchased Execucom's IFPS (Interactive Financial Planning Software) package, which provides a link between all corporate PCs and the central mainframe.

This computer link has allowed the company to centralize its financial planning function in the following two ways:

1. **Corporate staff reworks all the profit forecasts submitted by local units.** Operating entities are required to submit quarterly earnings forecasts, as well as annual budgets and long range forecasts, to parent headquarters for detailed analysis. The corporate planning director explained the rationale this way: "The local entities do not have an appreciation of the overall effects of funds flow on the parent company's books and cash position. We therefore do this critical analysis at corporate headquarters."

The profit plans submitted by foreign operations are thoroughly reviewed at parent headquarters to pinpoint their financial impact on the company. Automation allows corporate management to perform this review quickly and efficiently because IFPS provides for automatic downloading of information from the central mainframe to PCs located on the desks of each corporate planner.

2.  **The threshold level at which corporate staff analyzes new project proposals is low.** Any project proposal of more than $500,000 from a local unit must be submitted to corporate headquarters for detailed analysis. This is a very low threshold level for such a large firm. Says the corporate planning director, "If I have a manufacturing plant that I want to build or expand upon, all decisions must be made at corporate headquarters. IFPS gives us a tremendous amount of support on many variables: Price, market share, market volume and general economic conditions are all rolled together with a cost-of-goods model to allow us to make better projections." Thus, corporate planners are equipped with the up-to-the-minute tools for sensitivity analysis, obviating the need for local management to get heavily involved in the decision process.

### Automating for Decentralized Planning

Despite the general trend toward centralized financial planning, some firms are moving in the opposite direction. Furthermore, they are using the same automated tools to achieve their objective of local unit autonomy. A good example of this approach is provided by a computer firm with annual sales of over $10 billion and more than 700 operating units worldwide. According to the firm's corporate director of financial planning, the company uses a decentralized bottoms-up approach to planning that ensures local management's commitment to earnings objectives. "To get this commitment, profit center managers must have ownership of the plan. They must feel that it is theirs, that they've participated in it," explained the spokesperson. "You can't accomplish that by doing the planning at the top and passing it down to somebody. Human nature doesn't work that way."

But the firm does insist on a minimum level of central control. "Although we've decentralized the preparation of proposals, we haven't totally decentralized control. We can continue to maintain ultimate control thanks to our systems."

The firm's decentralized planning system is supported by a sophisticated satellite communications system that links a network of PCs at the country, region, and parent levels with the corporate mainframe. Most subsidiary financial officers have PCs on their desks, so they can do their analyses and then upload the information into the mainframe. Corporate analysts, in turn, can download from the mainframe to their PCs for further review.

In line with its overall commitment to decentralization, the company leaves the choice of financial planning software entirely up to local managers. In practice, however, most planning managers rely heavily on a well-known software package because of its simplicity.

Most importantly, the firm takes advantage of its computer infrastructure to decentralize financial planning in two critical areas:

1. **Operating budgets.** The company's forecasting cycle begins at the lowest level—the plant site—with each plant electronically transmitting its upcoming year's profit plan to a country or regional office. Financial plans then work their way up to corporate headquarters, where they are consolidated, and not usually reworked. At the end of the process, the information that corporate staff looks at is considerably less detailed than at lower levels, usually in the range of three to four lines.

2. **Project investment analysis.** Parent headquarters restricts its role in this analysis. Primarily, headquarters sets hurdle rates and lets local managers determine if corporate standards are being met. Corporate usually steps in only when a project exceeds $10 million. For example, expenditures for land and buildings are usually authorized by corporate staff. "When you're going to put up brick and mortar, that's a permanent kind of decision as opposed to putting in a piece of equipment in an existing facility. Most everything else, we would not review on a project-by-project basis at corporate," notes a spokesperson.

## FINANCIAL DECISION-SUPPORT SYSTEMS

Once a company decides to automate financial planning and selects the appropriate organizational structure, it can then begin to consider the broad array of hardware and software options available on today's market. And, although each planning function can be separately automated, most advanced automated systems integrate accounting and treasury databases, as well as mainframe and microcomputers, permitting firms to use a variety of hardware and software to massage their financial planning data.

Such decision-support systems (DSS) are the *Star Wars* of financial planning; they are the cutting edge of computer and telecommunications technology applied to the finance function. Enthusiasts rave about the benefits of DSS, from their enhanced reporting capabilities to improved analysis; and ultimately, better, more informed decision making by planners. In the words of one financial planner sold on DSS, "The technology is now available. Why not use every tool at your disposal?"

The survey identifies four basic types of DSS applications: data retrieval from a central database, ratio and regression analysis, sensitivity analysis and financial modeling, and input from external databases. As can be seen in Table 3–5, the corporate appetite for DSS will grow dramatically over the next three years; in some cases, more than doubling.

Choosing the proper software to implement these DSS applications can prove a difficult task. Dozens of brands exist. The following section explores how companies can evaluate the various features of DSS.

In addition, Tables 3–6 and 3–7 contain information about the

**TABLE 3–5**

**Percentage Use of DSS Applications by Respondents***

| Application | At time of survey | Three-year projection |
| --- | --- | --- |
| Easy retrieval from central database (ability to answer ad hoc queries) | 36 | 76 |
| Ratio analysis and regressions | 35 | 65 |
| Sensitivity analysis and financial modeling | 40 | 69 |
| Input from external databases | 22 | 49 |

*Numbers may exceed 100% because of multiple responses.

**TABLE 3-6**

**Most Popular Mainframe/Mini DSS Systems**

| Package name | Vendor | Customer base |
|---|---|---|
| IFPS | Execucom Systems | 1,500 |
| FCS | Thorn EMI Comp. Software | 1,400 |
| Foresight | Compro Financial Systems | 550 |
| System W | Comshare | 275 |
| CA-Fin Planning | Computer Associates | 250 |
| Empire | Applied Data Research | 200 |
| Simplan | Simplan Systems | 130 |
| Model | Lloyd Bush & Co. | 125 |
| Express | Information Resources Inc. | 120 |
| Strategem | Integrated Planning | 65 |
| EIS | Boeing Computer Services | 41 |
| XSIM | Interactive Data | 20 |
| | Other | 600 |

Source: International Data Corp., *Software News*, September, 1986.

**TABLE 3-7**

**Decision Support Package Options**

| Package | Development language | Mainframe | Mini | Micro |
|---|---|---|---|---|
| IFPS | FORTRAN | X | X | X |
| FCS-EPS | Assembler | X | X | X |
| Foresight | FORTRAN | X | X | X |
| System W | Pascal | X | X | X |
| CA-Fin. Planner | Assembler, SPF | X | | |
| Empire | FORTRAN | X | | planned |
| Simplan | PL/1, Assembler | X | X | X |
| Model | FORTRAN | X | X | X |
| Express | AED | X | X | X |
| Strategem | C | X | X | planned |
| EIS | FORTRAN | X | | X |
| XSIM | AED | X | X | X |

Source: Real Decisions Corp., *Software News*, September, 1986.

most popular DSS mainframe systems: Table 3-6 lists vendors and indicates market shares; and Table 3-7 describes package development languages and indicates what size system it runs on—mainframe, mini, or PC.

## Evaluating DSS Software

To choose the best DSS package, firms must first carefully evaluate their priorities and conduct a thorough investigation of available software. This section presents an evaluation system developed for a Big Eight accounting firm, which can be adapted to meet your firm's specific needs.

The evaluation should start by reviewing the requirements of the business application in terms of computer tools, people, and other resources. The staff performing the review should develop a list of desired software capabilities or features corresponding to the requirements of their applications. An example of this process follows:

| Business Application Requirements | Software Features |
|---|---|
| 1. Data in small volume is primarily entered at the terminal. | Data collection |
| 2. Financial data consists of numeric and text format. | Data management; text processing |
| 3. Reporting formats are fixed for the most part, but requirements for ad hoc display of data will increase, especially for senior management reporting. | Reporting features; graphics |
| 4. Financial calculations—such as NPV and IRR—and statistical computations—such as moving averages—are used commonly in the application. | Built-in financial statistical calculations |
| 5. Accounting relationships vary by SBU. Consolidation of results is required quarterly. | Modeling language |
| 6. Users are mostly novices with no previous computer programming experience. | Ease of use; vendor support and training |
| 7. Two or three users in the same department may run the application at the same time. | Technical characteristics |
| 8. Application will be developed jointly with MIS who will provide technical advice and maintenance. | Vendor support and maintenance |

9. Application database will eventually     Technical
   tie in with other mainframe databases.     characteristics

10. The cost of developing the application     Cost
    should not exceed a budgeted amount
    of $X$ thousand dollars.

Next, the firm should rank each business application requirement in order of priority or assign it a relative weight. For example,
suppose that requirements 3, 5, and 6 are considered high priority.
This means that the evaluation of the software should focus on
reporting/graphics features, modeling language, ease of use, and
vendor support and training. Of course, this does not preclude a
review of the other priorities by end-users and MIS personnel. These
software capabilities include:

- Data collection
- Data management
- Text processing
- Financial/statistical functions
- Technical characteristics
- Cost

At this stage, a checklist of questions for each of these categories
can be drawn up by a group of two to three users and systems
personnel.

Examples of questions for the top three categories are as follows:

**Reporting/graphics**
- Is there an automatic display layout for tabular information?
- Can footnotes be added to reports?
- What is the maximum number of levels of subtotals?
- Can plots or charts be generated through simple commands
  without reloading data?
- Is there an option that can be engaged with simple commands to
  present data in scales or on axes?

**Modeling language**
- Are model lines or spreadsheet cells numbered, named, or both?

- Does the software check each model line for correct syntax when it is typed?
- Are the line-editing capabilities in the modeling language or external to it?
- Can the user process multiple sets of *what-ifs* during a single execution?
- Is the model broken down into smaller subroutines that can easily be inserted into larger programs?

**Ease of use**

- Can the user input data without programming knowledge?
- Can the application be developed through a series of menus or predefined instructions?
- Is the language in plain, clearly worded English?
- What user aids exist in the software (e.g., HELP commands)?
- Does the format allow for both column and row manipulation?

**Vendor support and training**

- What is the degree of support provided by the vendor in the local office?
- How often is the software modified and improved?
- Is there an active user group?
- What is the overall reputation of the software?

The evaluation staff can assign a numerical score to each category, and can compute an overall score on a weighted-average basis. The software product that ranks higher then becomes the leading candidate.

The key ingredient to a successful evaluation process is a thoughtful identification of what the system is expected to do in business terminology. Needs should be set in order of priority to establish a screening criteria on the many software candidates. Only then can the company examine and evaluate specific functional and technical features. Once the needs have been identified and criteria measured, user and MIS management can reach a mutual decision.

## Case Examples: Corporate Applications of DSS Packages

Several years ago, a multinational retailer with outlets in the United States, Canada, and Germany was reeling from the failure of one of its major divisions. Awash in red ink, the firm was forced to close more than 30 retail outlets.

Chastened by this crisis, the firm's management vowed to prevent another costly disaster through highly coordinated, responsive financial planning and performance evaluation. According to the firm's assistant controller for financial planning, "When we went belly up with that division, better financial systems became mandatory to figure out where we were going." As part of the effort, the firm set out to automate every aspect of its operating budgeting process—from financial forecasting to internal performance reporting and evaluation—to help forge a strategy to return the corporation to profitability.

Management decided to purchase a DSS package that would store data in a central database and allow for downloading to personal computers. After looking at several packages, the firm decided to go with Execucom's IFPS. Explained the company's spokesperson, "We needed a system that met our needs for rapid change, that was user-oriented and not an MIS product. We chose IFPS because it is state-of-the-art. It allows us to capture the numbers once at the source without having to constantly reprocess them." Even better, "It had already been accepted by over 1500 companies and 80% of the major business schools in this country. That said a lot about it."

Despite this enthusiasm, company planners admit that it took time to automate the financial planning function. The process has been a gradual one, phased in over several months. For example, the company first applied the new package to budgets and monthly forecasts, enabling the firm to receive critical information on each of its profit centers. "Each of our seven divisions has 50 or 60 profit centers; and each center provides a detailed P&L statement, balance sheet, and cash flow statement. IFPS has allowed us to define profit centers; and business segments better, and to store all of the data in one central location."

Before the new system was implemented, the company was run as a loose affiliation of companies. Each profit center was a fairly autonomous unit and reported financial forecasts on an ad hoc basis. What corporate staff faced at that point was a mountain of sporadically reported information. IFPS allowed management to establish a standard report format corporate-wide for budgets and other financial plans and to require timely reporting on a monthly basis. The new system consolidates all reported information automatically.

After controlling its forecasting, management was able to set its sights on efficient performance evaluation. IFPS includes a feature that goes to the accounts reported in the monthly financial statements, and graphically depicts them in a return on investment (ROI) tree format. This is now done automatically for each of the firm's several hundred profit centers. The diagram allows any financial planner in the corporation to use his or her own PC to access ROI information from the corporate mainframe and compare results against any other company unit. It has also permitted corporate headquarters to standardize ROI hurdle rates corporate-wide. According to one corporate planner, "People need a clear target to focus on. We set a rate of 11% ROI, and we measure performance against that."

The assistant controller for financial planning considered ROI analysis critical to the firm's success. He maintained that, "ROI is one of the most important management tools available to increase productivity and accomplish change within an organization. It promotes communication at all levels, allows management to focus on what *can* be done and also focuses on what *will* be done to produce the results required."

The next step for management was to inform the divisions and regions of the reasoning behind the individual goals set for each operation. "We stressed that ROI is not just a single number or aggregate," said the assistant controller, "but an interrelated series of profit and loss outputs and balance sheet inputs that must be disaggregated by the ROI tree to be used effectively as an operational tool."

The assistant controller explained that "since this is completely automated and integrated into the management process, we can do a lot of *what-if* analysis. For instance, what will the impact be on ROI if we lower expenses by 2%, and inventory by 5%? In our case, these small, manageable changes will increase ROI from 8.7 to 10.6%. The

ROI analysis allows nonfinancial operations to understand the impact of various decisions on their ROI and the total corporate ROI. This promotes a more cooperative attitude on meeting goals."

The company's commitment to DSS has paid off handsomely: In 1986 the firm achieved a corporate-wide return on investment in excess of 11%. According to the company's assistant controller, "With IFPS, we have a clear picture of who the profit contributors are, and we can reward maximum ROI generators. Better divisional goal setting has helped us to reach our corporate goals."

In sum, the company achieved five primary benefits from their investment: parent headquarters now receives data much more rapidly, analysts have easier access to financial information, communication has improved at all levels of the corporation, staff costs are stable, and financial planners can use the data for better decision making.

A chemicals conglomerate with 75 foreign subsidiaries and over 30 divisions uses a mainframe-based version of EXPRESS for cost-reporting analysis at corporate headquarters and for a cost allocation model at group headquarters. According to the firm's assistant controller, "The highest priority was given to the consolidation and data collection end. Before EXPRESS, we were using three different languages. But our data continued to grow in size and complexity but not in the way of functionality. There was no chance of functional enhancement. Then we decided we needed to give more value to not just consolidation and collection, but to DSS—analyzing, reporting, and presenting data."

In response to this decision, a committee of users and MIS personnel examined four different DSS packages. They also compiled a list of fourth-generation languages for programming, database inquiry, and graphics. Then they hired a consultant to recommend some packages. "We found that two systems didn't have the power we wanted. We considered a consolidation package plus a fourth-generation language. But we found that the functionality was limited—it was too batch oriented, it was hard coded, and it needed reportion flexibility. We were already sour on the third package; it didn't have an English orientation and programming flexibility. So we ended up with an EXPRESS prototype. Its two basic uses are corporate consolidation, and planning and analysis."

Data enter the EXPRESS system every month from the 75 reporting locations. The larger European subsidiaries transmit through a telecommunications network to corporate's computer center. Smaller subsidiaries with poor telephone service—for example, Brazil and Argentina—tried to transmit their data electronically but electronic transmission took more time than that required to telex the data and have it reinput at corporate headquarters.

Of particular importance to the operations analysis group is the process of evaluating the net contribution of subsidiaries, which is standardized corporate-wide and expressed in dollar terms. Explained the company's controller, "The inflation and exchange rate relationship washes out to get you back to dollars. We don't set a higher hurdle rate for foreign subsidiaries. Management decides whether they're earning a premium over the standard rate which is sufficient for the country."

The controller at corporate headquarters sets the contribution rate and relies on recommendations from the operations analysis department. Said the director of operations analysis, "We apply our cost accounting to the S&P 400 companies to try to figure out what is the rate that people can earn consistently over time, and use that as our target. We get that data from an external database of current cost information for 1600 companies. The other way we determine contribution is to figure out what our overall cost of capital is and build up from that level so that over the long term we can satisfy our shareholders."

The operations analysis group also looks at more traditional measures such as working capital levels, balance sheet management measures of days outstanding for accounts receivable and payable, inventory turnover, and the nominal level of operating profit before taxes versus forecasts and budgets. It reports every month and a half to the VP International, who then gives feedback to the subsidiaries.

As a result of having the EXPRESS system, subsidiaries are now able to better assess their own performance relative to their asset base. Commenting on the impact of the system, the spokesperson noted: "For example, the petroleum equipment group has not been meeting its hurdle rates lately because of market conditions. What the system does is to give them the additional incentive to downsize their business to make it appropriate to their market share, by getting rid of assets not essential to the business, so that they won't be charged for them."

The EXPRESS system has also been applied at the group level. The most active user is the agricultural chemicals group, which manufactures insecticides and herbicides. The group accesses EXPRESS via the company's mainframe and uses two models: a consolidation program and a cost allocation model. The consolidation program was developed four years ago in-house and it is used to produce monthly volume, sales, and profit margins. Stated the director: "All of the reports necessary for corporate reporting are written in EXPRESS so it is now in a highly automated form. It's a fairly large database. We've segregated operations in several departments and we look at several product lines. There is therefore a fair amount of detail."

The director's group looks at 15 to 20 line items allocated across five or six product lines and two business units. The data from the units are analyzed on PCs and then input manually into the EXPRESS model. Just a few lines are transmitted to corporate headquarters—essentially bottom line results and some intermediate items such as sales, gross profit, and operating profit.

The second EXPRESS application is an allocation model developed a year and a half ago. The group is segregated into domestic and international marketing, and also has a manufacturing area and an R&D staff. The model allocates nonbusiness unit expenses to these business units to assess their performance on a full cost basis. It also allocates expenses to product line so that profitability can be reported on a product line basis. The EXPRESS model has enabled the group to set targets for ROA and net contribution that can be examined across product line in the regions or business units.

Since instituting its current cost accounting system via EXPRESS five years ago, the firm has been able to:

- **Reduce excess cash substantially.** In fact, the firm pinpointed $350 million in surplus funds that it has put to use for intercompany lending and short-term investments.
- **Identify and sell unnecessary assets, such as real estate.**
- **Streamline businesses and consolidate plant facilities.**

## OPERATING BUDGET AND CONTROL

### Automating Operating Budgets

Many firms realize that good operating budgeting—or profit planning, as it is called at some firms—can spell the difference between survival and success in a competitive global marketplace. As one planning director put it, "Most of the 'great corporations' spend a fair amount of time in the future planning to stay profitable." Operating budgeting consists of two basic procedures: forecasting anticipated earnings and funds requirements, and evaluating actual results against budgeted targets. Thus, operating budgeting is the cornerstone of any effective financial planning system. It is indeed a crucial method for anticipating and controlling the ongoing business of a company.

For this reason, operating budgeting is typically the most highly automated of any of the functions covered in this chapter. As can be seen in Table 3–8, a significant minority of survey respondents have already largely computerized key aspects of profit planning, and the degree of automation will more than double over the next few years.

### Forecasting Earnings

Of all the areas of financial planning, forecasting earnings ranks at the top of the list in automation. Indeed, over the next few years a majority of respondents to the survey will be highly computerized for forecasting earnings, while only 8% will not be automated at all. The financial planning director of a diversified capital goods manufac-

**TABLE 3–8**

**Percentage of Respondents with Highly Automated Operating Budgeting Systems**

| Function | At time of survey | Three-year projection |
|---|---|---|
| Forecast earnings | 24 | 52 |
| Forecasting funds requirements | 17 | 46 |
| Performance evaluation | 21 | 50 |

turer explained the trend this way: "My number one forecast item is how much money am I going to make. Everybody is keyed in on earnings per share."

For companies with automated accounting and control systems, the transition to computerized earnings forecasts can be a smooth one. The reason: Such firms already receive computer-to-computer transmission of data on monthly P&L statements, balance sheets, budgets, and short-term forecasts from individual subsidiaries or from divisional headquarters. As one planning manager put it, "Our forecasting database is identical to our reporting database. The automation of earnings forecasts is a natural outgrowth of the automated reporting of actuals."

Corporate's role in this process is to consolidate and review the reported totals. "We compare actual results to goals, and determine if forecasts are realistic," declared one director of financial planning. To ease this task, a growing number of firms are investing in decision-support software that allows planning staff to download information directly from the corporate mainframe and run different earnings scenarios. The time savings achieved through automation can be tremendous. According to the spokesperson for a United States multinational corporation, "Previously, to analyze a single account down to the unit level was a couple-of-days' task, involving quite a few telephone calls. Now it's a number of minutes to run a report. With our system, we can go down within the corporate structure, take any account, and run it out for all 150 of our entities."

The program of an extremely diversified United States concern with over $2 billion in annual sales serves as a good example of how to automate every step of a monthly earnings forecasting process. The company has about 40 foreign units worldwide, with regional headquarters in Europe, Asia, and Latin America.

During the first and last months of each quarter, individual business units are required to forecast their earnings for the rest of the year. These forecasts are transmitted via computer to the respective regional headquarters, where the data are analyzed and then stored in the corporate mainframe.

Parent headquarters has established a fully integrated series of computer programs for forecasting earnings. FOCUS™, a leading fourth-generation language developed by Information Builders, Inc., is the tool of choice for data retrieval from the corporate mainframe. In fact, corporate made the decision to invest in FOCUS in response to demands from business unit managers for rapid access to data stored in the mainframe.

Once the information has been retrieved, corporate planners work on networked microcomputers. They use spreadsheets to conduct fundamental analysis, and IFPS to create complex models tailored to specific divisional needs and to report intracompany financial plans.

So far, management is pleased with the results of the IFPS package. In the words of the firm's financial planning manager, "IFPS allows users to create models to suit their own specific needs or make their job easier. But the spokesperson cautioned against trying to do too much: "You can get into something that's so elaborate that its trying to forecast information based on sunspots, or you can take a real down-to-earth approach and use the model for aggregating earnings information."

### Forecasting Funds Required

According to the survey results, forecasting funds required is also slated for increased automation. Over the next few years, the percentage of respondents that are highly computerized for such forecasts will more than double from 17 to 46%. The financial planner of a capital goods firm explained: "Funds required is my number two priority in terms of automating profit planning. How much money I am going to need comes just behind how much money I am going to make."

As in the case of forecasting earnings, funds requirements are generally tied to the monthly reporting of actuals. The manager of international treasury operations of a manufacturing concern described the data he receives as follows: "We can look at the cash flow changes, working capital changes, capital spending, earnings level, and depreciation, and we have a complete funds statement similar to the sources and uses of funds statement that you would see in any financial report."

With this information in hand, corporate planners can use spreadsheets on PCs to project future funding needs based on current and expected cash flows. Planners often work closely with the treasury department in this area, with the treasury staff concentrating on short-term funds requirements and planners projecting medium- and long-term needs.

For example, one manufacturer has developed a combined earnings and funds required forecasting system that permits both short- and longer-term projections. This system for determining future cash flows consists of: (1) A monthly short-term funds forecast for the upcoming four weeks based on projected cash receipts and disbursements, which is analyzed by treasury staff, and (2) a quarterly, long-term funds forecast based on previous years' financial statements, which is the responsibility of the corporate planning department. The firm's corporate planning director explained the process: "The actual planning begins at the 30 strategic business units. From there, the data is transmitted via computer to our five operating groups. Each group maintains its own piece of the database and sends a copy of the information to corporate. At corporate we have a broad picture of the company as a whole."

The role of the corporate treasury and planning departments is to review group forecasts. Noted one financial planner, "There has to be some place in the organization where somebody takes a look at the whole thing. At corporate, we compare actual results to goals using a spreadsheet, and figure out how to reach goals if we're not attaining them. We look at two years worth of quarterly data, which drops a quarter as we input the current actual data."

Automation of funds required forecasts has led to significant benefits for both treasury and financial planning. The firm's treasurer pointed out, "We are getting better, more timely cash flow and cash requirements information thanks to automation. Before we automated this procedure, we were receiving reports haphazardly and they were often delayed. By the time we received data and could do anything with it, we had lost too much time." Planners benefit by having easy access to a huge amount of detailed forecast data. "This morning we had a request from our insurance division for payout projections for 1987 by business unit," related the director of financial planning. "Because of our system, all we had to do was run a funds report by business unit. We gave them the information in a few minutes." In sum, automation of these functions has led to accurate and timely responses.

## Performance Evaluation

The final link in the operating budget process, effective performance evaluation, ensures that operating budget objectives are being met. By measuring subsidiaries' forecast versus actual reported earnings each month, financial management can determine how well existing operations are performing, boost operating efficiency, make timely modifications of corporate objectives and strategies, and allocate resources productively.

At the same time, firms need to calculate a wide variety of ratios for evaluating performance, including return on equity (ROE), return on assets (ROA), return on sales (ROS), return on investment (ROI), and return on total capital (ROTC), which can help translate bottom-line results for each unit into standardized and easily comparable financial data.

Given the importance of performance evaluation, it is no surprise that respondents to the survey are heavily automating the function. According to the survey results, 21% of companies are now largely computerized in this area, and within a few years the figure will increase to 50%.

The most sophisticated firms are attempting to establish automated performance evaluation systems that are fully integrated with financial reporting and forecasting procedures, and that modify information to suit local operating conditions. A good illustration of this trend is provided by an international pharmaceutical organization with over 100 legal entities in 55 countries worldwide.

When the company started shifting its international financial operations from a regional to a centralized structure two years ago, it had to reorganize its system for evaluating subsidiary performance as well. Under the old system, this evaluation took place through four regional "satellite management centers." Each region reported its data monthly, either by computer in the developed areas or on hard copy from other centers. However, when many of the financial functions of these satellites were centralized at parent headquarters, the international group was compelled to upgrade its computer facilities to handle the enormous increase in information. It started by transferring the computer system used for the Latin American group to the international group headquarters.

The firm then took advantage of the opportunity to develop a highly sophisticated and automated evaluation system that was fully integrated with the financial reporting and forecasting system. With a program to adjust financial results to include volume, exchange, product mix, and price impacts on performance, and a network of terminals throughout the international group, the system now provides management with a much clearer picture of subsidiary performance. "What we've got here," stated the international controller, "is a system that brings up financial statements and analysis of all our markets for any given month at the push of a button."

Each subsidiary now transmits 500 to 800 line items directly to the international group on a monthly basis. The information is consolidated on a minicomputer and then stored on a mainframe at corporate headquarters. For performance evaluation, about 200 line items are maintained in the database, and are segmented according to markets and product lines. The corporate MIS staff was instrumental in developing this database; five corporate DP professionals and one analyst from the international group spent six months creating it.

The setup provides international staff with financial data quickly and efficiently. "The entire system collects the information and presents it to us in financial statement format every month. It also stores data which can be pulled up onto the screen. We have a track of performance since 1983," noted the spokesperson.

The system is straightforward. For example, by simply typing the correct password into an office terminal, managers in the international group can call up the following menu on their screens:

- **Business Breakdown**

  by product division (5) or by region (9)
- **Financial Statements**

  1. P&L statement
  2. Expense reports
- **Accounting Period**

  1. Monthly
  2. Yearly
- **Types of Analysis**

  1. Budget versus actual (month or year-to-date)
  2. Actual (this year) versus actual (last year)

International planners can look at financial results from a product-line or geographic perspective. In the case of sales statistics, for example, managers can go as far down as major product group results or individual country performance and manipulate the data. Said the spokesperson, "We take statutory records and massage them, and reclassify, reallocate, and reassess them to prepare our own management statements."

These financial data are accessible to all areas of management in the international group, including finance, marketing, and operations staff. "The system goes up to the very highest level. At the executive level, a lot of end-user information is canned, menu-driven material." Senior executives use the system to quickly gauge actual performance against budgeted amounts. "If they want to see the German statement of earnings, they can see it. If they want to see all the intergroup sales for Germany for a given month against budget or against last year, they can pull it up onto the screen." Financial analysts in the international group also access performance data.

In addition to making information available to the full spectrum of management, the company's system is also notable for its use of a special category called VEMP—Volume, Exchange, Mix, and Price—that allows management to distinguish each element's impact on operating results. A good example of VEMP in action occurred recently in Nigeria. When the naira was unexpectedly devalued, the international group staff isolated the impact of exchange on operating performance. "We forecast how the devaluation would affect operating results. As a result of the devaluation we had lost 12 points of sales growth. We knew that we'd have to get more volume or increase prices to make up for it."

By having performance data so easily available, executives can gauge a unit's actual performance by considering all of the variables that comprise VEMP. Explained the spokesperson, "When we review the performance of Nigeria, we now take into account that the naira devaluation has had a considerable impact. To overcome a major devaluation is very difficult to do, but if the manager still has good volume (units sold), good mix (profit margin) and prices (rate of increase), he is measured both on total performance and the fact that exchange conditions have changed."

This action does not guarantee that performance will necessarily improve drastically in Nigeria. "The system is not used as a stick to force people to do something better. It's just used to distinguish these elements to better describe a set of events that has occurred. What it does ensure is that the international group and the field staff will have a better idea of actual operating results."

The official inflation and exchange rates used in setting VEMP amounts are usually generated by the field offices. In spite of the centralization of the finance function, the local units still have a better grasp of local economic conditions, and their forecast rates are input into the system for determining the macroeconomic impact on performance.

The firm has benefited from its investment in a state-of-the-art performance evaluation system in the following ways:

- **More people are using the data for decision making.** "In the past, we used to produce two thick books that nobody looked at," explained the controller. "Now, we can get laser printouts of 100 major products and we can look at them by country or by markets within the product."

- **Managers can act more quickly on the numbers.** "We have faster, more efficient reporting. The information is easily accessible, so our managers can respond to changes in business more rapidly."

- **Data takes into account world realities.** VEMP makes modifications for macroeconomic events. One common corporate-wide set of instructions is used to factor in volume, exchange, product mix, and price fluctuations.

- **Staff size is down.** As a result of the move toward centralization and upgraded systems, staffing requirements have been considerably reduced. "In the international financial area, we have 75 people. Before, we used to have 35 at each of our four satellite management centers."

For the future, the firm hopes to upgrade its system to take on the task of managing worldwide totals. This system would also allow other corporate departments, including treasury and tax, on-line access to performance information. Explained the spokesperson, "Greater interaction among departments is bound to increase overall productivity."

## CAPITAL BUDGETING

The capital budgeting process encompasses a variety of planning activities with a time horizon of more than one year, which is an increasingly difficult and critical exercise in today's environment. Extremely volatile currency and interest rates, political upheavals, and the sudden imposition of exchange controls all pose threats to what once were secure overseas investments. One financial planner recalled a classic example: "During the Falkland Islands conflict a few years ago, we had a real dilemma about expanding operations in Argentina. The locals promised a good rate of return, but risk of nonpayment dramatically increased. We eventually decided that the ongoing business seemed good enough to risk the investment—but it was an agonizing decision."

This survey shows that a fast-growing number of companies are turning to automation to cope with these uncertainties. As one financial planning manager explained, "The biggest risks about projects nowadays are the assumptions. By automating, you can determine which of the assumptions are the most sensitive. This produces more and better data to use and rely on."

As can be seen in Table 3–9, survey respondents agree with this assessment: Over the next few years, they will more than double their use of computers for such key capital budgeting functions as project investment analysis and long-term portfolio planning, and will increasingly automate the forecasting of financial trends and political risk analysis to buttress their decisions.

## TABLE 3–9

**Percent of Respondents with Highly Automated Capital Budgeting Systems**

| Procedure | At time of survey | Three-year projection |
|---|---|---|
| Project investment analysis | 21 | 42 |
| Forecasting financial trends | 8 | 19 |
| Long-term portfolio planning | 5 | 13 |
| Political risk analysis | 1 | 3 |

## Project Investment Analysis

Project investment analysis encompasses all discounted cash flow forecasting methods such as net present value (NPV), internal rate of return (IRR), and payback period. Once a project has been proposed, finance staff must conduct sensitivity analysis. For example, what happens to the IRR on a project should prices degrade rather than hold constant? Other variables include price, market share, market volume, general economic conditions, and political risk (see the box on pp. 105–106).

According to survey results, the use of computers for analyzing capital project proposals will rise dramatically over the next few years from 21% of respondents to 42%. This tremendous surge can be attributed in part to the spread of PCs to all aspects of financial planning. For example, one leading firm in the high-tech industry with annual sales in excess of $5 billion and offices in over 60 countries has long employed automation in its formal project analysis process. According to a spokesperson, "We've been using automated IRR models for 18 years. They used to be on a mainframe system but now they're done on PCs. We've been able to download P&L statements and balance sheet information to the PCs, using fourth generation languages, since 1982."

In this company, the ease of access and *what-if* capabilities provided by PCs has enabled senior management to standardize new project analysis corporate-wide. "We decided that since we have so many units scattered around the world, it would be better to require a standardized format from each of our major groups." This regimented approach was facilitated by a highly computerized internal telecommunications system that allows all of the groups to dump reports directly to a central mainframe.

The analysis process works as follows. Twice a year, the corporate planning department evaluates current costs of capital and, based on those figures, determines an appropriate hurdle rate for new projects. "We factor it up a little to make sure that we're in the top quartile of high-tech firms," remarked the spokesperson. This rate, which generally ranges from 14 to 18%, is transmitted to the group level through the internal communications network.

On a quarterly basis, five American and three international groups send proposals for new projects to headquarters through the same network. The number of proposals submitted varies widely but, in general, the groups seek approval only for projects over $10 million. As one corporate planner explained, "Our groups tell us the things they intend to commit in the following quarter. We may take issue with something and ask them to provide us with more detail. I don't tell them 'you can do this and you can't do that,' but we are trying to maintain control of the total level of capital investment."

The financial analysis performed at the group level, however, is dictated by headquarters. "We have standardized IRR calculations that we require the groups to do on projects. That is the key measurement. Analysts use spreadsheets as a desk tool for doing those calculations. They compare these calculations with our hurdle rates. The easy availability of computers within our organization has made this comparison a relatively easy process that any of our groups can perform."

Because of the highly competitive nature of the computer industry, capital investment is usually driven by overall strategic business concerns. For this reason, the firm goes beyond quantitative factors in its review of proposed projects. Group managers are expected to explain their ratio analysis and present qualitative reasons for adopting a given project. By having the quantitative analysis standardized corporate-wide, parent company officials can more easily study the qualitative aspects of the proposals.

### Forecasting Financial Trends

When analyzing proposed projects or developing long-term portfolio plans, companies factor in forecasts of such key financial trends as inflation, interest, and exchange rate movements. The survey shows that a growing number of firms—from 8% of respondents currently, to 19% over the next three years—are turning to automation to assist in the forecasting process and to provide an electronic link with other aspects of the planning function. The widespread availability of external databases is a driving force behind the move toward computerized financial forecasting: 22% of respondents indicated that they receive information from outside vendors now and 49% will use external forecasts within a few years.

However, these developments are having a major impact on corporate economics staffs: Automation has led to severe cutbacks, and even group eliminations in this area. According to one planning director, "A couple of months ago the corporate economist was fired. Top management made a decision that an economist wasn't needed because of the availability of external databases."

Some firms are using automation to help redefine the forecasting function by integrating it with more practical aspects of financial planning. A large high-tech conglomerate, serves as a good example of how a company can use automation to accomplish this goal. The company's senior management was firmly convinced of the importance of maintaining a corporate economics staff. At the same time, they felt strongly that radical changes were necessary to improve the department's productivity and relevance for the company. As one tenured economist at the firm stated, "What made us valuable is the fact that we knew the company well, and it would be difficult for an outside forecast to serve the same purpose. What we had to do was restructure our departmental objectives to meet corporate needs."

In the past, the corporate economics department was seen as an aloof and separate entity. Now, through better integration of the economics department with the financial function, the corporate economic staff has become a more relevant factor in capital budgeting analysis. They are involved in capital budgeting in two primary ways:

1. **They prepare a summarized list of standardized economic assumptions, which are distributed corporate-wide.** The economics department now concentrates on those parts of the economy perceived as most crucial in the long run, such as real growth of the economy, interest rates, and inflation. To distribute the forecast data, staff relies both on in-house publications and computer networks.

2. **They respond to ad hoc queries from local project analysts.** Automation has made it easier for corporate economists to get involved in the analysis for new project proposals. For example, if a review is under way to evaluate committing funds for a major

plant expansion in a certain country or region, an economist may be requested to estimate long-term product demand, inflation rates, or currency fluctuations. In one case, the Mexican subsidiary requested inflation forecasts before submitting their proposal for expanded operations to corporate headquarters. Said the economist working on the project, "My predictions were much higher and more realistic than those of the local staff. This changed their projected ROI, both in dollars and in local currency."

## Long-Term Portfolio Planning

Long-term portfolio planning addresses critical strategic issues: the impact of potential acquisitions, divestitures, and project investments on corporate profitability. Despite the necessity of such big-picture analysis, many firms have not yet devoted resources to computerizing the function. In fact, only 5% of firms are currently highly automated for long-term portfolio planning.

A common excuse for not automating is that long-term portfolio planning demands too much subjective input from a broad range of corporate departments. For example, a planning officer of a mainframe computer manufacturer stated that, "Long-term portfolio planning is a complicated activity that involves many people. Each year we look at the strategy for each of our businesses, including future product lines, of product volume, business area estimators, and technical people looking at product development. It's not just one or two guys who sit down in a room with a computer and decide when we're going."

Despite such resistance, the survey shows that over the next few years 13% of firms will be highly automated in this area. Currently, the main use of computers for long-term planning is PC-based analysis of mergers, acquisitions, and divestitures. For example, a $1 billion international consumer goods producer recently had to devise a divestment strategy for a shaky food services division. For assistance in assessing the impact of divesting the division, the firm turned to a PC-based software package. In the words of a spokesperson, "The package allowed us to use spreadsheets and input various selling prices to determine the divestiture's influence on earnings and earnings per share. We were able to run many iterations and figure out the best sales price for the unit."

On the other hand, a rapidly expanding telecommunications conglomerate comprised of seven separate firms is going beyond this relatively simple computer application for long-term portfolio planning. The firm is developing a state-of-the art optimization model to assess the company's portfolio of investment opportunities and provide a much-needed link between such planning and project analysis. The reason behind this need is that traditional systems usually rank or select one project over another. That is, projects are not assessed as an integrated whole. But the company's Capital Program Management System (CPMS) is, according to the director of capital development, planning "an optimization model that takes into account the synergies created by different projects given various constraints." The firm's planning department can thus evaluate alternative capital portfolios and see how well they meet both short-term and long-term financial requirements.

To analyze the interrelationship between several projects, known as investment clusters, the net present value of each project, subject to 50 constraints, is projected out within a five-year planning horizon. Management chose to evaluate net present value because it is a well-accepted measure of a firm's wealth. The various constraints are broken down into two broad categories:

1. **Resources**, including such items as labor hour limits, equipment delivery capacity, forecasts of equipment prices, and forecasts of demand for products and services.

---

### AUTOMATING POLITICAL RISK ANALYSIS

The survey shows that just 1% of firms are highly computerized for political risk analysis, and projects that figure will rise to only 3% over the next few years. The reason: Most companies do not believe that it is possible to create an objective model for analyzing what many managers consider to be a very subjective decision.

However, one chemical goods firm with over $4 billion in annual sales has created a very practical, PC-based political risk model for rating countries as potential investment sites. The model is "relatively simple," according to the corporate economist who created it. "We look at changes in government (movement toward conservatism or liberalism), the government's attitude towards foreign investment, its attitude towards remittance of funds (dividends or any other capital flows), the degree of export/import controls, and the government's attitude towards Western companies in particular. We use a scale of 0–10 for each of these variables."

When major changes occur, the relevant numbers are adjusted. "If there were a military government elected in Columbia, we might change the overall government rating from a six to an eight," stated the economist. "I feed in the new number with the already existing numbers and we come up with a weighted average."

The company has rated 15 countries which include the firm's 13 most strategic locations. These include Western Europe and a few of the emerging industrial nations, plus India and South Africa. "Most of the countries we've rated have the economic infrastructure to support considerable investment by our company," noted the economist.

2. **Financial,** including the amount of capital available, the percentage of internally generated funds and other limitations affecting the funding side of the investment. These constraints are gleaned from standardized financial data corresponding to pro forma statements regularly used in the company's financial planning system. For each planning year, 20 items of company financial data are required, including interest rate estimates for short- and long-term debt, debt retirement schedules, proscribed debt/equity levels and the effective income tax rate.

A huge database is necessary to perform the analysis in the CPMS. "We have something called a central office profile that describes the current plans now and for the next ten years. Marketing and service people are looking at the same data as planning people. We spend a lot of time on the data model. Defining common data elements was a major undertaking."

For example, the corporate planning staff recently analyzed five alternative project proposals generated by one of the operating companies. They used CPMS to evaluate capital funds required for the various projects by, for instance, comparing *Project A* with *Project B*, *Project A* with *Projects B* plus *C*, and so forth. The net present value of each of these investment clusters was then calculated. When a portfolio was finally selected, the decision resulted in a dramatically more efficient use of the company's financial and operational resources: Total capital for the chosen projects was reduced by 3% (with the same level of service) and engineering labor hours were slashed by 30%.

The benefits of the system to the firm as a whole were summed up by the spokesperson: "People now have access to the same information—common tables for discounting cash flow, access to current plans. Management can now test certain assumptions about net income—for example, what happens if we increase our requirement for net income next year; what would the investment portfolio look like? With the capital program management system, you can take data and analyze how it fits in with the overall direction for the company."

## CAPITAL STRUCTURE AND STRATEGY

When financial managers raise capital for long-term investments they have to make sure that their funding decisions follow the dictates of corporate debt/equity policy. Then they can go out and look for the least expensive sources of long-term funds in the marketplace.

Automation facilitates this process by permitting managers to review historic financing costs, consider the dilution effect of adding more equity, and evaluate the impact of dividend payout. Computers also help track the capital position of other firms in the same industry and plot various *what-if* scenarios for future financing strategies.

Despite the importance of these procedures, capital structure decisions are far less automated than other areas of financial planning. As can be seen in Table 3–10, less than 10% of respondents to the survey use computers heavily for critical aspects of the function.

The two major reasons for this trend were best explained by an

**TABLE 3–10**

**Percent of Respondents with Heavily Automated Capital Structure Systems**

| Procedure | At time of survey | Three-year projection |
|---|---|---|
| Long-term borrowing | 9 | 17 |
| Debt/equity structure | 8 | 16 |
| Dividend policy | 2 | 6 |

American financial planner: "Since capital structure decisions are subjective, long-term decisions, they aren't easily automated. On top of that, the people who make recommendations on capital structure are from a high level in our organization, and they don't use computers on a regular basis. Until the majority of senior managers get used to using PCs on a regular basis, quantitative analysis will take a backseat to intuition."

But a small vanguard of sophisticated companies are already computerizing capital structure decisions. And survey results indicate that the number of largely automated companies will double or even triple over the next few years in the functional areas discussed below.

**Long-Term Borrowing Decisions**

To make long-term borrowing decisions, companies must compare funding costs among different instruments and markets, as well as between internal and external financial alternatives. This procedure requires considerable interplay between treasury staff and financial planners. As one director of financial planning described it, "There is a distinction between *whether* we should borrow long-term and *how* we'll do it. The planners get involved with whether we should do it. The actual decision about how to follow through is a treasury function."

One firm that has successfully applied automation to long-term borrowing is a United States holding company that oversees a variety of industrial businesses. Recently, the firm's international treasury staff and financial planners combined forces to make a decision on whether a French affiliate should buy a European headquarters building or enter into a leaseback agreement.

Due to the centralized finance function in the firm, corporate staff had the final say on the project. According to the international treasurer, "The subsidiaries never make the decision on their own. Corporate's role was to review the basic assumptions made by the French company and to ask some very pointed questions." In this case, the French affiliate favored the leaseback option because of a corporate-wide policy of measuring foreign subsidiaries according to their return on assets employed. Corporate planners naturally wanted to consider both sides of the coin. To do this, they used a PC to run "the buy versus lease scenarios at least 15 times, because the assumptions kept changing. To crank that out by hand would have been really onerous." The firm also consulted with several French banks and American accounting experts.

In the process, the planning staff discovered that according to FASB 13, any leasing arrangement would be considered a financial lease, which would have to be shown on the balance sheet—thus eliminating any potential performance evaluation gain from leasing. "Once they were able to eliminate the question of reducing the assets, it became a bottom-line decision: Given a reasonable set of assumption, which was cheaper?"

At this point, treasury staff took over. Also using a PC spreadsheet, they compared fixed versus floating-rate financing and tried to determine where France was in its interest rate cycle. "As an independent decision, we decided to go with 12-year fixed financing," declared the spokesperson. "We felt that interest rates were at a cyclical low and would go up in the next few years."

The final decision to go with fixed-rate financing was facilitated by the use of a complex computerized model. "We look at financing alternatives by inputting a growth factor for the unit, various costs of funds and withholding rates, and alternative dividend repayment ratios to determine the overall impact on capital structure. Without this model, we could never have performed the analysis so quickly and efficiently."

## Debt/Equity Structure

Determining the appropriate mix of debt and equity for global operations can be a tricky task for multinational firms. Management must decide whether to standardize its capital structure corporate-wide, determine optimal rates for major operating divisions, or establish specific targets for each operating unit. Firms must then constantly monitor debt levels to ensure that corporate goals are being met.

At a diversified consumer goods firm, senior management keeps track of debt/equity ratios on a regular basis thanks to automation. "We are centralized for treasury management," stated the firm's director of financial planning, "which means that any debt decision is made here. We have a target ratio of 65 equity:35 debt. Given that, we are constantly looking at that calculation to see what our new cost of capital will be. We do it on a current basis and on a longer-term basis for acquisitions and capital expenditures. From that cost of capital, we build up to a targeted return on capital employed that is required by our operations to cover the taxes, corporate expenses, and the required return that our shareholders need. We use a spreadsheet that builds up from the various pieces to the required return."

Unlike most firms, which review debt/equity structure only occasionally, this conglomerate reviews debt/equity ratios each month. According to the director, "We don't change the debt/equity ratio, but we want to know the impact of the current market on our cost of capital. We realize that we couldn't survive and do the work we do without being automated in this area. We've made some significant acquisitions in recent years which added debt, and we had to know how much equity to issue."

## Setting Dividend Policy

Dividend planning may be divided into the two broad areas of setting the proper payout ratio on common stock to shareholders, and determining the appropriate level of dividend repatriation from foreign subsidiaries to parent headquarters.

Compared with other aspects of financial planning, calculating payout ratios is relatively easy to conduct and is thus rarely automated. As the financial planner of one high-tech firm put it, "Dividend policy is a minor aspect of financial planning and a natural by-product of putting together a profit plan and a balance sheet." However, some firms are finding that the gathering of data for such decisions can be greatly simplified and improved by tapping into databases for information on short- and long-range cash flow forecasts, dividend payout ratios of other firms in the same industry, historical dividend ratios, interest rate histories, and market yields of capital market securities.

In the case of automating dividend repatriation policy, the argument for automation is more compelling. To formulate the best strategy, companies must predict interest, foreign exchange, and tax rates in the parent country and in each of its foreign subsidiaries. For example, a United States multinational has to make remittance decisions for 60 subsidiaries in the Americas, Europe, Africa, and the Asia/Pacific region. The complexity of keeping track of that volume of data was described by the firm's financial planner: "In 60 countries everything is going up, down, and sideways every minute of every day. You've got to have some way to organize that information and set your priorities." To that end, the firm developed a PC-based spreadsheet with a global funds matrix that enables the planner to decide when to remit by forecasting the future dollar value of local funds. It tells how much the company should be willing to pay to bring local currency home (in terms of a discount on local currency, a withholding tax, or any other cost involved in bringing the funds out of the country).

The spreadsheet incorporates assumptions on interest rates, tax rates, and currency trends in each country from which a remittance is due. These are used to compute an attrition rate—a number that indicates how local investments will perform over a six-month period in dollar terms. The spreadsheet's inventor explained its value this way: "It's very important to quantify the capital-attrition factor. That's something that has to be worked out for each local currency. If a dollar in the local currency was remitted, can you calculate the composite effect of interest, income tax, and devaluation on that remittance? What is the ratio between the dollar that was remitted and the dollar that was not? That gives you a very easy rule for decision making."

"You've got to do it on a composite basis rather than on simply what the devaluation potential might be," added the manager, "because you can have countries with a low tax rate, a high interest rate, and a high devaluation rate. Just the fact that it's a high-devaluation country doesn't necessarily mean that the funds should be flowing out. It's got to be weighted by the other two."

"The best way to visualize it is to say there's an uphill and a downhill pipeline. If it's an uphill pipeline from that country to the United States, then the funds really are doing better by remaining in the country. If it's a downhill pipeline, then you will try to redouble your efforts to increase remittances."

The matrix is based on a simple remit/don't remit decision rule. Funds are remitted if the dollar after-tax return on six-month bank deposits is greater than the local currency after-tax return, adjusted for expected devaluation; funds are not remitted if the dollar after-tax return on six-month bank deposits is less than the local currency after-tax return, adjusted for expected devaluation. In other words: if $i(1-T)$, in dollars, is greater than $i(1-T)d$, in local currency, remit; if $i(1-T)$, in dollars, is less than $i(1-T)d$, in local currency, don't remit. [$i$ = interest rate; $T$ = tax rate; $d$ = devaluation rate]

The spreadsheet contains the following data:

A. **List of countries.**

B. **Six-month nominal investment rate.** A six-month term was chosen because it represented the average maturity of the company's global excess cash investments.

C. **Tax rate.** This is the tax rate applicable to interest income in the countries listed.

D. **After-tax investment rate.** This is the six-month local currency yield adjusted for taxes.

E. **1 + D.** The calculation begins with a $1 local currency equivalent. This column shows the yield on $1 after six months, before adjusting for devaluation.

F. **Last six months' devaluation rate.** Although not part of the calculations, these numbers provide a quick check on the currency forecast in column G. If the projections for devaluation in the next six months are dramatically different from actual devaluation in the last six months, the manager should be prepared to justify the difference.

G. **Next six months' devaluation rate.** These are taken from various external sources.

H. **1 – G.** This shows how many cents are left from each dollar after six months, before interest and taxes.

I.  **Composite effect.** This adjusts the after-tax return on a six-month investment for devaluation. It shows what $1 deposited locally would be worth in six months.

J.  **Ratio of local currency value to United States value.** This is the slope of the remittance pipeline. A number greater than one indicates an uphill slope from the subsidiary to the parent—in other words, a remittance that should be left in local currency. A number less than one shows a downhill slope: Excess liquidity should be pulled from the subsidiary. The lower the number, the more the corporation is losing on local funds and the more important it is to bring funds home.

K.  **Six-month attrition rate.** A negative number indicates a positive return. The number to beat is the United States attrition rate. The larger the positive number, the greater the loss to the company on local-currency funds.

By using this information wisely, the company can set time priorities and evaluate the cost of remittance alternatives.

### Automating Capital Structure Decisions: The State of the Art

A multi-billion dollar telecommunications giant has few peers in its commitment to sophisticated decision-support systems. After an extensive search for an outside vendor in the late 1970s, the firm decided that XSIM, available through Chase Econometrics/Interactive Data Corp, was the most powerful software package that fit its requirements.

By using XSIM, the firm now has access to all of Chase's databases. Such access to external sources of data was considered critical to supporting top management in making strategic decisions. The firm also currently taps into two other external databases—Data Resources Inc., and Standard and Poor's COMPUSTAT. These three databases provide strategic and financial planners with complete economic and competitor information.

The system, which runs on a mainframe at the company's operations center, has been used to develop two general purpose tools for financial managers: the EDSS (Executive Decision Support System) and CDSS (Corporate Decision Support System). The EDSS is very simple to use, provides quick access to key financial items in the database and is used directly by senior management for data retrieval.

For complex sensitivity and statistical analysis, the staff relies on CDSS. A key component of this tool is a mainframe capital structuring model that includes 900 different equations, which treasury and planning analysts use to determine long-term capitalization policies. Its speed and accuracy is relied on heavily. For instance, "A couple of years ago we ran over 300 iterations in playing with debt/equity structure and dividend policy—do I need more shares, what coverage targets are appropriate?" stated the director of financial strategies.

Specifically, the company employs the model to help make decisions in the following areas:

- **Debt/equity structure.** The firm adheres to standardized corporate debt/equity targets. "We're trying to strengthen our equity ratios 44% by year's end because we are a weak A– rating and our policy is to become a strong A. By strengthening our credit rating, we hope to minimize our cost of capital," the spokesperson explained. The company uses the mainframe model to run alternative scenarios and arrive at target levels.

- **Dividend planning.** The company uses the model to determine how various changes in dividend levels, share issuance programs, and stock market prices will impact corporate earnings and debt/equity ratios. "Dividend payout affects your equity ratio. The more you pay out, the more equity that is drained out of the company. You can achieve your debt/equity ratio by constraining dividends or by issuing less debt. I can measure the impact of increasing my dividend by 10 cents a year versus 20 cents a year on reaching our targeted debt/equity ratio by the year 1990."

- **Long-term borrowing.** The spokesperson relies on a PC to analyze the shape of the company's liability portfolio's maturity curve, that is, "How much of a debt will be retired in each of the next 25 years to make sure that a new issue will not create a big spike?" The mainframe model is also used to run scenario analyses on worldwide financing options.

According to the spokesperson, the firm's decision support system cannot be justified on cost reduction alone, which is the usual rationale for most computer applications. "It does take less time to do an analysis, but the major benefit is that a good DSS allows you to assess critical data that simply could not be digested in the past. In an environment where billions of dollars are at stake, preventing one bad decision can justify the cost of our systems many times over."

## TAX PLANNING

Tax planning is an integral part of the entire finance function. As one tax director put it, "We're the last link in treasury and accounting decisions. They always have to consider the tax implications of their decisions so we need to interact with them efficiently."

Multinational companies must devote special attention to this area because they have several rapidly shifting tiers of regulations to consider. They must constantly evaluate local tax laws affecting overseas subsidiaries in addition to the parent state and federal tax statutes. As one spokesperson for a high-tech conglomerate put it, "When you're dealing with taxes, you want to be a little more careful about the recommendations you make. To really handle things, you need the capability of quick turnaround, which only the computer can give you."

Making decisions faster is only one of the benefits reaped from automating tax planning. Other advantages include improved relations between tax planning and treasury and accounting departments. And, in fact, many firms are establishing PC links to treasury and accounting databases to speed up that communication.

Staff reduction is another key benefit. According to one director of tax planning at a high-tech firm, "We'd probably have 100 people instead of 50 working in this area if we didn't have computers."

Despite the attractions of computerized tax planning, the number of firms that have acted on the issue is surprisingly low. According to the survey, only 8% of respondents are highly automated for tax planning. But the survey results also reveal that this situation will turn around over the next few years, and that the figure should more than triple to 26%.

There are two major reasons for this anticipated growth in computerized tax planning: (1) the growing complexity of international tax law, especially in the United States, and (2) the availability of PC software that can handle the unique tax profiles of each country and company. Let's examine these issues in turn and then consider a case study.

The first issue is the growing complexity of international tax laws, especially in the United States. The recent United States tax reform act completely altered how companies can use foreign tax credits, and has forced firms to rethink their worldwide tax strategies. As a result, firms are becoming more insistent that tax planning must be centrally coordinated, a task greatly eased by automation.

A chemicals firm with 75 overseas subsidiaries serves as a good example of how firms can use automation to centralize tax planning. Since 1984, the company has required its operating units to transmit all basic financial data—P&Ls and balance sheets—through a computer to parent headquarters, where the information is then stored in the corporate accounting database. All European operations send the data first to regional headquarters, which relays information to corporate. Subsidiaries in other parts of the world transmit directly to headquarters.

The information stored in the mainframe is downloaded to PCs so that the tax department can test different scenarios about the impact of alternative tax and exchange rates on such critical matters as dividend repatriation policy. According to the firm's manager of international tax planning, "We now have a system of data gathering so we can make informed decisions about dividends. Before computers, we'd say, 'Sure, send us the money back to the States.' Now we can look at the tax consequences. The ROI on the computer system for tax planning has been fantastic."

But the transition to a highly automated centralized tax planning function has not been entirely smooth. In the words of a spokesperson, the company is "very highly entrepreneurial, which leads to problems in information gathering. There's a long lead-in time from the foreign units over to here. There are all sorts of problems with data transmission. We get all sorts of interesting excuses as to why the numbers didn't get in."

But despite these problems, and especially because of the new tax law, the firm remains committed to automation and centralization.

According to the spokesperson, "The new tax law means that we have to start from scratch with the software. There are so many changes made that it's like starting from square one. We'll have to have more contact with the foreign units to see what's going on in terms of their taxes."

To accomplish these goals, the company is adopting a two-pronged strategy. First, the firm plans to standardize the software used overseas for the operating units' tax analysis. Initially, the international tax manager hopes to send software developed by a Big Eight firm to the more active subsidiaries. Second, the company is attempting to upgrade the link between the international tax planning unit and the corporate treasury and accounting departments by installing a PC network. Currently, these groups communicate inefficiently with paper. In the future, the company predicts, "There'll be a PC set up in every person's office tied in to the mainframe. We won't have to wait to get data printed for an overnight run."

The second major reason for predicted growth in automating rests on the availability of improved software packages and PCs that can handle the unique needs of tax planning. Until recently, most tax planners were often dissatisfied with existing software and often lacked the expertise to develop their own. The attitude of one planner at a major chemicals firm is typical: "If you can find a computer program that can handle taxes in foreign countries and domestically, you've got yourself a winner. I haven't found anybody who can do that."

The main problem is that each firm has a unique tax profile. Therefore, any software package has to be tailored to the peculiarities of a company's tax situation in a particular country. For example, a firm in France might be taking advantage of an incentive program that effectively lowers its tax rate by 5%. But an off-the-shelf model would need a lot of work before it could reflect this circumstance. As one tax planner pointed out, "If a treasurer wants to bring $100 million out of France, there is no general model to quantify the tax implications of a dividend decision. Simply automating a rate change won't give you the answers."

But times are changing. Sophisticated software packages are now being created so quickly that many companies may be overlooking opportunities for efficient applications of tax automation. According to a spokesperson for one Big Eight firm, "Our market research shows there is a tremendous lack of awareness as to what's available. When people say they're automated for compliance, they generally mean they have a way to get the calculations put on the form."

Two of the more popular kinds of software marketed today are tax treaty databases for broader strategic tax planning and tax compliance software to help firms calculate the implications of specific tax programs and incentives.

Touche Ross's World Tax Planner is a good example of a PC-based tax treaty database. The program includes the tax rates of 185 countries updated monthly—individual withholding taxes on dividends, interest and royalties, plus tax treaty information on 800 pacts. The software can provide 15 alternative scenarios for remittance decisions and print out the calculations behind the recommendations.

For example, if a firm wanted to repatriate funds from Spain, the program would calculate the tax rate on dividends remitted from Spain as well as what the difference would be if the funds were remitted indirectly through other countries such as Germany or France. The recommendation would be based on the database of taxation treaties and laws regarding dividends in the particular countries.

According to one user of the package, the director of tax planning for a multinational retail group, "The system is unique. It's the only one that integrates all of the treaty network around the world to help a firm decide about transferring funds, making new investments or any other cross-border transactions. Of course, even though the software is updated monthly, you have to verify the tax laws and do a follow-up with your local people." However, the package has improved the firm's turnaround time on making decisions and has been especially important because the company is thinly staffed for its centralized finance function that handles the tax planning for all of its foreign operations.

The big issue now for tax compliance software is the new tax law. In the past, Big Eight accounting firms were able to offer compliance packages in anticipation of new laws. For example, in 1984, in response to the pending Foreign Sales Corporation law, Price Waterhouse offered MAXIFSC, which was designed to aid compliance. But the complexity of the new tax law dwarfs other tax legislation in its range, and complexity makes it difficult for firms to automatically produce new software.

Under the new legislation, income will be siphoned into passive and active income baskets, with separate baskets for royalties, interest, dividends, and rents. For many firms with multiple foreign subsidiaries, the new law will require hundreds or even thousands of baskets. Because most tax software is PC-based, storage of such voluminous data could be somewhat problematic. Said the director of corporate software at one Big Eight firm, "We have some people that have as many as 5000 baskets. The only limit to the number of baskets you can have is the amount of hard disk space on your PC."

### Case Example: One Company's Approach to Computerized Tax Planning

A high-tech firm with 35 overseas entities has devised an on-line mainframe-based tax planning system to communicate quickly and accurately both internationally with overseas operations and interdepartmentally between the tax planning function and corporate treasury and accounting. The firm has used the system for four years and, in the words of the firm's tax planning director, has made tax planning "more reactive. There is now better communication between accounting, treasury and tax planning. People can't keep the key data in their desk drawers. Anybody can access it through their terminals. If you know how to manage the mainframe, you can change assumptions a lot more quickly and get a printout in regard to those changed assumptions. If you had to do it manually everybody would throw up their hands and say 'that's not possible.' " PCs are not used for this function because of the capacity and power requirements for compliance tasks.

Data from each of the 35 countries are electronically sent to three regional headquarters, which then transmit information to corporate headquarters. The data are culled from the controller's reporting system on the 10th and 11th workdays at the end of the month. The company chose this periodic reporting scheme because they discovered that they could not do dividend planning at year-end. They had to monitor it on a monthly basis.

The tax department reviews the incoming data and then discusses the tax implications with tax staff overseas and treasury staff in the United States. The level of computer use at this stage then depends on the issue or subject. Intercompany pricing and distribution of profits on a legal entity basis is heavily automated. The data reports are generated directly from the controller's computer, which allows tax planners to recommend changes for intercompany pricing. They also use the database for dividend planning, but that requires further manual manipulation and a fair amount of discussion with the treasury people after data is received from the controller's staff.

The spokesperson remarked that the system has enabled tax related decisions to be made much faster: "For example, on dividend planning, we can quickly come to a conclusion on which dividends should be repatriated from which of our 35 foreign entities. The treasury people have to look at their cash balances and their forex cover included in their own system. If they end up being too long on dollars in a particular country than in local currency they may start a campaign for dividend repatriation to strip out excess cash. Automation makes it easier for us to honor their request."

In the past, the firm used a Big Eight software package to help determine one of the major issues of foreign tax planning—how to allocate domestic expenses to foreign-source income according to what was permitted under the 61-8 regulations. The software package was critical to these decisions because it helped in the choice of how to minimize United States tax liability. Included in the package were the earnings and profits of each of the countries and the taxes paid according to each of the companies' earnings. The staff liked this planning tool because they could change the assumptions once all the data was into their database. Then, different analyses could be run.

Each year, the package helped the firm to examine the key issue of whether to allocate expenses to gross receipts, to net income, or to adjusted gross income. The tax rates were provided by the firm because the tax director believed that an outside CPA firm would know the statutory rate but would not necessarily know which tax planning opportunity the company had taken advantage of—its rate could be higher or lower than the one stipulated in the package.

But gradually the firm grew to believe that using the software package was overkill. Noted a spokesperson, "We found that on audits, the IRS officials were doing their calculations on the back of an envelope. Since that worked out to our advantage we stopped using the Big Eight database. The IRS may get more sophisticated—they have new PCs and the agents are supposed to use them. Right now they're using them as word processors. When they start to use them as true computers we might revise our strategy."

On the compliance side, the firm is currently buying a service called CORPTAX, which allows it to massage the federal and state returns that are printed off that database. The package permits the tax department to change assumptions on state income tax returns depending on the current state of the law. Commented the tax director, "On the one hand, states have become aggressive for foreign-sourced income, for example unitary tax. On the other hand, many companies have challenged them in court and have won. You need to do more than just read the code and the regulations. You have to understand what's happening in that state and be on the cutting edge of the new judicial developments and what people are setting up as audit issues against the various states. What we do is perpetually keep in the loop with a number of outside organizations and then input that into the return before it's finalized. We have inputs from our database, load it into their database and give instructions with regard to various assessments and they will print off data that ends up being the return."

The tax planning director anticipates that the new United States tax reform act will change the way its foreign earnings are reported and dividends are remitted. Although the firm has not fully formulated its strategy, they have decided to change the dates on which foreign taxes are reported and the dates on which foreign earnings are exchanged into United States dollars.

In sum, this firm's experience with automating has been mixed. The external readjustment dictated by the new tax laws, as much as the internal tendency to become too sophisticated for the needs of the business, has forced the firm to reevaluate its automation strategy. Their response has been a clearer and more concise use of resources along with a continued open mind about automation.

## SUMMARY

Automating financial planning is projected to run a close second to computerizing reporting and consolidating accounting data in the next few years. According to the FERF study, the percentage of firms giving top priority to automating the financial planning function is expected to swell from a base level of 10% to a respectable 37%. In tandem, the number of firms that will commit to automating this function will triple. This phenomenon is backed by some summary statistics; North American firms are leading the automation pack (21% highly automated), as are firms with over $2 billion in annual sales (20%), and intermediate goods firms (21%). The study also reveals that, like the treasury function, financial planning is a function that will become more centralized with automation (refer to Chapter 1 for a discussion of centralized, decentralized, and regionalized approaches to corporate organization). When asked to assess automation's impact on organization, 38% of the respondents expect that financial planning will become more centralized at parent or regional headquarters because of automation, whereas 18% feels that automation will make their firms more decentralized.

Given the components of any effective financial planning system, FERF respondents believed that the hierarchy of automation was as follows: in operational budgeting—forecasting earnings, forecasting funds requirements, and performance evaluation; in capital budgeting—project investment analysis, forecasting financial trends, long-term portfolio planning, and political risk analysis; and, in capital structuring—long-term borrowing, debt/equity structure, and dividend policy. Aside from these key parts of the planning system, automation is also spreading to tax planning with limited success.

There are two recurring themes that affect the automation of these components directly—the availability and quality of software packages to evaluate this data and the corporate commitment to subscribe to databases from which to draw auxillary data and in which to store company-specific information. While many companies have been eager to purchase software to assist in financial planning, the paucity of adequate resources has been alarming until recently. And, due to the unique needs of each company—especially those which are multinational and have currency translation, devaluation, and tax concerns in units around the globe—it has been exceptionally difficult to find packages that meet the express needs of each company. As was discussed in Chapter 1, the costs associated with tailoring a program to meet special requirements can be exhorbitant. Thus, the high degree of reluctance to automate this front is completely understandable and justifiable on the bottom line. However, the cost of databases has not been a deterring factor.

Rather, they have counterbalanced the software problem to a degree. Due to the fact that the accounting function is so highly computerized and that it rests easily in databases, the way has been cleared for companies to buy into commercial databases and to make room for the nesting of their own in corporate systems.

The first step has been accomplished easily, and only the problem of overmassaging the data that exists can be related to the second. The general mode of operation, however, is the same in most companies. Databases with both commercial and proprietary information are loaded onto mainframes in a central facility, and planners (and whatever management chooses to do) downloads the data sets needed for a specific inquiry onto a PC, where it is fed into a spreadsheet and analyzed. The results of the analysis are generally used for discussion and the results, if satisfactory, are uploaded for further review.

Consequently, the analysts are eager for good software that can be easily adapted to company needs, and the planners are delighted in the generally used system of downloading information from a mainframe. The inadequacy now lies in the data, which, due to the nature of the game, is never static.

# PART 2

# Automating Treasury Management

# CHAPTER 4

# An Overview

## INTRODUCTION

It is no wonder that efficient treasury management has become a paramount concern for multinational companies. In their drive to maximize internal use of funds, reduce borrowing costs, and minimize foreign exchange risk, firms face several formidable challenges. For one thing, interest rate and currency swings have become increasingly dramatic and unpredictable. For another, the liberalization of money and currency markets in Europe and Asia, aided by rapid technological advances, is creating a truly global, integrated financial marketplace where firms can use and apply the latest financial tools. This radically changed world financial environment seriously complicates the treasury function, posing new opportunities and risks that can save, or cost, companies literally millions of dollars.

In line with these developments, few areas of corporate finance have received as much attention in recent years as treasury and treasury automation. To solve complex cash and currency management problems, for example, respondents to the survey are turning to computers. The percentage of firms with highly automated treasury operations will triple from 16% to 52% in a few years, the highest projected growth rate for any area of the finance function examined in this study. And, at least 90% of respondents will introduce computers in some part of their treasury operations over the same time frame.

The experience of a multinational corporation in France illustrates the trend toward treasury automation. This $7.5 billion equipment manufacturer operates in all major regions of the world. Until the early 1980s, the firm was flush with cash, funding itself primarily through advance payments from large OPEC and Third World customers. All billings for exports, which account for about two thirds of the company's sales, was done in francs. The resulting rosy financial picture showed no major borrowings, no currency exposure, and, therefore, no need for sophisticated treasury systems.

That all changed with the worldwide recession. With OPEC wealth declining and the debt crisis in many developing countries ballooning, the firm watched its healthy cash inflow from export sales dissipate. Almost overnight the company had to become a heavy borrower in both its domestic market and in the Euromarkets. Additionally, its overseas customers began to demand billing in other currencies besides the franc, forcing the company to work with nearly 20 monetary units.

Deeply in debt and facing massive currency exposures, the firm brought in a new finance director with experience at an innovative American firm. The CFO described his mission: "We have one goal as a company: to make money and make it fast. And treasury management means money."

The finance director swiftly mapped out an overhaul of the firm's treasury system. As an integral part of the process, he introduced sophisticated automated systems for treasury management. The domestic subsidiaries were given terminals linked to a microcomputer system at corporate treasury. This system was then connected directly with seven concentration banks used by the company to administer a centralized cash pooling system. The banks provided electronic balance reports, transaction initiation capabilities, and automatic account reconciliation. On the international side, the CFO implemented a multilateral netting system and used a Netherlands-based finance company to handle financing and exposure management for the American, European, and Asian subsidiaries.

The CFO is confident his massive investment in computer systems will pay off. "We will have easier reconciliation, better control, lower forex and borrowing costs, and reduced funds transfers. But what you can quantify in savings through good treasury management is only a fraction of what you can save by improved liquidity and exposure management. This cannot be calculated; nobody knows how much automation can save you."

## The Appeal of Automation

Corporate fascination with automated treasury systems began in the late 1970s and early 1980s with the deteriorating economy and high interest rates. Research reveals six primary reasons for this attraction: pressure on profits, the desire to limit treasury staff, the need for hard data, the growing sophistication of global markets, the paucity of systems now available, and marketing efforts by software vendors. Let us touch on each of these subjects briefly.

First, to help boost sagging bottom lines, many firms are seeking improved treasury operations. For example, a United States electronics firm set up a highly automated in-house factoring company in Geneva in the early 1980s. In a single year, the center showed profits of $600,000. The center also saved the corporate group $750,000 in reduced foreign exchange losses, $150,000 in funds transfer costs, and $333,000 in lower borrowing expenses. The combinations of profits and cost efficiencies thus totalled nearly $2 million.

Second, computers can help ensure that treasury department staff size does not grow exhorbitantly when confronted with a greater volume of information and a higher degree of complexity in the financial markets. For example, the treasurer of a rapidly growing $2 billion United States high-tech manufacturer estimated that his nine-member staff would increase to at least 14 people if they did not use computers. In the same vein, because of its automated system, a Swedish auto giant needs only a skeletal staff to record 25,000 foreign exchange transactions per year and to generate bank confirmation letters.

Third, at the heart of every efficient treasury management lies the gathering and management of accurate information. Companies cannot hedge currency exposures unless they know about them and they cannot develop investing and borrowing strategies unless they have timely information at all stages of the cash cycle. "Treasury management is entirely dependent on information," said a bank treasury consultant, "and that is why computers can play such a dramatic role."

Fourth, computers and electronic services help treasurers keep pace with the growing sophistication and complexity of global financial markets and intracorporate cash flows. One international finance manager summed up the situation this way: "There are a lot more problems, and a lot more ways to solve them than have existed in the past. All these new markets have opened up—the options markets, interest rate futures, stock and currency swaps. Pushing a pencil on the back of an envelope is becoming a less sophisticated way of doing it—and a less accurate way."

Fifth, because accounting and control typically receive first priority in financial automation, there is a low degree of treasury automation now. Therefore, more opportunities exist to streamline operations. "Treasury has remained an untapped area for automation," declared a bank consultant. "It therefore has the greatest opportunity for putting automated systems in place. It is now going through a rapid growth period and catching up with where a lot of the other parts of the institution already are."

Finally, intense marketing efforts by banks and the media spotlight have focused on financial software applications. As the treasurer of a United States manufacturer put it, "It's the buzzword these days. Treasury management systems seem to be the thing. Once the word gets around, it's just like designer clothes or anything else."


### Looking Ahead

To start helping companies understand automated treasury systems, this chapter will present an overview of the subject. It will first examine what types of companies are the best candidates for computerized treasury management, and then discuss two critical issues: how firms are automating the reporting and analysis of treasury data, and what hardware and software decisions they must make to do so. The chapter concludes with two contrasting corporate approaches to automated treasury management.

Subsequent chapters will focus on computerizing four key areas of treasury management:

**Cash management:** Chapter 5 explores how companies use computers to upgrade every aspect of the cash cycle; from reporting and forecasting, to receivables and disbursement management; short-term borrowings and investments; and banking relations.

**Currency management:** Chapter 6 examines the state of the art in automated forex reporting and forecasting, monitoring currency contracts, and making transaction and balance sheet hedging decisions.

**Cross-border treasury systems:** Chapter 7 discusses the latest computer applications for the full range of cross-border techniques and vehicles—leading and lagging, cash pooling, netting, reinvoicing, and in-house factoring.

**Electronic banking:** Chapter 8 details sophisticated banking services specifically designed to support the treasury function, including automated balance reporting, electronic transaction initiation, and treasury workstations.

## WHICH COMPANIES COMPUTERIZE GLOBAL TREASURY SYSTEMS

Although many firms are, or will be, automating the treasury function, not all are proceeding at the same pace. The survey reveals that the level of treasury computerization differs among companies according to the following key variables: size, domicile, type of organizational structure, and industry type. The following paragraphs enlarge on the specifics of each of these.

### Size of Company

As can be seen in Table 4–1, large firms, measured both by number of foreign operating units and level of sales, are spearheading the move toward highly automated treasury systems.

The assistant treasurer of a software design company explained

**TABLE 4–1**

**Percent of Respondents with Highly Automated Treasury Systems**

| Sales | At time of survey | Three-year projection |
|---|---|---|
| Over $2 billion | 25 | 55 |
| $500 million - $2 billion | 18 | 62 |
| $200 million - $499 million | 13 | 50 |
| Under $200 million | 4 | 32 |
| **Number of Foreign Units** | | |
| Over 40 | 24 | 61 |
| 21-40 | 20 | 65 |
| 11-20 | 11 | 52 |
| 6-10 | 11 | 42 |
| 1-5 | 17 | 46 |

this trend: "The larger the company, the stronger the need for a complete and total system. It's primarily a function of size in terms of currency exposures, cash flows, and investment activity." Although the larger companies will continue to lead the pack over the next few years, the survey also reveals that a vanguard of small and medium-sized companies are planning to adopt computerized treasury management techniques. These firms are generally poised for strong growth and are taking steps now to automate their treasury procedures before the function gets out of control.

## Country of Domicile

North American firms show a much higher degree of automation in treasury than European or Asian companies, as shown in Table 4–2.

The explanation for this trend is that much of the advanced computer technology, especially in the micro-based systems that are

**TABLE 4–2**

**Percent of Respondents with Highly Automated Treasury Systems**

| Location | At time of survey | Three-year projection |
|---|---|---|
| North America | 21 | 54 |
| Europe | 11 | 49 |
| Asia | 0 | 46 |

so critical to treasury management, was developed in North America. North American firms have thus been acquainted with and exposed to computers that have ready business applications longer than companies in other regions. However, as the table shows, times might change. The pace of growth of automated treasury systems among European and Asian firms is projected to be exponential over the next few years. According to the survey, Europeans will increase their use of highly automated systems more than fourfold, while Asian companies, who have no systems now, will buy in to almost 50% use.

### Global Treasury Organization

Centralized and regionalized companies tend to be more automated for overall treasury management than decentralized firms, as shown in Table 4–3.

Companies in which control of treasury operations resides at parent or regional headquarters need computers to manage the overwhelming amount of data required by centralization. As a finance officer at a large United States services firm put it, "When our growth rates were high, we could tolerate a policy of decentralization. But now we see that we must have more central direction. And one of the first things to do when a company like ours centralizes is to set up a good cash and currency exposure reporting and forecasting system—an underlying framework so that you can build up a good treasury management system. So we are beginning to look into computers."

## Industry Type

The survey shows that with the exception of high technology companies, the various industrial categories are basically on par for the

**TABLE 4–3**

**Percent of Respondents with Highly Automated Treasury Systems**

| Type of organization | At time of survey | Three-year projection |
|---|---|---|
| Centralized | 17 | 55 |
| Regionalized | 17 | 60 |
| Decentralized | 14 | 45 |

**TABLE 4–4**

**Percent of Respondents Who Have Highly Automated Treasury Systems**

| Type of Industry | At time of survey | Three-year-projection |
|---|---|---|
| High technology | 20 | 56 |
| Intermediate goods | 16 | 60 |
| Capital goods | 16 | 50 |
| Consumer goods | 15 | 47 |
| Service | 14 | 50 |

current and projected levels of treasury management automation, as shown in Table 4–4.

High-technology firms currently rank high in treasury because they manufacture the hardware and software used to computerize the function. As the spokesperson for one such company explained, "We're a software firm. We need to be on the leading edge of technology, and to show our products in the best light we need to be able to tell customers not only that this company and that company use our stuff, but we use it ourselves."

## COMPUTERIZED REPORTING AND ANALYSIS OF TREASURY DATA

Although specific computer applications exist for each aspect of treasury management, the general process can be divided into two basic elements. The first is subsidiary-to-parent reporting of cash and currency information, and the second is massaging and manipulating data for analysis, decision making, and management reports. These are examined in detail in the sections that follow.

### HOW AUTOMATION IMPACTS TREASURY ORGANIZATION—AND VICE VERSA

The processes of centralization and computerization sustain and support each other at most firms. Not only do centralized companies tend to be more automated, but advanced computer technology makes centralizing operations easier than ever before.

The survey reveals that 65% of firms have a centralized treasury function, which is a higher percentage than for any other aspect of finance covered in this study. The reason is that centralized companies reap the twin benefits of economies of scale and the concentration of treasury expertise.

For instance, a United States glass manufacturer recently created a highly automated regional treasury center in Europe. According to one company manager, "There's just two people in that office, so we really needed automation to get a handle on things. Prior to that, we didn't have any centralized treasury management. The controller of each of the different subs would go out and do his own foreign exchange transactions and manage his own cash and banking relations. So it made for a lot of small transactions performed on an occasional basis. He explained his firm's rationale for automating: "This system will pull a lot of it together. We'll cut down on the number of transactions and we'll get better rates due to the larger transactions."

The foreign exchange manager of a highly centralized United States automaker argued for the pooling of expertise, in that effective treasury management requires a company to "put talented people together to practice the state of the art. The kind of talent you need, to stay at the edge of what is the state of the art in dealing with these issues, is a scarce commodity. You can't get it located around the world for you. You can't have 55 different people at different subsidiaries stay closely in touch with the financial community."

As firms become more familiar with hardware and software capabilities, they can rationalize global treasury operations and obtain these benefits for themselves. According to the statistics, 45% of respondents believe that treasury management will become more centralized thanks to the use of computers. Again, this is higher than for any other area of the finance function. Additionally, for those respondents already centralized, computers have an even stronger affect: 54% of centralized respondents and 53% of regionalized respondents reported that the increased use of computers had centralized treasury operations even further.

The finance director of an electronics firm explained why computers had this impact on his firm: "With the developments

> in telecommunications, electronic banking and computer soft-
> ware in general, you need less and less decentralization because
> information is available to one point." That one point, a com-
> puter system, will be discussed later in this chapter.

## Subsidiary-to-Parent Reporting

Timely, effective reporting is the lifeblood of any treasury management system. As Table 4–5 shows, companies currently retrieve data
from subsidiaries primarily through mail, telexes, facsimile, telephone, computer-to-computer links, or computer diskettes. However, the percentage of respondents using computer-to-computer
links to receive treasury information from subsidiaries will increase
from 14 to 39% over the next few years, while those collecting data
with computer disks will grow from 4 to 13%. Use of other, more
traditional, communication modes will fall markedly over the same
time horizon.

A number of factors account for the current low level of automated reporting systems. Many foreign subsidiaries, especially those
in less developed nations, still do not have access to sophisticated,
dependable hardware and software and must rely on the traditional
data transmission modes. Furthermore, some nations lack adequate
telecommunications facilities and reliable bank reporting services,
so that even traditional methods may be plagued with difficulties. A
Philippine MNC, for example, must rely on cars, trucks, jeeps, and
even canoes to gather information from its 120 sales offices and 17
regional headquarters. To facilitate data transmission, according to
the firm's treasurer, the company is attempting "to tie all of our area
offices together by citizens band radio because there aren't telecommunications everywhere."

**TABLE 4–5**

**How Foreign Operating Units Report to Corporate Treasury***

|  | Computer link | disk | Tele-phone | Mail | Telex | Fac-simile |
|---|---|---|---|---|---|---|
| At time of survey | 14 | 4 | 22 | 65 | 50 | 27 |
| Three-year projection | 39 | 13 | 15 | 41 | 33 | 21 |

*Total may add to more than 100% due to multiple responses.

An unfavorable regulatory environment may also prevent the development of effective computer systems. For example, Brazil imposes restrictions on the import of foreign-made computers, and Korea tightly regulates the cross-border flow of computer information.

Even when these technical and regulatory issues are overcome, the installation of telecommunications links may be thwarted because of organizational sensitivities. For example, because such links give headquarters more direct control over information and performance, local personnel—particularly those in recently acquired firms—may resent or even fear this invasion. Said the assistant treasurer of a decentralized natural resources firm: "My hands are pretty much tied. A lot of our companies have been acquired on the basis that they would remain independent. They believe that subsidiaries should be autonomous financially, too. They refuse to give up their power."

Finally, in some countries' companies are unable to establish cross-border links because staff with telecommunications skills are unavailable or extremely expensive. But in spite of the myriad problems, the benefits to be obtained from a computerized reporting system generally make the task worth the time and effort. Interviewed survey respondents enumerated the following advantages to direct telecommunications links with foreign subsidiaries:

First, they cited the advantage of speedy data transmission. Computer-to-computer reporting systems remove inefficiencies in the communications process because companies can avoid lost time in the telex or mail rooms on either end, and there is less chance of garbled messages. There is also no need to rekey (and possibly miskey) data. As the assistant treasurer of one United States multinational remarked, "We have a very lean treasury staff and want to avoid the redundancy of someone in the home office inputting manual subsidiary reports. It's a waste of our time."

Second, they noted that they have easier access to data. Because computer links offer two-way communication, corporate treasurers do not have to wait for subsidiaries to compile and telephone or telex their reports. As the treasurer of a capital goods manufacturer said, "The point is that you can get a lot of data in different formats and access it a lot easier to get what you want, not what someone else wants to give you."

Third, they agreed on the benefit of lower costs. Once telecommunications lines are established, a major advantage of computer links is transmission cost. But to ensure cost-effectiveness, firms should put subsidiaries on-line on a case-by-case basis. For example, one United States manufacturer prepares cash and exposure forecasts based on daily sales orders generated by the group's subsidiaries and agents for cash forecasting purposes. Sales orders are input into the system in one of three ways, depending on the subsidiary's size. In countries with high commercial volume, orders are sent in via computer between subsidiaries and headquarters. For lower-volume countries, a cheaper system is used, in which telexed information is automatically input into the mainframe without manual intervention. In very low-volume countries, sales reports are sent by telex and input manually into the computer. In short, the purpose matches the medium.

### Information Analysis at Headquarters

Any subsidiary information a parent receives needs to be consolidated, massaged, and augmented with data from other areas to provide a sound basis for effective decisions. The survey reveals that treasury staffs use computers for the decision-support functions shown in Table 4–6.

### Financial Modeling

Often referred to as *what-if* analysis, computerized financial models project the consequences of an assumed change in one or more

**TABLE 4–6**

**Use of Decision Support Services**

| Types of service | At time of survey | Three-year projection |
|---|---|---|
| Financial modeling | 20 | 47 |
| Retrieval of information from a central database | 16 | 53 |
| Input from external databases | 15 | 43 |
| Statistical analysis | 14 | 43 |

variables. They are used by treasury staff to compare borrowing and hedging options given specific interest rate and exchange rate forecasts. The modeling package employed by one American MNC, for example, instantly recalculates all cash and currency positions based on projected swings in exchange and interest rates. The model, in effect, helps financial staff to anticipate possible problems, and to avert future crises. For that reason, 20% of survey respondents use these tools now and 47% will do so in the future.

For many companies, the foremost application of computer models is for cash flow forecasting. For example, one firm has developed a cyclical model of its business. According to the international finance manager of this consumer goods firm, "We take historical information on what happened to the balance sheet throughout the year, what levels of inventory we can expect at different times. The model uses all that information to forecast our cash flows. For a company like ourselves, that can be vital because we are subject to very sharp seasonal variations."

One company that needs a very sophisticated modeling package is a Philippine copper firm. According to a company spokesperson, the company has to consider "government requirements, restrictions, foreign exchange, and both internal and external factors." In response, the firm built a computer model to enable the finance staff to conduct sensitivity analyses of factors, such as copper prices, refining costs, foreign exchange movements, and inflation and interest rates. The results allow analysts to do extensive what-if exercises. And, to forecast currency movements, the firm depends primarily on inflation rate differentials. "If the inflation rate here is so much and the United States dollar is getting stronger by a certain percentage, then we try to calculate how much the peso will depreciate," says a spokesperson. Once the finance staff has chosen the scenarios that seem most probable, the computer generates a full forecast for the following year.

### Retrieval of Information from a Central Database

Many companies want not only current reports from overseas units but access to historical treasury data and information. Software programs that allow easy queries into database storage files permit treasury staff to construct such complete overall pictures of a company's financial situation. According to the statistics, 16% of respondents currently use computers to access information from a central database and that number will rise to 53% over the next few years.

A treasury manager of a United States automaker explained the benefit of his company's centralized treasury database: "One of our jobs is to act as general financial staff. If a question comes up, which may boil down to our chairman wants to know something, we need to be able to get at the information quickly. Without a central computerized database, how do you get it in a standardized format that's understandable and has been checked for errors so that it doesn't take an entire day of someone working full time to answer a single question?"

However, a database with subsidiary input and treasury-specific information should not be the only source of data for treasury management. The accounting department and other areas of the company may receive and store valuable treasury management information, and it is becoming increasingly apparent that linked computers can allow treasury staff to explore and exploit these and other realms. As put by a treasurer's assistant at a high-tech firm that is seeking to integrate its stand-alone treasury computer system with its mainframe database, "It's just part of the total systems concept. There's going to be less paper involved, and when you want a specific number, you just call it up from the database instead of leafing through pages and pages of computer printouts." (For more on micro-to-mainframe links, see page 146).

Access to other databases may reward treasury with sources of information long forgotten by the accounting department. Recalled one treasurer whose company went through an extensive forex study; "Eventually, the controller's organization was the source of most of the component export/import data by country and currency world-wide. They didn't even know they had it."

The ability to retrieve accounting data also saves treasury personnel from rekeying information into treasury's computer system. An analyst at one consumer goods conglomerate explained that he wanted a hookup with accounting because, "One of the things treasury gets involved in is reporting to lenders, monitoring all the long-term note agreements and covenants. I would ideally like to access that data directly with my terminal, rather than have to manually input it myself and then massage it into the format required by lenders."

In addition to borrowing information from accounting, treasurers can explore other potential in-house sources of data on production, marketing, or sales. For example, the finance department of one large chemicals and textiles firm is using borrowed data. According to the assistant treasurer, the system was originally established "to give us precise data on every new order in every part of the world. The information was used for inventory and production management, for purchases of raw materials, and to solve shipping problems." But the finance department quickly realized that the data had applications for credit management: "A little while after the order-entry system began, we started using it to check customer credit limits and, combined with receivables information, to produce collection reports."

### Accessing External Databases

Aside from internal data, financial executives need to know about the outside world and market opportunities. Computers can provide speedy on-line access to such information which may give alert treasurers a jump on time-sensitive data.

Almost anything, from real-time financial quotes to the full text of the *Wall Street Journal* to econometric forecasts to company financial reports, is available in external databases. Without these tools to discover financial regulations, currency movements, borrowing costs, and investment yields, treasurers must make time-consuming telephone calls or wade through reams of printed text. As a result, the number of respondents using such services is predicted to jump from 15 to 43% over the next few years.

The potential savings treasurers can reap from real-time access to currency and money market rates were highlighted by the experience of one treasurer of a United States MNC. "At the time of the last French franc devaluation," he said, "I noticed a comment on the screen, looked into things a bit more and, within an hour, took out a Euro-franc loan. The next day the franc went down. I think we saved roughly a quarter of a million dollars on that one. Just that one shot paid for the service for the next few years."

The market for treasury information is dominated by Reuters, which launched its Monitor service in 1973; and Telerate, which joined forces with Dow Jones and Associated Press, to provide a comparable service in the late 1970s. These are not the only service companies, however. Citibank, for example, offers a comprehensive service which offers its subscribers market rates, company financials, country economic and regulatory information, and world news garnered from a variety of other service companies.

### Statistical Analysis

Computers also give treasurers the ability to carve up massive volumes of data easily. According to the survey, 14% of respondents currently use computers for complex statistical calculations, and that number will increase to 42% in the next few years.

A good example of this type of application is offered by an American consumer goods firm. Its foreign exchange manager receives exposure reports from each subsidiary, which he then runs through a statistical consolidation program to give him a concise picture of which currencies he's exposed to and for how much. By inputting exchange rates, he can see the dollar equivalent. "Our exposure in yen and marks are pretty fixed numbers month to month," the manager explained. "What changes is the exchange rate. When my management asks me, 'What's the exposure?' I want to give them a dollar amount."

A valuable application of statistics that can save a company money and administrative headaches is credit analysis. The Korean subsidiary of a United States MNC, for example, faced with an extremely risky operating environment, automated its credit analysis procedures along the following lines. After gathering customer data from banks, company reports, newspapers, and company directories, the company feeds the data into a computer program, which in turn generates a list of ratios that include gross income/sales, current ratio, quick ratio, net worth/total assets, debt/equity, fixed assets/ net worth and long-term liabilities, sales per employee, and sales growth. The computer compares the ratios to industry averages stored in its database. Depending on its deviation from these averages, the customer receives a ranking from zero to 100 points.

A similar manual procedure is followed for a general rating, based on more subjective considerations such as management reputation and prospects for growth. The point total for each category is added and divided by two, and the company is assigned a ranking based on that average. The appropriate ranking is then entered into the customer's computerized credit file and is used to set terms and limits. The rankings are updated once a year.

## WHICH COMPUTERS COMPANIES USE

After deciding which aspects of treasury management should be computerized, firms must choose the appropriate hardware for the assigned tasks. As Table 4–7 demonstrates, the most obvious trend in treasury automation is the move away from the stand-alone micro-computer to use of a microcomputer networked to a mainframe.

The following sections discuss the pros and cons of using the most popular treasury management computers—mainframes and micros.

### Using a Stand-Alone Microcomputer

Treasury automation has been intimately intertwined with the development of the microcomputer. According to the survey, 49% of respondents today use a stand-alone microcomputer for treasury management, which is 20 percentage points higher than the rate for the PC's nearest competitors—mainframes and minis. But as treasurers begin to demand more than micros can offer in terms of memory, processing power, and links, the number of stand-alone micro users will shrink to 15% over the next few years.

**TABLE 4–7**

**Computers Used for Global Treasury Management**

| Type of system | At time of survey | Three-year projection |
|---|---|---|
| Micro without access to mini/mainframe | 49 | 15 |
| Direct use of mini/mainframe | 29 | 24 |
| Micro with access to mini/mainframe | 26 | 69 |
| Do not use computers | 13 | 6 |

The reasons for the current preeminence of microcomputers include programming flexibility, low cost, and enhanced control. Taking these trio of benefits one at a time, let us first examine the flexibility issue. Micros excel at key treasury management tasks such as report writing, rearranging data, preparing graphs and summarizing data. Analytical software that a treasurer can design, greatly enhances the worth of the PC. "If you have someone interested in it, you can develop a lot of good programs," observed one treasurer. On the other hand, the size of mainframe operations makes building interactive programs a technically complex and expensive job.

Second, with the rapid developments in PC technology, the cost of fairly powerful microcomputers has decreased steadily. An adequate system, complete with software, modem, monitor and printer, can be purchased for $2000 to $3000. A mainframe computer, by contrast, costs at least $150,000 to $200,000. And as timesharing and maintenance costs rise, the micro becomes an even more attractive option. As one treasurer summed, "Mainframes are very expensive and micros aren't, so we try to maximize the use of micros to avoid investing in memory extension for the mainframe."

Third among the benefits is that feuds over system control are legion in corporate lore. The treasurer of one electronics firm complained that, "If we try to get something from the EDP department, we have to wait a half a year, one year, two years. They will say, 'This is not so important; your job is low-priority.' PCs are easy to program and there is no delay." Indeed, microcomputers let treasury staff program and maintain their own computers, instead of submitting projects that may be queued at the end of a long list of pending MIS jobs. "Our informational needs change pretty rapidly," noted the treasurer at one fast-growing high-tech firm. "We're revising report formats all the time. It's nice not having to go to MIS to get the simpler things accomplished."

### The Allure of Mainframes/Minis

The survey reveals that a significant minority of respondents, 29%, use mainframes and minicomputers for treasury management. Not surprisingly, the larger firms adopt this strategy more than the smaller firms: 39% of respondents with more than $500 million in sales use mainframes or minis, as compared to just 20% of the smaller firms. Similarly, 41% of firms with over 40 foreign units, and 49% with between 21 and 40, rely on mainframes and minis, compared with 22% for those with less than 10, and 18% of those with less than five.

Four main advantages to using a minicomputer or mainframe system are the ease of communications, the enormous processing power, the amount of standardization among users, and the greater security. To substantiate the claim of ease of communications, one manager said, "In an international environment, lines of communication are extremely long. We chose a mainframe system because we wanted to cut the time it takes for our subs to communicate important information to headquarters. The volume of information is too high for us to rely on a microcomputer system." For instance, when one PC communicates to another, the sub must call the home office to make sure their PC is turned on and is in transmission mode. That means a long distance phone call, which is not convenient when there are major time differences between the two offices.

Second, the enormous processing power and storage capability of mainframes is legend. One major explanation for treasurers' shift away from stand-alone microcomputers is that they continually butt against the limits of micro memory. Mainframes and minis, on the other hand, store a tremendous amount of information and make millions of calculations with stunning speed. Moreover, many minicomputers and mainframes have superior multitasking capabilities. With most microcomputers, the user must finish one task before starting a new one.

The third benefit of mainframes is the high degree of standardization among users. A common complaint among micro users is the lack of standardization among PCs throughout the company. A mainframe system can ensure international compatibility, and make interfacing with the accounting databases easier; these abilities mesh with long-range MIS goals.

Lastly, mainframes offer a high degree of security. As the micro worked its way into corporate treasury, data security was a large issue. As one treasurer griped, "The disadvantage of a PC is that you have to focus on internal controls. A mainframe is much more powerful, and it has built-in controls." Materials stored on a diskette or hard disk can be tampered with by merely turning on a machine. With mainframes, passwords and directory structures can confound all users except those who know the system. However, as micro technology has advanced, security mechanisms have become more sophisticated. A recent development is the so-called *Smart Card*, a disk with a processor without which the machine cannot run. By removing the disk, the system is locked.

## Linking Microcomputers to Mainframes

For many treasurers, micro-to-mainframe networks represent the best of both worlds. They can take advantage of the enormous storage power of mainframes and the convenient programming capabilities of micros. Links enable treasurers to use a corporate database simply by electronically transferring (downloading) data to the micro. Thus, the biggest trend in treasury computerization over the next few years will be to link microcomputers to mainframes; the percentage of survey respondents doing so will more than double from the rate of 26 to 69%.

Because computer-to-computer links are complex, many firms transfer data by printing hard copy of information in mainframe databases and rekeying that information into the micro. However, with a programmed link, the data can feed directly from the mainframe into the microcomputer, thus preventing retyping errors, saving time, and increasing treasury's control over central data. Said the treasurer of a United States consumer goods manufacturer: "The chief advantage of borrowing information from an existing mainframe database is that the data and the system already exist. There is less duplication of effort or cost. It can be massaged into any format required."

A good example of a treasury system that electronically downloads data from the mainframe is that of a Canadian natural resources firm with extensive international operations. The firm's EDP department has built an interface between the accounting mainframe and the finance unit's micro, permitting easy access to detailed information on all billing procedures and accounts payable. According to the company's treasurer, these data are the "key to our whole cash management exercise. We can go back and retrieve the last six months of production of an oil field and a full list of all their customers and how much they owe so that we can do our forecasts.

We use a PC to retrieve data from the mainframe and interpret it any way we want."

Other companies use micros creatively to turn simple time-sharing systems (i.e., renting memory in a service company's computer) into valuable treasury management tools. For example, one United States electronics company upgraded the automated system at its factoring company by trading dumb terminal (that is, a terminal with no memory capacity) access to the time-sharing computer for PC/smart terminal access. "We now have our own microcomputer with a printer, disk drive, and the modem, so that we will be able to work locally with the programs that are in storage here," explained the treasurer. Treasury staff pull data from the mainframe and run the information through a variety of cash management programs on the micro. The system reduces costs by allowing the firm to buy inexpensive microcomputer hedging packages and spreadsheets, thus avoiding time-sharing connect charges during the day, when the rates are very expensive. The time-sharing system is accessed only for that short amount of time when data is pulled down. Consequently, the firm pays the time-sharing service for storage, direct connection with the computer (which is relatively brief), and printing that is done at the service center site.

An alternative application of a micro-to-mainframe link is to upload from a PC to a mainframe. This is especially applicable for bank balance information, which is obtained directly from foreign subsidiaries, domestic banks and, occasionally, foreign banks. A standard use is to input treasury information directly into accounting. It goes from the banks through a treasury workstation (which can be a minicomputer), where the data are manipulated, and then over to accounting records.

Establishing direct links between a micro and mainframe is not always easy, however. Many software houses market networking packages, but these have typically been beset with technical bugs. The problem is that computer links are more complicated than wires running between two machines; they are viable only if the software that converts or translates machine-readable data is compatible. Despite the important role that computer links play in the design of treasury reporting systems, they remain one of the major technical challenges facing many corporate MIS/EDP departments. According to a manager at a capital goods producer, "Links are the messiest area. There's not a nice clean product out there to use. Sometimes you have to use four or five different things to make them work."

## TWO CASE EXAMPLES: CONTRASTING APPROACHES TO TREASURY AUTOMATION

The following two case studies illustrate many of the themes and issues discussed in this overview on treasury management. In the first case, a centralized French firm has used purchased and in-house systems to speed treasury operations on its mainframe-based system. It has recently introduced microcomputers and uses them in tandem with the mainframe for what-if analyses. In the second case, a United States conglomerate with a contrasting decentralized approach to business operations uses the cash pooling administration and cash management software at a single bank, external to the company, to organize its treasury function.

### Letting the Company Do the Work

A French textiles manufacturer has built a computerized system to handle a broad array of treasury management responsibilities—from pooling cash and selecting the best investment and borrowing instruments to preparing forex reports for the central bank and monitoring bank compensation. The system began 10 years ago when, in automating its sales and credit and collection functions, the firm implemented a sales order entry system on a mainframe. That system monitors daily sales orders generated by the group's subsidiaries and agents, both inside and outside France.

The company took its next step three years ago when it purchased a microcomputer to track its total foreign exchange position, currency-by-currency, and to plan hedging and foreign currency funding strategies. They input data for the computerized exposure management system manually from the sales order entry program and from subsidiary reports that include borrowing and lending positions, receivables and payables, full cash positions and forecasts.

The firm developed its exposure management package in-house because it "couldn't find one in the market that was quickly and easily usable," explained a spokesperson. "We work in a lot of currencies in a lot of countries, making it very complex." In addition, to comply with forex regulations, the firm needed a program that could automatically generate reports required by the Banque de France.

For domestic treasury management, the company purchased sophisticated software for its mainframe-based system. According to the assistant treasurer, "It's a full treasury system, giving us everything we need to manage our cash in France. It calculates cash positions, lets us do what-if analysis, the whole thing." The company bought the basic package from a computer service company, and then in-house finance and software staff tailored it to meet the company's specific requirements. "It was a good program, but we had to link it to our administrative structure, reporting systems, bank accounts and so on."

The company uses this software package along with an automated balance reporting service, offered by a computer service company, to run a cash pooling scheme among the firm's 24 domestic subsidiaries. The balance reporting system, which is linked directly to the mainframe, monitors the firm's 40-plus domestic bank accounts and consolidates data from eight different French banks for input into the mainframe. The software program then identifies "the cash position of each company at all their banks. If we find that a company is long in one account and short in another, the computer will produce funds transfer instructions to pool the net amount in a single location." Excess funds from the various companies within the group are first moved into one of seven divisional concentration accounts and then concentrated in a central account managed by headquarters staff. "We keep the divisional accounts separate because we want to identify very clearly the industrial units of the group, to keep their own identities. But we can move the funds around as easily as if they all came into one account."

The firm also uses the system to calculate its operating units' upcoming borrowing requirements and to conduct what-if analyses that compare the various funding and investment alternatives, based on cash and interest rate forecasts. To do so, the computer stores information on the full range of available borrowing and investment vehicles, and updates interest rates daily. According to the assistant treasurer, the software package helps "the company compare borrowing options very quickly—for example, foreign versus domestic ones. For instance, the computer takes into account that interest has to be paid in advance on American-dollar bankers acceptances. It also tells us which are the highest yielding money market instruments when we have surplus funds."

Finally, the firm purchased a domestic cash management program that calculates all of its business with its banks, so that, in the words of the spokesperson, "When the banks come in here and complain that we do not give them enough business, we can show them figures on checks, drafts, collections, forex business, and so on. [This is necessary] because the banks, especially the United States banks, want more noncredit business." Moreover, the program checks bank charges because, notes the spokesperson, "French banks make a lot of mistakes. So we must check value dates, commissions, and the calculation of interest rates. By doing this we save six to eight million French francs per year." The firm has automated this aspect of its cash management "because it is a completely crazy job to do manually."

As with many other companies, the firm continues to upgrade its system and tack on new packages and electronic bank services. Its plans include improving its computerized scheme by linking the mainframe and the microcomputer, thereby eliminating all manual intervention. The company also will link its European operations by terminal to the headquarters mainframe, giving subsidiaries access to the central database.

## Letting the Banks Do the Work

A United States chemicals and capital goods conglomerate has managed to avoid the trouble and expense inherent in setting up a state-of-the-art treasury system. Instead, through a strategy that is "beautiful in its logic and simplicity," according to the firm's treasury manager, the company intends to use its banks to reap the rewards of automation.

The company's solution stemmed from its decentralized, constantly changing organizational structure and high volume of information needs. "We couldn't come up with a system that would meet all of our requirements," stated the manager. "When we design systems, we have to consider a number of things. First, we are constantly buying and selling companies to manage our portfolio of businesses. From a systems point of view, we have to be able to cope with that. Second, we want to avoid interfering in the operations of the businesses as much as possible. We try to avoid generating an enormous workload for reporting, for example. Third, because of the hands-off policy, there is a proliferation of legal entities of this company overseas. We are not like other companies that merge all their overseas operations under one roof." However, continued the manager, "We still want systems that bring together all the companies in any particular country, and to do things in each country in the name of the parent." But when the firm tried to manage its cash and exposures centrally, the profusion of overseas legal entities caused a plethora of problems. For example, pointed out the manager, "If we wanted to consolidate cash in a country with a lot of legal entities, in the past we had to create a lot of intercompany loans. One legal entity is cash-rich, another is cash-poor. We were creating dozens of loans."

To overcome these self-imposed obstacles, the company struck upon a two-pronged strategy. First, "We produce on a country-by-country basis a legal entity, which might be an existing legal entity, bearing the parent's name, which serves as the finance company or holding company of the group for participation in a cash pooling system." Second, the manager went on, "By concentrating all our cash management activity with a single bank, it is possible to take advantage of the bank computer system for a lot of the reporting and consolidation."

Under this new system, whenever a local entity makes a deposit to its account, it feeds into the cash pool. The money is not actually moved, however, and the subsidiary's account balance still reflects that deposit amount. But the pooling system means the cash is available for all legal entities in a particular country. As the treasury manager put it, "If you have a net borrower in the system, an offset is automatically made between the amount one legal entity has and the amount another entity needs. From the local point of view, it looks like he had a bank account that earns interest or is charged interest on the basis of its cash balance."

By concentrating the cash pooling administration and cash management details with a single bank, according to the manager, the firm reaps the gains from its simplicity. "Instead of having to pay for setting up a complicated internal reporting system, and go through the incredible programming effort to produce a consolidated report, and then have to go through all the administration of moving money around between legal entities with intercompany loans, the pooling system and the commitment to a single bank enable us to consolidate cash on a daily basis and have the bank generate the reports. And all this happens without moving any money."

In essence, the company has organized the treasury function up front, as opposed to putting a reporting system in place and then organizing the treasury activity. They can use the bank system to consolidate cash and net their position, thereby eliminating that administrative activity. They can also use the bank system to provide foreign exchange data and cash balances of each individual legal entity, thereby using it not only as a cash management reporting system, but also as a foreign exchange reporting system. Yet, this is all done without having complex reports from business units, without having to develop a lot of internal software, without a massive investment in hardware.

The system thus "has incredible implications," according to the manager. "By virtue of having all this information already organized, it is much easier to take that and interface the system with a PC workstation to consolidate all our worldwide information. Instead of going out and creating a computer monster that calls 4000 banks, all with individual communications protocols, we have a treasury management system that takes maximum advantage of the existing level of computerization at the banks. And then when we implement a workstation package, we only have to worry about communications protocols with one bank in each country."

This changes the logic behind treasury automation, declared the manager. "There is a lot of overengineering going on out there. One of the selling points of the workstation packages is that you don't have to change any of your banks to do this. And people run out thinking that's great and they buy it. Then they're stuck with this communications protocol problem and anybody who has ever dealt with PCs knows what I'm talking about. The bank changes a comma to a semicolon and you can't access your cash balances. This will be a much easier system to administer because there's only four or five different protocols that you have to worry about."

So far, the firm has only set up its 20 Canadian units on the system.

Plans call for the Netherlands and the United Kingdom operations to be up by the end of the year. The company then intends to move through the individual countries in which it has significant operations, those in Europe specifically, and convert all its operating units to the new system.

## SUMMARY

Cash and currency management, even in a company that operates with only one currency, can be a tangled web. With the introduction of manageable computer hardware and software over the past decade or so, firms have turned increasingly to these machines and their associated programs to collect, sort, and analyze treasury data. This statement is supported in whole by the FERF study, which shows that the percentage of firms with highly automated treasury operations will triple in the next few years, and that nine out of every 10 firms will have automated at least some portion of those operations during the same time frame.

Large firms, measured both by number of foreign operating units and level of sales, are spearheading the effort and, by and large, most of these are North American based. European companies are also making inroads on automation, and an unprecedented growth is due among Asian companies who, at this point, have almost no automation in place. From an organizational perspective, centralization and automation are practically synonymous. The synergy created by the economies of scale and staff expertise at large centralized firms almost defy the use of manual procedures.

Automation of treasury functions can be evaluated in two steps—the first being how information is reported to parent companies, and the second being how it is used. The FERF study evaluated six types of reporting media—mail, telex, facsimile, telephone, computer-to-computer transmission, and exchange of diskettes. Most foreign subsidiaries currently use the least sophisticated of these methods (as well as various modes of messenger service), but project that at least one in two will use some means of electronic transmission in the near future. The blockades to modernization include proscriptive legislative and trade embargos of electronic media. The latter concern, how data is used once received, revolves mainly around databases and analyses. Over half of the firms surveyed believe that they will devise or purchase an analysis system centered on a core database (into which they can feed data, and from which they can extract selected samples for analysis); almost half project that they will subscribe to an external database (from which they can extract nonproprietary information). For the time being, however, such scenarios are more in the planning phase in most companies than in the progress stage.

The experience of companies that have made the plunge into automated treasury systems offers good insight into the nature of the computer business in general today. For the most part, firms that have been in the business for some time are making the switch from using mainframes as the sole computing source to using micros that are networked to mainframes. Although mainframes are wonderful for data storage, their cost as processors is exhorbitant. By using them primarily for storage and not for processing, and using micros as the processing tool, all hardware is used effectively. Conversely, firms that began automating their offices solely with micros are now networking them for greater efficacy.

# CHAPTER 5

# Improving Cash Management Through Automation

## INTRODUCTION

The star of cash management began rising in the late 1970s, when soaring global borrowing costs, high inflation rates, and severe recession forced companies to take decisive action to protect corporate profits and preserve sales. In those circumstances, many companies found that the best and easiest way to minimize financial costs and risks was to improve their cash management systems. Indeed, in that period and in current times, effective cash management systems and strategies did, and can, save alert companies millions of dollars each year by reducing borrowing needs, funds transfer costs, and tax obligations. As one treasurer put it, "Without cash management, we would be losing money. It's the difference between profit and loss."

Parallel with this increased interest in cash management, corporations became enamoured with automation. The vision? In the words of a treasury manager, "Information at the push of a button, your bank balances ready and waiting first thing in the morning—the computer makes everything handy." The impact on cash management? "Incalculable." An independent treasury consultant agreed. "Cash management was meant for automation. Computers have a role to play in every aspect."

In fact, the survey shows that cash management, along with its close relative, electronic banking, is the most highly automated area within the global treasury function. As shown in Table 5–1, over a third of respondents have already highly computerized at least some aspects of their cash management systems.

The current low interest rates, especially in the United States, have seemingly dulled the luster of cash management and the automation of the function for the time being. Because cash management thrives in times of inflation and high interest rates, the present situation is very static. As the finance director of an American high-tech firm put it, "It just doesn't appear that important to us now. Of course, we still look for obvious inefficiencies in our cash management practices, but we just don't think the payback is there for an investment of thousands of dollars in computer technology when interest rates are so low." A frustrated marketing manager of electronic cash management systems agreed: "You remind them of the past and you warn them about the future, that interest rates might rise again, but that is very nebulous. It takes a very open-minded individual to sell that idea to."

**TABLE 5–1**

**Percent of Respondents with Highly Automated Cash Management Systems**

| Function | At time of survey | Three-year projection |
|---|---|---|
| Reporting | 25 | 57 |
| Forecasting | 13 | 45 |
| Credit analysis | 10 | 21 |
| Receivables | 37 | 54 |
| Payables | 39 | 56 |
| Investing | 10 | 27 |
| Borrowing | 10 | 27 |
| Bank costs/relations | 5 | 20 |

In this financial climate, industry seers are also speculating that automation itself will radically alter, or even eliminate, the traditional tasks of the cash manager. As computerized information flows and transaction initiation catch on within companies, between banks and companies, and among unrelated firms, the traditional cash management definition of reducing idle balances, speeding receivables, delaying payables, and maximizing returns may become archaic. "Once you go to electronic transmission of all business trading documents," prophesied a cash management director of a United States automaker, "and once you go to electronic payment and electronic receipt of payment, then the historical roles disappear. There can be no acceleration or deceleration of receipts and payments. It will essentially be instantaneous. You will know with greater precision how much money is available on any given day and that will allow for optimization strategies. You'll get to the absolute minimum of idle cash."

On the positive side, the survey clearly shows that the reports of the death of cash management are greatly exaggerated. As Table 5–1 reveals, a majority of respondents plan to install highly computerized cash reporting, receivables, and payables systems over the next few years, while also planning to double their automation of the other functional areas of cash management. These respondents also cite four major reasons they are committed to this automation:

First, many companies are not banking on continued low interest rates. The downward slide of the dollar, and the Fed's concerted efforts to prop it up, have many treasurers concerned about rising rates again. As one cash management consultant put it, "Interest rates are not going to stay low forever, and a change today effectively reduces costs in the future."

Second, treasurers believe that even with low rates, automation of cash management can still result in substantial interest savings and gains. One corporate cash manager said it best: "If I can whack 20 days off my DSOs (days' sales outstanding) with annual sales of $500 million, that's still a lot of money. It depends on the size of the cash flows; that's where you generate the savings. Even if rates are at 5.5%, I'm still saving over a million dollars. That's good enough for me."

Third, many cash management professionals believe that automation of the function slashes administrative and banking costs. Some system savings are totally unrelated to the current level of interest rates. Computers reduce staff, for example, or at least keep them from growing. For example, an Australian subsidiary of a United States company cut its credit and collection staff in half by automating the function—while, at the same time, reducing DSOs by 14 days. And, lastly, many companies believe that cutting costs is not the only reason to automate cash management. Many companies turn to the latest cash management tools to improve managerial control and decision making. In the experience of one pharmaceuticals firm, "The real savings can't be quantified. With an automated system, we know exactly where everything is. We can make borrowing and investment decisions much more accurately. We can control our cash management."

For companies that want to improve their cash management through automation, this chapter examines the corporate use of computers in every step of the cash cycle, from reporting and forecasting through receivables management, payables management, short-term investment and borrowing, and banking relations. Figure 5–1 shows these relationships clearly. Through case examples, the chapter also shows how companies cut costs and upgrade control

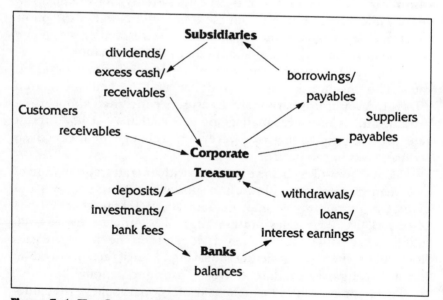

**Figure 5–1: The Corporate Cash Flow Cycle**

by computerizing cash management information flows, credit analysis, invoice processing, payment initiation, debt and investment decisions, and monitoring banking charges.

## WHICH COMPANIES ARE AUTOMATING GLOBAL CASH MANAGEMENT?

Most aspects of cash management in many companies will automate to some degree over the next few years. However, the survey reveals that the extent of critical cash management functions does and will vary markedly, depending on a company's size, domicile, and organizational style. For instance, in line with the general trends in treasury management automation, the survey shows that larger companies rely more heavily on computers than their smaller counterparts, both currently and in the future. This is shown in Table 5–2.

As shown in Table 5–3, the patterns are very similar to those of treasury management automation in general: North American firms, with their technological edge, lead the world in computerized cash management, although Asian and European companies will be closing the gap in the years ahead.

The type of organization of the global treasury function also has a decisive impact on automating the cash management function. Table 5–4 displays the survey data on that issue.

As shown in the tabular data, both centralized and regionalized firms are projected to computerize at a much faster pace than companies with a decentralized approach to cash management. The reason, similar to that discussed in Chapter 4, is that to reap the economies of scale offered by centralized or regionalized cash management, companies find automation a critical tool. For example, the cash manager of a capital goods manufacturer spoke for many colleagues when saying, "The automation of our international treasury function really ties into the establishment of our regional treasury center (in Europe). They need computers to process all the data the subs are sending in and our communications system lets us check up on what actions they're taking. At the same time, we realized that with a six-hour time difference, we can't manage our worldwide cash from [the United States]."

**TABLE 5–2**

**Percent of Respondents with Highly Automated Cash Management Systems**

| Size | Reporting Cash Positions | | Managing Receivables | | Managing Payables | |
|---|---|---|---|---|---|---|
| | At time of survey | Three-year projection | At time of survey | Three-year projection | At time of survey | Three-year projection |
| Over $2 billion | 34 | 68 | 40 | 51 | 47 | 56 |
| $500 million–$2 billion | 28 | 63 | 39 | 55 | 43 | 57 |
| $200 million–$499 million | 23 | 57 | 33 | 51 | 30 | 49 |
| Under $200 million | 12 | 38 | 36 | 58 | 33 | 61 |
| **Number of Foreign Operating Units** | | | | | | |
| Over 40 | 24 | 64 | 46 | 66 | 53 | 65 |
| 21–40 | 25 | 62 | 24 | 42 | 26 | 46 |
| 11–20 | 29 | 60 | 42 | 52 | 39 | 52 |
| 6–10 | 25 | 58 | 42 | 60 | 42 | 59 |
| 1–5 | 26 | 53 | 36 | 51 | 40 | 57 |

**TABLE 5–3**

**Percent of Respondents with Highly Automated Cash Management Systems**

| Domicile | Reporting Cash Positions | | Managing Receivables | | Managing Payables | |
|---|---|---|---|---|---|---|
| | At time of survey | Three-year projection | At time of survey | Three-year projection | At time of survey | Three-year projection |
| North America | 33 | 62 | 40 | 57 | 45 | 60 |
| Europe | 13 | 48 | 34 | 52 | 35 | 55 |
| Asia | 11 | 58 | 29 | 42 | 18 | 42 |

**TABLE 5-4**

**Percent of Respondents with Highly Automated Cash Management Systems**

| Type of Organization | Reporting Cash Positions | | Managing Receivables | | Managing Payables | |
|---|---|---|---|---|---|---|
| | At time of survey | Three-year projection | At time of survey | Three-year projection | At time of survey | Three-year projection |
| Centralized | 27 | 61 | 39 | 58 | 40 | 61 |
| Regionalized | 16 | 63 | 23 | 43 | 23 | 43 |
| Decentralized | 24 | 48 | 38 | 48 | 41 | 49 |

## CASH REPORTING AND FORECASTING

Effective cash monitoring and forecasting is critical to the success of any cash management system. Treasurers need reliable and timely information from their banks, subsidiaries, and other departments at corporate headquarters to keep their bank balances low, cut borrowing needs, trim outstanding accounts receivable, and improve payables management. Adept reporting also allows both parent and regional headquarters to assess the performance of local cash managers. Equally important, good forecasting keeps cash managers on top of changes in the cash position and helps them develop a coherent and profit-maximizing investment and borrowing strategy by anticipating excesses and shortfalls.

The treasurer of a United States equipment manufacturer summed up the importance of good cash reporting and forecasting this way: "The key to cash management is information. You can't manage cash if you don't know where your money is and when it is arriving. If you don't know that, there's no way you can manage your cash, because you can't know whether you need additional money or whether you have money to invest."

To improve the efficiency of treasury reporting systems, many companies are installing computer hardware and software at local, regional, and/or headquarters levels to store and manipulate treasury data. According to the survey, 25% of respondents have largely automated their systems for reporting cash positions and 57% will have done so in the next few years. Ninety-one percent of companies will have introduced computers to some aspect of their cash reporting over the same horizon.

The treasurer of a United States metals manufacturer thus spoke for the vast majority of his peers when he said, "Without an automated system, you cannot have the up-to-date information you need to perform good cash management. Everything takes too long and there are too many errors. The old ways just aren't good enough. Everything suffers. Collections are slow. Payments are missed. Bank reconciliation is messy. In today's world, you need computers to run a cash management system."

## Reporting Domestic Cash Positions

At the local subsidiary level, the starting point for any effective cash management reporting system is the daily cash position report, which shows the day's starting bank balance position adjusted for anticipated cash flows for that day. This includes sales receipts, investment earnings, and loan proceeds. Much of this information can be gleaned from electronic bank reports, so many North American firms, given the superior electronic balance-reporting services available in the region (see Chapter 8), often have no need to set up separate, internal reporting systems for domestic subsidiaries.

In areas with less-developed electronic banking systems, a greater need for efficient internal reporting systems to link domestic subsidiaries exists. For instance, an Italian MNC set up its own automated reporting system when faced with inadequate electronic balance-reporting services. The firm contracted a United States computer services company to install an on-line reporting system that links its 20-plus domestic operating units with corporate headquarters. Each unit enters its profit and loss information and currency exposure positions through a terminal on a daily basis. The figures are then instantly transmitted to a computer at headquarters, where a software package converts the data into cash management reports on payments to suppliers, receipts from customers, bank balances, and short-term borrowings. The package also uses operating units' input to provide a three-month rolling forecast. Working with the timely data in this system, treasury staff shift liquidity and match currency exposures within the corporate group based on each unit's data.

## Case Example: One Subsidiary's Automated Cash Reporting

The experience of a German subsidiary of a United States food producer offers a good example of how to computerize a domestic cash reporting system. After auditing its cash management activities, this subsidiary learned that it was encountering significant delays during the collection process, that its banks were not honoring its value-dating agreements, and that it was consistently in overdraft in one bank while piling up surplus funds (at a low interest rate) at another. A report on the review concluded that "an effective information system that can *plan* rather than *react* to problems will improve both the decision-making process and the profitability of the company."

To achieve these goals and to avoid costly mistakes, the firm called in consultants from a United States bank. This team recommended installing a computerized daily cash management reporting system that was supported by sales and customer account ledgers and directly connected to the firm's banks. The system checks expected receipts against planned disbursements, working as follows: By 10:00 A.M. each day, the firm's finance department receives the previous day's ending balance and details of all incoming receipts in excess of 50,000 Deutsche marks. The bank balance is then reconciled with the book balance, including unrecorded disbursements and anticipated receipts. The finance director receives the report and, therefore, is apprised of all required disbursements and maturity of short-term debt. Investment strategies can then be developed to use the expected receipts most effectively and to roll over short-term debt and investment portfolios.

In establishing this automated system, the company set the following goals, which are worthwhile considerations for any company with similar problems. They are divided into banking and internal concerns.

## Banking

1. Monitor the collection and mobilization of customer receipts by banks to ensure that negotiated value standards are being provided.
2. Ensure that collected funds have been credited to overdraft positions on a timely basis.
3. Determine the gross and available balance of cash and overdraft positions to develop either investment or borrowing strategies.

## Internal

1. Provide a rationale for determining the amount and timing of intercompany transactions to achieve a balance between cash, debt, and foreign exchange exposure strategies.
2. Revise daily customer aging schedules based upon established terms of trade and clearing arrangements.

The computerized reporting system developed by the company to meet these five objectives is illustrated in Figure 5–2. The top of the figure shows the types of information the firm stores in its computerized database, including internal sales and purchasing reports, cash forecasts, aging of receivables and payables, and borrowings and investments. The company also obtains money market information from external sources and balance and transaction data from its banks. By tapping this comprehensive database, the company's computer can generate the cash management reports, shown at the bottom.

## Using Computers for Cross-Border Reporting

Treasurers who want to improve their ability to manage global cash resources centrally or, at least assess the performance of overseas financial managers, are also turning to computerized systems. Headquarters must be able to monitor trends in bank balances and costs, bad-debt expense, outstanding receivables and payables, borrowings and investments, and forecasts to catch problems before they get out of hand. Table 5–5 illustrates how parents receive various types of cash management data from overseas units currently and how they project they will obtain this data in the near future.

The table shows that computer-to-computer and tape/diskette transmission are the only methods that will increase in use over the next few years. Bank balance and activity data top the list targeted for such automation because of the large cost savings corporate treasury can achieve by minimizing idle funds and regulating subsidiary banking relations. Payables and credit and collection data are at the bottom of the list because these functions are generally handled by subsidiary managers and the treasurer only needs to check them monthly or quarterly to evaluate local performance.

One example of a computerized reporting system that helps parent headquarters keep tabs on subsidiaries' actions is provided by a United States capital goods manufacturer with extensive operations in the Far East. "Even though we're very decentralized," explained a spokesperson, "and upper management just receives

## INPUT DATA (Stored in Data File)

Weekly sales reports

Weekly purchase reports

Weekly cash receipt and payment forecast

Aging schedule, intercompany transactions

Aging schedule and update, outstanding accounts receivable and payable

Investment file

Borrowing file

Current day transactions

Monthly cash receipt and disbursement forecast

Bank balance reporting by account and bank

Available balance (Value-date terms)

Transaction breakdown (debits and credits)

Bank statement, ledger balance

Money market rate reports, daily rate information

## OUTPUT REPORTS (Produced from Data File)

Daily receipt and payments schedule: actual versus forecast analysis

Previous day receipt and payment (actual)

Consolidated cash receipt and payment forecast: revised rolling 10-day cash forecast

Available investable or overdraft balances by currency/account

Bank borrowing schedule
or
Investment schedule

**Figure 5–2: A Cash Management Reporting System**

## TABLE 5-5

**Transmission Methods for Key Cash Management Functions (Percent of Respondents)**

| | Bank balances activity | Liquidity reports/ forecasts | Short-term borrowing | Short-term Investment | Payables Information | Credit/ collection |
|---|---|---|---|---|---|---|
| **Computer-to-Computer** | | | | | | |
| At time of survey | 8 | 8 | 7 | 6 | 6 | 5 |
| Three-year projection | 32 | 29 | 26 | 25 | 21 | 21 |
| **Telex** | | | | | | |
| At time of survey | 39 | 35 | 34 | 34 | 20 | 24 |
| Three-year projection | 25 | 21 | 20 | 21 | 13 | 16 |
| **Mail** | | | | | | |
| At time of survey | 38 | 45 | 40 | 38 | 46 | 45 |
| Three-year projection | 19 | 25 | 24 | 23 | 29 | 28 |
| **Facsimile** | | | | | | |
| At time of survey | 19 | 21 | 17 | 17 | 13 | 14 |
| Three-year projection | 15 | 15 | 13 | 13 | 8 | 11 |
| **Telephone** | | | | | | |
| At time of survey | 14 | 9 | 9 | 10 | 6 | 8 |
| Three-year projection | 10 | 8 | 6 | 8 | 4 | 5 |
| **Computer tape/disk** | | | | | | |
| At time of survey | 3 | 2 | 2 | 2 | 3 | 2 |
| Three-year projection | 10 | 10 | 8 | 7 | 7 | 7 |

monthly reviews of local operations, we want to know what's going on, we want to know fast, and we do not want to be surprised."

To achieve this goal, the company set up a reporting system in the mid-1960s for large subsidiaries in Australia, Japan, and the Philippines; and for sourcing operations in Hong Kong, Malaysia, and Singapore. All the units are now fully computerized and transmit monthly reports through the firm's own time-sharing network either to corporate headquarters (for subsidiaries) or to individual product divisions (for sourcing operations). To avoid any possible government constraints on cross-border data transmissions, the Asian units process all data locally. In addition to full financial statements for accounting purposes, local units also provide information on balances, currency exposures, borrowings, investments, days' sales outstanding and aging of receivables.

Once the processed data is received in the United States and consolidated, the parent's treasury staff can retrieve reports, such as cash flow and working capital analyses and projections, from the computer. The firm then carefully scrutinizes the data to ensure that subsidiaries are following corporate guidelines. For example, the spokesperson explained that borrowing limits have been set for each unit, "and if our group in the Philippines is getting near the top of the band, we're going to find out why. We set targets and goals on all these cash management items and monitor them very, very closely."

As with this company, many other firms want to monitor subsidiary cash management performance, but don't want to place a heavy reporting burden on overseas units. Therefore, some headquarters treasury staffs, such as the case of an Italian automaker, use available accounting data for this purpose. In this company, treasury uses software that, according to its CFO, "automatically converts the accounting data—our subsidiaries' P&L statements—into cash flow information." The program manipulates the data "using parameters that we feed in, such as average payment terms to suppliers, average payments from customers, and so on." It then generates daily, weekly, and fortnightly cash forecasts. Each month, it also produces a rolling three-month forecast that shows actual results for the current and previous two months. Said the spokesperson, "The model quantifies our expected cash flows. This is critical to our whole system."

## Case Example: A Cross-Border Treasury and Accounting Reporting System

To check on both its regional treasury center and local European units, a major United States chemicals company established a fully integrated financial reporting system on a mainframe at its European regional headquarters. The company wanted to avoid loading a myriad of reporting responsibilities on local managers so it sought to merge the treasury system with the accounting system. The treasury staff, however, faced enormous difficulties in tapping into the accounting system. The key problem was that the system had been developed to create historical data for the controller before the years when cash management became a critical concern. As a result, information in a form that the treasurer could use easily, and cash management reports had to be assembled manually.

In the mid-1970s, the company began a multi-step program to turn this system into an integrated, on-line accounting and treasury management system. It hoped to improve both the accounting and the cash and currency management functions. The company's first step was to establish on-line order and billing capabilities. Terminals were installed in each sales location, allowing customer orders to be electronically reported to the order and billing department in regional headquarters and to manufacturing plants. This allowed the company to create five-week cash forecasts based on due dates or on customers' historical habits. In addition, billing was generated automatically by the release of a shipment.

The second step, completed in 1982, was to integrate accounts receivable with the general ledger and to put them on line. Order and billing, accounts receivable and the general ledger modules are now interactive and can be operated from the same terminals and computer. The third step, near completion, is to put the accounts payable ledger on line.

Information received by the reporting system is sent to the United States parent from regional headquarters and used for a variety of cash management functions, from monitoring credit terms and forecasting cash positions to analyzing short-term borrowing scenarios. According to the spokesperson, the recent improvements mean that "we can look at any accounts receivables in Europe or

Africa. When we look at the account of a customer in Finland, we get on the screen here, the same information that they get in Finland."

The accounts receivable module contains the daily sales information for each European sales office, which is vital to credit management. With this system, the individual sales offices can access the database to get a real-time statement for every customer, including the overall balance outstanding, the amount overdue, the aging of accounts, the amount invoiced to date, and payments received to date. The regional headquarters can do the same from its centralized computer, which monitors the region's $200 million in customer exposure.

The accounts payable module monitors due dates of payments to suppliers. And, by consolidating the accounts receivable and accounts payable modules, the accounting system is able to generate daily cash-balance reports by currency and by bank. In short, the reporting system helped the treasury staff to improve credit and collection, the timing of disbursements, and cash reporting and forecasting.

Although system development was expensive, the savings have been impressive. "If I had to make an assessment," said the assistant treasurer, "our savings on both the accounting and the cash management modules were between $300,000 and $500,000 from a systems development standpoint, let alone in terms of operational savings." The main benefit is a reduced accounting staff. Because everything is done automatically, the company's accounting staff spends less time preparing entries or reconciling them when they receive invoices. Furthermore, the treasury department can process payments in a much more accurate and efficient way.

## Forecasting Cash Positions

As the previous examples demonstrate, forecasting goes hand in hand with cash reporting. By having subsidiaries create cash forecasts, and by using data generated by internal accounts payable and accounts receivable systems, as well as from bank balance reporting systems, corporate cash managers can develop accurate cash forecasts. Forecasts enable cash managers to manage bank balances, project financing requirements, make investment decisions, and match anticipated inflows and outflows. As the treasurer of a United States consumer goods company summarized, "Cash forecasts are the most important tool for monitoring and controlling corporate cash. Without them, good cash management is simply impossible."

By turning to computer applications—whether it be through simple spreadsheets or sophisticated software packages—a treasurer can ensure better and more timely forecasts. As one corporate treasurer explained, "We have a computerized cash forecasting model that projects monthly cash needs six months out by subsidiary and by currency. The advantage of computerizing the reporting and forecasting is that these figures can be accessed quickly and frequently as needed." According to the survey, the percentage of firms adopting highly automated forecasting systems will soar from 13 to 45%, with 87% of companies computerizing some aspect of their forecasting in the near future.

A good example of an automated cash forecasting system is provided by one United States manufacturer that insists on detailed cash forecasts from its domestic subsidiaries to structure its borrowing program. The subsidiaries submit eight-week forecasts with a rolling forecast for the next four quarters. The elements of the forecast include profits before interest, interest, depreciation, inventory, receivables, payables, capital expenditures and dividends, and long-term debt payments.

The subsidiaries send reports to the firm's mainframe at headquarters, and include a number of financial ratios; for example, turnover, sales versus DSOs, sales versus cash disbursements outstanding (CDOs). "I see the reports to be consolidated and the consolidated report by unit and by total," noted an assistant treasurer. "For instance, I can tell you right now that in the first quarter of next year we will have generated $2.5 million in cash; in the first half—$9.5 million."

The longer-term forecast helps the manager in two ways. First, "There are no surprises. It helps me anticipate my borrowing needs and investment capabilities. If one person is going to need $20 million, I need to plan for that." Second, the manager continued, "What the units are going to generate or require will affect our consolidated corporate forecast for interest expense. I can get a rate forecast from any of the economic publications put out by the banks, but I need to know my borrowings to budget for my interest expense."

The eight-week forecast gives the manager an immediate picture of the way the business is going. "We have a commercial paper program and the eight-week forecast lets me make sure that I have maturities to match my receivables. For example, about half of our domestic business is with the auto industry. We have tracked their payment habits on our computer and they usually pay the first three days of the month and around the 15th through the 18th. I get big receipts those two periods. I want to make sure I have commercial paper maturing those days so I can pay it down on those days. Otherwise, I'm borrowing—I have borrowings outstanding—when I have all this money. I could invest it but you still lose the spread between bank loans and deposits."

## COMPUTERIZING CREDIT AND COLLECTION PROCEDURES

Multinational corporations face a variety of receivables obstacles that can cost hundreds of thousands of dollars each year—slow-paying customers, poor mail and bank clearing systems, and complex value-dating arrangements that can tack days onto the collection cycle. Computers help firms bring their receivables management under control by enabling them to monitor every aspect of the function closely, thereby trimming excessive days' sales outstanding (DSOs) and minimizing the staff time and errors involved in manual procedures. For these reasons, 37% of respondents to the survey have already highly automated receivables management and 54% plan to do so within three years.

Savings from receivables automation can be enormous. A subsidiary of a United States paper manufacturer, for example, set up an automated receivables function several years ago to handle its 50,000 accounts. At that time, the firm had bad debts worth 1.2% of the net value of its sales, and DSOs of over 100. To address this problem, the new computerized system maintains credit histories on its customers (permitting instant checking on credit limits) and automatically generates invoices when sales data are entered. It also sends out dunning letters to customers that do not pay on time. As a result, the firm has reduced its bad debts to just 0.45% of its sales and its DSOs to 72.

This section will examine how companies are achieving such impressive results by automating the nuts and bolts of receivables management, from monitoring performance through internal reporting and analyzing credit risks to accelerating debtor payments. The section concludes with an instructive example of one firm's successful computerized credit and collection system.

## Monitoring Receivables Management

To keep tabs on subsidiary performance, most companies require local managers to report DSOs, aging of receivables, and bad debt expense. Sophisticated firms also prepare reports on customer payment patterns, major delinquent accounts, discounts or penalties, credit terms, and so on. By computerizing the internal reporting process with data such as this, firms can build a database that stores, and can be tapped for, full details on the credit terms, rating, and history of each customer, as well as detailed entries for each transaction.

A United States steel producer, for instance, faced with a growing number of bad debt and customer defaults in the accounts of its French subsidiary, provided them with a real-time receivables system. According to the company's treasurer, "The collections were on a computer for several years, but reports were only generated every 15 days. The new system allows us to interrogate the computer at any time, whenever the subsidiary treasurer wants to. He can have his receivables situation every day, to inform the salesmen of their customers' positions so they can try to get payment." The computer is also programmed to signal overdue accounts and new orders that put customers over their credit limits.

Close monitoring of receivables also can help headquarters' cash managers evaluate collections at the local level. For instance, a treasurer of a decentralized American capital goods producer receives receivables reports in this manner: "Our four lockbox banks send the details of our lockbox receipts to our central receivables processing center via courier. The center applies the payments to each one of the accounts at each one of the divisions."

Once the processing center enters that data into the computer, the cash manager can access it to generate a number of reports—aging of receivables, DSOs, and receivables breakdowns in terms of gross amounts and percentages. Noted an executive at the company, "I can see those numbers every day. I can pull numbers by division or by total. We have one program that shows me the largest dollar amount of the longest overdue payment—the absolute worst account. That's my criterion for pulling the whole receivables report. We generally won't harp on the divisions to do something, but when it becomes a problem, then we'll step in."

## Automating Credit Analysis

Because sloppy monitoring of customer credit risk and payment performance increases DSOs and the chance of defaults, the percentage of companies that will try to correct those problems by highly automating customer credit analysis will grow from 10 to 21% over the next few years. Such firms are using computers to store customer information from both outside credit agencies and in-house data on invoices and payments. As the treasurer of a United States MNC put it, "You have to have current accounts receivable on-line to run a strong credit department. You are always either extending credit to a new customer or an existing customer. With an existing customer, you have to make sure his account is current—what's outstanding, whether he's holding back payment, whether you have problems with him. You need day-to-day, on-line receivables information. You need quick access to that data."

For new customers, firms can research creditworthiness through on-line access to credit-rating agencies or through alternative in-house procedures. A West Coast trucking firm, to cite an example of the first type of approach, subscribes to one such service that shows company balance sheets and payment records as well as general background and history. This data is available to each unit in the firm through electronic mail that can be printed, on request, on preformatted forms. This way, each unit can handle its own credit analysis.

The second type of approach includes gathering customer information from in-house files, credit rating agencies, banks, suppliers, newspapers and other sources; and using that data to calculate objective statistical indicators that help set credit limits. A subsidiary of a United States steel producer, for instance, uses a microcomputer to calculate credit limits based on what the company's credit manager called "classic balance sheet analysis. We look at the working capital, days in inventory, the full financial picture of customers."

Credit analysis at a Canadian manufacturer goes even further. After culling customer credit data, the firm uses the computer to yield the following: profitability ratios (net return on capital, total assets, and turnover); liquidity ratios (cash, quick and current ratios, DSOs, and stock turnover); financial or solvency ratios (debt/equity); fixed asset cover; reserves; and past payment performance. The firm's computer program then assigns numerical values to each of these categories with the following maximum point totals:

| | |
|---|---|
| Liquidity | 25 points |
| Fixed-asset cover | 20 |
| Profitability | 20 |
| Payment experience | 15 |
| Solvency | 10 |
| Reserves | 10 |

In combination with a further calculation of net worth and turnover, the point totals are used to develop credit limits. The computer takes the sum of ten percent of net worth and three percent of sales turnover, and divides it by two to arrive at a base. For example, for a firm with sales of $20 million, a net worth of $10 million, and a point total of 85, the base figure would be calculated as follows:

$$\frac{(\$20 \text{ million} \times .03) + (\$10 \text{ million} \times 10)}{2} = \$800,000$$

The firm then applies the following formula:

$$\text{Base figure} + \frac{(\text{base figure} \times \text{point total})}{100} = \text{credit limit}$$

Consequently, the hypothetical firm's credit limit is determined to be:

$$\frac{\$800,000 + (\$800,000 \times 85)}{100} = \$1,480,000$$

The computer logs this figure in its database, enabling the firm to check customer credit with the push of a button when an order arrives. It also signals credit managers to stop shipment if the client is over its limit or paying slowly. All the data on the credit limits are updated annually.

## Case Example: Computerizing Credit Analysis

One United States retailer has an exceptional need for tight credit monitoring because over half the company's $14 billion in annual sales are made on credit. The company accepts eight forms of payment, including four major credit cards, of which there are at least 152 million cards in circulation. The size of the potential customer base is staggering.

To minimize losses from credit card fraud and delinquent debtors, the company installed a network of computers in its stores with real-time access to a credit database that is maintained on one of the company's nine mainframe computers. "We authorize every credit transaction," stated the banking manager at the firm. "We don't care about floor limits, if it's over $50 or whatever. If there's a card coming up to the register—any card—it gets authorized." The company maintains active files of its own cards and of the major bank card networks. "We're not going against just derogatory files, an electronic version of the paper list of all stolen or lost cards reported. We're going into the active files."

Authorization occurs when the customer goes to make the purchase. The clerk types in the card number, purchase amount, item code, date, and other billing items. That information is transmitted through the Series 1 computers to the host mainframe, where the data is compared to the resident computer files. "They get one of three responses at the register," explained the banking manager. "One is the okay, which comes up most often and takes about five seconds. Then there's two variations on the hold. One is: Send them up to the credit office. The other is: Call a floor manager over to look at the driver's license or other form of identification to make sure that it is still the customer that holds the card." After the transaction is verified, the computer updates the customer credit file. "All the billing information is maintained, for credit and for inventory purposes. We know the merchandise they bought."

One of the major advantages of the company's on-line system is that it not only prevents use of stolen or lost cards, but also allows the company to stop and check suspicious cards. "We know the profile of a hot card," declared the manager. "If someone comes into the store on a spree and makes five purchases in excess of $100, that's unusual behavior. If the card has not been used for a long time, sometimes we'll put a stop on it just to make sure it's still our customer that has the card. And, there are credit limits. If a purchase goes over the limit, it's a local management judgment whether to allow that purchase or not, although at that point the customer is told this will be the last permissible purchase until he's paid down below a certain limit."

## Refining Internal Billing Procedures

The traditional collection cycle begins with the receipt of the customer order. After an order has been approved for delivery on the basis of agreed credit terms and a review of the customer's credit standing, the billing process starts. During this segment of the cycle, the order is processed and shipped, generally by the warehouse (or in the case of a service company, service is initiated or rendered), the shipment data is entered into an internal information system, and an invoice is generated and delivered to the customer. Because billing is the one stage that is completely under the company's control, billing delays can be described as self-inflicted injuries. Fortunately, automation can speed up and monitor these internal processes.

For instance, one treasurer located a source of billing delays in his company's Australian subsidiary's widely scattered sales offices, because they sent billing information to headquarters in Melbourne by "courier or even mail." To reduce the turnaround time, they introduced a new EDP system, and put in a mainframe. Under the new system, all sales offices have on-line hookups with the central computer in Melbourne, and sales agents key in orders daily, automatically invoicing their customers.

The savings that such automated receivables processing can provide is also illustrated by the case of a German subsidiary of a food producer. The firm's order-to-invoice procedures consumed six to ten days because the distribution warehouses took excessive time transmitting invoices to the treasury department at corporate headquarters. The company reduced the time required to process orders and mail invoices to just one or two days by installing on-line computer terminals at its warehouses. In addition to reduced clerical costs, the firm calculated that by accelerating the collections cycle, its new system generated the following in interest savings:

Average daily sales X five days' savings X overdraft rate = annual savings

Dm300,000          Dm1,500,000          6.75%          Dm101,250

## Dunning Customers Electronically

Many companies are also automating the final phase of the collection cycle—the handling of delinquent accounts. Customers that refuse, or are unable, to pay on time can undermine even the most sophisticated receivables system. To cope with delinquent accounts, companies must maintain a system that tracks slow-paying customers and duns them on a regular basis.

One consumer products company with extensive European operations, for example, has such a system. The firm's computer generates a weekly receivables report showing current and previous transaction status and received remittances. That information feeds into a billing reminder software package that generates dunning letters according to the following schedule:

Day 1—Delivery/invoice date

Day 14—First letter

Day 28—Second letter

Day 35—Third letter

Day 49—Fourth letter

An example of a more rigorous collection program is provided by a United States services company. When the firm was confronted by the often lackadaisical payment habits of its United Kingdom customers, it set up a computerized system with its British subsidiary to track overdue customers and produce reminder letters automatically.

The firm's attempts to minimize outstanding receivables starts even before the first invoices are sent out. According to the subsidiary's credit manager, "When a client opens an account, the system sends out a letter from our department, stating the terms and how they are to pay. We literally, but very politely, get on them as soon as they open the account." Once payment comes due, the computer generates letters demanding payment on a two-week cycle. After four weeks, the customer is turned over to a collection agency. "While we have been criticized by a number of people for being nasty and impatient," commented the credit manager, "customers are in the habit of paying us. They know from the start that if they don't pay us quickly they will get harassed. So, we have a very high success ratio."

### Case Example: A Computerized Export Credit and Collection System

Receivables management is difficult enough for purely domestic sales. But that is only half the battle for MNCs with significant export sales. Such firms must not only establish procedures to protect the company from country risk, but must also deal with such pitfalls as foreign exchange controls and poor credit rating information on foreign customers. To make matters worse, export payment instruments are more complex than those used for domestic sales, and the collection cycle is usually longer, which leaves more time for delays.

A United States chemicals MNC has developed a computer system to upgrade control over its export collections by integrating an enormous amount of detailed receivables data and presenting it in the shape of *Form A* (see Figure 5–3). This customer status report contains a wealth of information, including the credit line assigned to the customer (CR LINE) and the date the credit line was assigned (C/L Date). If the C/L Date is 12 months old, the order is automatically referred to the credit department. The form also shows the payment terms (TERMS) used for the customer. In this case, they are 120-day sight draft documents against acceptance. If an order comes through with different terms, that order is kicked out for review by the credit manager.

Another feature is the Dun and Bradstreet Rating (DB Rating). In this case, the client company is not quoted in D&B. The form then identifies whether the importer is a subsidiary and notes the risk class assigned by the credit manager. In this case, the space is blank indicating this is not a subsidiary. "We have three classifications—*A*,

## Form A

| FSCP | | CR LINE: | 900000 | C/L DATE: | 070985 | MGR | J-AS |
|------|--|----------|--------|-----------|--------|-----|------|
| REMIT 982199 | | TERMS: | 120 SD/DA | DB RATING | NQ | -RISK | C |
| PARENT 00000 | | INV YTD: | 903108 | FST SALE | 09/82 | DUN: | 10X |
| | | INV PYR: | 1154000 | LST SALE: | 072785 | STAGE: | 0 |
| | | HYBAL: | 752358 | LST CASH: | 081385 | LTR1: | 999999 |
| | | HI PYR: | 685597 | PO BOX: | PHILA | LTR2: | 000000 |
| | | ACTION DATE: | 082885 | STATEMENT: | S | OK: | 75600 |
| 28258/28269 | | PAYS-DISC: | 000% | PROMPT: | 096% | LATE: | 004% |
| PD26AGLB99 | | AVG ELP DYS: | 165 | DAYS LATE: | 1 | CUR MO: | 3 |

LST  -3  2  -2  1  1  2  -4  1  1  0  2  11

| FUTURE | CURRENT | 1-30 | 31-60 PD | 61-90 PD | 90+ PD | BALANCE |
|--------|---------|------|----------|----------|--------|---------|
| 331296 | 187306 | 192910 | 0 | 0 | 0 | 711512.00 |

PAGE 1 of 2

### OPEN ITEMS

| INV DATE | INV NO | REFERENCE | AMOUNT | TERMS | DUE DATE | SBU | LTR |
|----------|--------|-----------|--------|-------|----------|-----|-----|
| 03/13/85 | 000-28258 | PN/2060 | 40000.00 | 120SD/SA | 082585 | 095 | |
| 03/13/85 | 000-28289 | VP/792 | 36200.00 | 120SD/SA | 082385 | 095 | |
| 03/14/85 | 000-28247 | VP/797 | 39200.00 | 120SD/SA | 082385 | 095 | |
| 03/19/85 | 000-28276 | VP/799 | 38400.00 | 120SD/SA | 082385 | 095 | |
| 04/01/85 | 000-28269 | VP/780 | 39110.00 | 120SD/SA | 082485 | 095 | |
| 04/18/85 | 000-28349 | VP/797 | 35200.00 | 120SD/SA | 091685 | 095 | |
| 04/18/85 | 000-28350 | VP/795 | 36700.00 | 120SD/SA | 091685 | 095 | |

UPDTE?    RETURN?    PAST?    CLSED?    STMT?    GOTO: _____

Figure 5-3: Example of a Customer Status Report

*B,* and *C,*" remarked the credit manager. "If this were an *A* risk, then orders under our credit approval system would clear automatically, regardless of the credit line assigned to that customer. We don't want to see those orders."

The report also shows the dollar amount of invoices for that customer for the current year (INV YTD) and the prior year (INV PYR). This reveals whether business with this customer is increasing. It then gives the date of the first sale made to the customer (FST SALE) and the date of the most recent sale (LST SALE). It shows the highest outstanding balance the customer has had this year (HYBAL) and last year (HI PYR), and identifies where the customer should send his check (PO BOX). The company has a lockbox (a bank-operated post box for speeding collections) at that location.

A very useful feature of this system is the automated dunning cycle. Considering customer and country practices, the credit manager assigns a dun date (DUN) to each customer, showing the number of days after the due date that dunning should commence. Said the credit manager, "If we decide, for example, that a bill with a maturity date of September 4 will be paid in seven days, it will automatically come out of our system if it is still unpaid on September 11. The dun dates depend on the payment practices we have experienced in a country. For example, we review accounts more quickly in the United Kingdom than in Ecuador because we know that there will be a long delay in Ecuador. This way, we won't waste our time dunning customers before they are likely to pay."

The form also shows what stage the customer is in if dunning has started (STAGE), and whether the first or second letter or telex has been sent, and the date it was sent (LTR). The credit manager noted, "The computer would automatically generate a dunning letter. But we don't use letters for international sales. We use telexes. But, I would telex the customer directly only on rare occasions. In most cases, we will go to the subsidiary and let them go to the customer."

In addition to a dunning date, the credit manager can manually input an action date. "I may want to go into an account on a particular date to check something out. If I want to see that account next Monday, I will enter that date and it will appear on my action list for Monday. I can also enter a note showing why I want to see the account." In this example, the credit manager set 8/28/85 as an action date for following up on invoices that were due prior to that date. The printout shows in the space for notes, on the left side of the form, that the invoice numbers 28258/28269 marked for follow-up were paid on August 26 to lockbox 99. Thus, the credit manager will not have to follow up those invoices on August 28.

The form also shows that a statement is mailed every month to the customer and identifies the amount of orders that have been approved but not yet shipped and billed (OK). The balance outstanding plus the OK balance should be less than the credit limit or else the order is automatically kicked out for review.

The next line records the percentage of payments the customer made by taking a discount, paying promptly, and paying late. The credit manager explained his approach: "If the customer's not paying a substantial percentage promptly, we will go to him to find out why. We can also check against prior records to see if the percentage of late payments is increasing. This shows that you may have a credit problem with that customer."

Also tracked automatically are the average number of days that elapse prior to payment (AVG ELP DYS); the average number of days the customer has been late in payment (DAYS LATE); the number of days he was late on his payments this month (CUR MO); and the average for each of the prior 12 months, starting with this month (LST). Negative numbers show that the customer paid ahead of schedule.

Next, the form shows the balance outstanding. It shows the total due over 30 days from now (FUTURE), and the amount due within the next 30 days (CURRENT). Then the form displays the amount past due for one to 30 days, 31 to 60 days, 61 to 90 days, and over 90 days, and the total past current and future due amounts (BALANCE). In this case, $192,910 is entered in the one to 30 days past due column.

The form then identifies all open items. It shows the invoice date, invoice number, customer order or reference number, amount of the invoice, terms of sale, and due date. The due date can be changed. The local bank tells the manager when the sight draft has been accepted so that he can go into the system and adjust the due date to agree with the bank's records. The items with due dates prior to the date the record is called, equal the amount past due. If interested in only late accounts, the credit manager can also request a report that shows only the past due information. The full report also tracks receivables by strategic business unit (SBU), and shows whether a dunning letter or telex has been sent on that specific invoice (LTR). In this case, the dunning cycle has not yet been initiated because there are no items over 10 days past due.

Finally, the report is updated every night to reflect new invoices and new payments. "The bank's computer talks to our computer at night and tells it that such and such items were paid to our account," explained the credit manager.

The credit manager elaborated on the example: "At the top of the form, it shows that we gave this customer 120 days sight draft; sight draft means when he gets the documents in his country. In this case, the country is Australia. There are approximately 40 days sailing time to Australia. When the shipment arrives, the customer accepts the draft. Then, 120 days later, he pays his bank and the bank wires the funds to us. On the average, it takes 165 days for his account to turn over with us, which is one day late. The form also shows how promptly he has been paying for each of the 12 prior months. We look at this to see if there is a trend showing that the delays are getting worse."

## COMPUTERIZING DISBURSEMENT MANAGEMENT

All too often, disbursement management—the flip side of credit and collection—is a weak link in corporate cash management systems. This is because, unlike accounts receivable, payables do not constitute working assets and thus have a less noticeable impact on profits and financing costs.

However, firms pay a high price for their failure to take a cogent, systematic approach to payables management. For example, one Hong Kong-based treasurer of a United States company was shocked with the results of an audit conducted on subsidiary disbursement management practices: "What I discovered was some companies would get an invoice, approve it, and pay it the same week. So, I emphasized that the payables were not to be made until they had to be made according to the general terms of trade in the area." So, to help its Japanese subsidiary follow this standard textbook approach, the firm installed an automated payables system. The result: an estimated quarter of a million dollars in annual savings. "It's a large operation there, there's a lot of money involved, and they were paying about 30 days in advance of terms. We saved all that money just by extending payment out to the full length of the terms."

According to the survey, a fast-growing number of companies are following this firm's lead. In fact, 39% of respondents have already largely automated payables management—the highest rate for any cash management function covered in this study—and 56% will do so within three years.

This section will explore how companies are automating three key areas of payables management: reporting, internal processing, and making disbursements. The section will conclude with a glimpse into a possible future world of paperless payments.

## Automating Payables Reporting

As with collections, the monitoring and reporting capabilities of computers can be used to alert companies to inefficiencies in corporate payables practices. For example, systems can track outstanding disbursements and cash disbursements outstanding (CDOs—the payables equivalent of days' sales outstanding) to see how well a payables department is meeting general payments guidelines. In addition, such reports can help companies assess the impact of disbursement timing on supplier relations and measure the impact of discounts or penalty fees on liquidity.

Computerized systems also help track disbursement float, which is the time it takes for a payment to reach a supplier and work its way through a bank clearing system. For example, the United Kingdom subsidiary of a United States chemicals firm is working on an in-house program to monitor clearing times automatically by comparing the dates checks are issued with bank statements showing when they are debited. A spokesperson for the company explained, "The real problem is that we don't know how efficient our suppliers are in presenting checks to be debited from our accounts. In the quickest settlements, we count one and one-half days' mail float plus two days clearing, for a total of three to three and one-half days. But some of our customers are very inefficient in presenting checks, and we get about 10 days in those cases. Until we know that we've got that 10-day float, we can't use it. We're building this computer program to figure that out."

A good example of a highly automated payables reporting system is provided by a United States building materials manufacturer. According to the company's cash manager, disbursements—including payroll and plant expenses—are fully managed from parent headquarters. But "All the documentation is done at the local level—matching invoices, preparing the paperwork, everything we need to get to the point where a check can be written." However, to coordinate its centralized payables strategy, the firm established computer links to keep headquarters in constant touch with its 25 operating units. "Our accounts payable function at the local level, processes payment information for use by our corporate accounts payable. They're a feeder mechanism; they channel payables information to parent headquarters."

The company can pull several reports off its on-line system. First, it can get an uncompared-item report. It is produced as follows: Upon receipt of goods, the dock supervisor compares the vendor's invoice with the contents. The invoice is stamped and forwarded to the operating unit's accounts payables staff, which enters the data into the computer system and runs a comparison program with purchase orders. Uncompared items, because of price, quantity, or description, are segregated and compiled in a special report. That report can then be accessed by the appropriate local manager who takes the proper actions.

Second, the system can produce a 501 report. Items of a capital nature, that is anything to be capitalized and depreciated, are the object of this special authorization report. "Let's say you were going to spend a million dollars on something," a local manager explained. "Our treasury people would be tuned in through a report we run called a 501, which is available to everyone in the approval process, including the cash manager." The report enables the cash manager to prepare for extraordinary items.

Third, the system can provide a vendor-payment detail report, which is produced daily by all 25 operating units and transmitted to headquarters. This keeps the parent informed of all purchases. The listing includes vendor name, address, amount due, and due date. "Since terms are generally 30 days," the headquarters spokesperson explained, "we have an excellent idea of our cash requirements."

Fourth, the system provides a payroll report. Every two weeks, each operating unit transmits its hourly payroll information to the parent. The system then cuts checks for salaried employees automatically.

These four reports are based on information fed from local companies to headquarters. But information can flow both ways. The operating units can obtain two reports prepared by headquarters. First, the units can receive a payment-status report. As checks are issued, the amount and check number are input into the system. The status is automatically updated when checks clear. Because many of the units deal with the same suppliers, payments to vendors are often lumped together in a single check. In that case, the cash manager explained, "The computer produces a listing for the vendor of all invoices being paid, and divides the aggregate payment among the individual invoices for the units' information." Second, the units can also see a budget-variance report. Once a month, the system compiles a statement informing managers of their current budget status. According to a division manager, "This helps us keep things under control. If we're going over, maybe I'd better look into it. But usually we know what's happening. However, the system has built-in tolerances and if a unit goes beyond its budget, it signals the cash manager at corporate headquarters.

According to the spokesperson, the automated and centralized payables system yields a number of benefits: "First, we can see the cash position for the company as a whole at the push of a button, which enables us to maximize cash deployment. Secondly, it's made bank management much simpler and more cost-effective. Because we've centralized, we use fewer banks and our costs are much lower. And we don't have unused funds sitting around in a lot of banks. Finally, we have multiple locations that don't have to worry about printing checks, issuing checks, and reconciling bank accounts. The computer system really saves them that staff time and effort because we can see all the information here and we do all those jobs here."

Another illustration of a sophisticated payables reporting system is provided by a United States consumer goods firm. The firm's reporting package has four components. First, to convert requisitions into purchase orders and to report that data to accounts payable, it has a purchasing control module. This module helps the purchasing department evaluate vendors based on price, quantity, and on-time delivery. It also gives accounts payable staff advance warning of upcoming disbursements. Next, to determine how to pay vendors, and who will do it, it contains control and structure data. This module defines how accounting entries will be accumulated and contains information on material specifications, banking channels, payment schedules, and account codes. To supplement this module, the system contains vendor data, including vendor numbers, names, and alternate payees. Finally, the system holds accounts payable data, which contains information on the following invoices: regular, prepaid, credit memos, debit memos, and contracts (e.g., rent).

The system also automates staff reports and internal processing tasks. Reports include current and future cash requirements by pay period and vendor, as well as ad hoc reports tailored to the needs of treasury staff. It also performs automatic check reconciliation.

---

### AUTOMATING FOREIGN DRAFTS

Drafts are checks drawn in foreign currency to pay overseas suppliers and employees. An automated system for foreign draft issuances provided by a subsidiary of a United States bank promises to relieve the problems usually associated with such transactions and to save companies money as well.

A microcomputer-based software package is the heart of the system. To start, the user chooses one of the available currencies. Then, the image of a check and a voucher appears on the screen. The user enters the date, transfer amount, and recipient in their appropriate places on the check, and inputs the control information on the voucher. The system then prints a check on check stock, ready to be mailed to the supplier. "We used to have to call our bank, order the draft, and then wait to get it back," commented one satisfied user. "At one point last year, it was taking about a week. Now, if we need a rush draft, we can do it right here."

The check data is captured for daily transmission to the bank's information processing center, where the balances, check numbers, and currency are checked electronically. The bank computer consolidates all the incoming draft data, and the parent bank's traders buy the currencies.

After the currencies are purchased, the check data is beamed by satellite to a branch of the parent bank in the

---

supplier's home country. The funds are transferred to an account of the bank's subsidiary at the local branch, enabling the branch to pay the check. Explained a spokesperson for the subsidiary, "The company issues the check today, we buy the currency tonight, and the money is available in our account two days later. That's the quickest anybody can do it, unless you transfer the funds from an overseas local currency hold account." The issuer, meanwhile, transfers the cash to the New York account of the subsidiary, which then uses the money to fund the various payment accounts it holds around the world.

The automated system offers the benefits of lower fees and enhanced control. Said one user, "Drafts certainly are lower-priced using the new system. It's under $10, and it's normally around $20 if you order a draft on the phone." In addition, because the computer consolidates the orders of over 100 corporations and banks, the cost of foreign exchange is cut.

Another benefit of the computerized system is that the company handles the draft from initiation to mailing the check. "We can depend on ourselves here," said one firm's cash operations analyst. "But when you call a bank, once you get your fingers out of the pie, you're depending on someone there to do the work." The system also generates a variety of convenient internal audit reports, which summarize issuances by currency, check number and American dollar amount, and expense code.

## Streamlining Internal Processing

The success of any disbursement strategy hinges on the ability of payables staff to execute internal procedures in a swift and orderly fashion. Without efficient processing of invoices and payments, companies run the risk of missing out on discounts, injuring supplier relations through chronically late payments, or, even worse, needlessly incurring additional financing costs.

To avoid these costly mistakes, and to reduce administrative expenses, a growing number of companies are turning to automated internal processing. Companies are finding that such systems reduce staffing requirements because they don't need people to prepare payments, match them to invoices, make sure an approval for payment has been obtained. In addition, reconciliation time is usually reduced considerably.

The money that can be saved by automating just one administrative aspect of the payables function was demonstrated by a bank consultant who audited the operations of an Australian manufacturing subsidiary. According to the consultant's analysis, the firm's manual check-processing costs included the following:

| Item | Unit cost |
|---|---|
| Stamp duty | A$0.10 |
| Bank processing charge | 0.18 |
| Check stock | .05 |
| Secretarial cost at 4.7 minutes per check | 0.90 |
| Total cost per check | A$1.23 |

In this study, about three quarters of the expense of manual check writing could be attributed to manual preparation. As a result, the consultant recommended purchasing a system that, at a low initial cost, would automatically print checks several times a month. The system could also be configured to automatically update the firm's computerized accounting records and cash forecast.

Another important benefit of automation is increased control over disbursement procedures. A cash manager of a United States firm described the virtues of an automated payables package obtained from his bank: "We keep track of our payables on an electronic ledger. Every time we issue a check, we have the amount, the magnetic code, the invoice number, and this is transmitted to the bank via terminal. Then, as the checks arrive, the bank compares them to our ledger, and if there's a match, they pay out. It really streamlines our payables. The advantage of the arrangement is better control and the fact the disbursement account is fully reconciled at all times. If for some reason we want to stop payment, that can be done over the terminal as well."

A major United States retailer has gone so far as to automate virtually every aspect of its payables—including an electronic ordering system. According to a company executive, "Not all our suppliers have this arrangement, but we'll set it up if we have sufficient volume and they're willing." Not only is the payables ledger updated when the order is placed but, at some locations, a wand reads a bar code to electronically record the arrival of goods at the loading dock. "The receiving desk makes note of any damage or shortage and this is included in a supplementary report." Informed of the receipt of goods, the system can then generate payment in the form of an electronic credit.

## Controlling Disbursements Electronically

Once the how and when of supplier payments are determined, these parameters can be programmed into a computer along with invoice and transaction details to keep payables staff informed of upcoming disbursements, and to enable them to devise the most cost-effective disbursement strategies. For a multinational corporation, the computer is the ideal tool to keep track of the world-wide variety of payment terms, instruments, and environmental practices.

For instance, a United States agricultural equipment manufacturer built a computer system for overseas subsidiaries to monitor all payment terms and instruments, and also to generate checks, drafts, and bank transfer orders for domestic operating units. Explained a treasurer, "All the suppliers are coded in the computer. Their outstanding invoices with the due date and the amount are recorded when orders are placed. The computer calculates how much is falling due every day and the payment methods to be used." When a payment is made, the computer automatically eliminates the invoice from the queue.

With the system, the treasurer can more precisely time disbursements to match cash outflows with inflows, thus optimizing borrowing and investment tactics. This would be a complicated procedure if done manually, because the company's production cycle causes extreme fluctuations in revenue during certain times of the month. A spokesperson clarified this problem: "I have more supplier payments falling due on the 10th and the 15th. So I try to match up receivables with the amount of disbursements that I know I have. I keep operations so that they have invoices on one side of the desk and checks on the other. You put the checks in when you know that you have the invoices covered. This is why we went from making disbursements at the plant level to making them by our centralized finance people—more finance control."

The savings resulting from using automated systems to control payments were highlighted by one treasurer of a United States chemicals concern. Since the company fully computerized the disbursements of its European subsidiaries, payables managers throughout the region are able to identify exactly when payments are due. According to the treasurer, "This is proving very beneficial in the United Kingdom, where we had a tendency to pay suppliers ahead of time. Now we can pay right on the due date. With weekly payments of five or six million dollars, we're saving a lot of money." Indeed, with annual Europe-wide disbursements of over $250 million, the company estimates that it saves $230,000 a year with the system.

Computerized payment systems also help firms keep track of special payment terms. For instance, many suppliers offer discounts for prompt payment, and one building materials manufacturer found that its automated system helped exploit these opportunities. The firm maintains a computer listing of all suppliers, invoices, and credit terms, and the software makes sure the company pays within certain time periods for certain suppliers. This takes advantage of discounts of up to three percent and saves the firm 20 to 30% per year.

On the other hand, one United States company turned to computers because it was constantly incurring penalty fees for late payment and was damaging supplier relations. Explained the firm's treasurer, "We were paying a lot of interest to suppliers for overdue payments—21% over the merchandise charges in some cases. That's where we were really losing. So we installed a computer system to make sure we pay everything on time."

However, the prospect of paying on time does not appeal to all companies. Many firms still resist automating their disbursement systems because they fear loss of disbursement float. As a treasurer of a French chemicals firm commented, "We find that the old, slow manual techniques are much better for us—if not for our suppliers." And, companies that want to delay payment can follow the lead of a United Kingdom firm that built payment delays into its automated payables system. According to a spokesperson, "We computerized our payables, but we made sure that we stayed as inefficient as ever. We've programmed the computer to ignore the due date on invoices and produce checks as of the date we normally pay suppliers—which is well beyond the stated terms."

Finally, companies are automating their disbursement systems to take advantage of electronic payment modes that are often more flexible and less expensive than paper-based methods. For instance, one United Kingdom capital goods company programmed a monthly payments cycle into its computer. Each month, the computer issues payments by generating BACS[1] tapes for most of the bills. If computer tapes containing payment details are submitted to BACS two days before value date, BACS processes the information and electronic payment is effected for same-day settlement on the specified value date. (For more on direct depositing and similar electronic payment services, see Chapter 8.)

### Future Vision: EBDI and the Demise of Traditional Cash Management

If Electronic Business Data Interchange (EBDI) gains universal acceptance, routine trading documents will soon be transmitted between the computers of suppliers and customers in all industries. Furthermore, as paper trails are abandoned, electronic payment systems, such as Corporate Trade Payments under the Automated Clearing House (ACH) system in the United States, will become more viable. In the process, the position of cash manager will be changed substantially.

As a first step toward a paperless environment, companies are realizing that they need to automate and standardize all intracorporate and bank communication processes. The problem is basically one of setting standards and protocols to be followed by everyone so that different computers can understand each other. A number of industry associations have attempted, with some success, to set standards, but EBDI represents the efforts of the American National Standards Institute (ANSI) to set national and international standards. However, negotiations with other countries and attempts to make industry standards compatible with ANSI standards have been

---

[1] Bankers Automated Clearing Systems, an independent company for direct deposit services owned by the major London clearing banks.

long and arduous. Although international links are now being set up, the institutionalization of EBDI is still in the planning stage.

The prime mover in the drive toward overall automation has been the American automotive industry. The Big Three have all set timetables by which vendor relations should be automated, and all are operating under the EBDI format developed by ANSI. Recent estimates predicted that the industry will be 90% paperless by 1990.

When that industry meets that goal, prophets of EBDI believe that a domino effect will ensue. For instance, General Motors deals with some 20,000 suppliers in the steel, glass, chemical, and rubber industries. Once the automaker automates relations with these vendors, some people believe that the vendors will turn around and try to automate their supplier relations. The subsequent ripple effect would draw more and more companies into the EBDI network. Predicted one expert, "EBDI will have the same impact on business in general that the telephone did when it became a viable business tool."

This has dramatic implications for the cash manager. The delay between when a purchase is made and when a cash manager is informed of it will be eliminated. As one industry spokesperson envisioned, "You transmit an on-line order to a vendor; the vendor ships the order; the shipping notice will be generated and electronically transmitted to the customer. That action will trigger the billing department to prepare an invoice and send it electronically to the customer." Thus, the cash manager will not have to wait for a battery of clerks to deliver a three-day-old status report. The cash manager could, instead, track the status of outstanding receivables and payables in real time from a terminal—honing cash forecasting to precision.

In addition, corporate resistance to automated payment systems under the ACH could be washed away by the impact of EBDI. According to the director of cash management at one of the Big Three automakers, companies have not embraced electronic payment systems to date because the economics are weak. "If you simply turn a paper check into a stream of electrons, you save a postage stamp, an envelope, and paper check stock." But with EBDI, the equation is altered drastically. "If the company communicates electronically such information as price quotes, purchase orders, purchase order acknowledgments, invoices, and so forth, to its suppliers," pronounced the manager, "then the addition of an electronic payment in a compatible format has the potential to automate the entire cash management function."

For one thing, the uncertainty that plagues all cash managers would be eliminated. "You will know with precision when you're paying out funds and when you're receiving funds," said an EBDI enthusiast. Added the automaker's cash manager, "There is sloppiness in today's system due to the uncertainties of check payments and receipts. As a result, you either overborrow or leave too much cash that's idle." When both supplier and customer use EBDI and the accompanying electronic payment system, the chance of misapplication of funds is significantly reduced.

Secondly, the role of float would disappear. Commented the treasurer of a consumer products firm active in EBDI, "Traditionally, the cash manager's role has been to accelerate receipts, decelerate payments, and minimize the amount of idle cash on hand each night. That is becoming obsolete—all those funny little manipulative games of the traditional cash manager will disappear."

Finally, the automaker's director of cash management speculated that the definition of the traditional cash manager would be forever changed: "The MIS function and the cash management function will be merged. Where the cash manager was traditionally on the treasurer's side, this role will blend and blur into accounts receivable and payable on the controller's side. The manager will become an information manager who will be more integrated into the information used by other parts of the organization—the purchasing function, the sales function. There will be someone perhaps called the EBDI manager. That is the proper role for today's cash manager to be assuming."

## AUTOMATED DEBT AND INVESTMENT MANAGEMENT

In the attempt to match cash needs with internally generated funds as closely as possible, almost all cash managers enter the credit or investment markets from time to time to cover temporary cash shortfalls or to maximize earnings on short-term excess funds. A growing number of companies are finding that they can use computers to improve the monitoring and analysis of both these short-term investment and borrowing opportunities. To this end, respondents to the survey will nearly triple their use of computers for these functions over the next few years—from 10 to 27%.

Easy-to-use electronic spreadsheets have greatly spurred debt and investment automation. One consumer products company, for example, stores investment information and banking data on its microcomputer and uses a spreadsheet to "track all the instruments we've entered into, their rates, when they mature," explained the firm's treasurer. "If you have a lot of investments, it is very inconvenient to keep track of all of them on paper. It's worth a little money to get them on a computer." Should the firm need to borrow, debt instruments are maintained in the same fashion. An example of the type of spreadsheet report is illustrated in Figure 5–4.

Computers can also be programmed to search out the highest-yielding investment or the cheapest borrowing instrument. An Italian auto manufacturer, for example, turned to automation to discover the wide number of potential debt instruments at its disposal. The firm uses a micro-based financial information system to answer what-if questions about, for example, conditions in domestic markets as compared to the Euromarkets. The firm's system also contains information on the various types of instruments available and indicates the least expensive option. To do so, it looks at the information the firm stores on all bank credit arrangements and their associated rates. "The computer searches the database for the least expensive credit lines to cover the projected cash needs," the company's CFO explained. "Then it identifies the best borrowing instruments for a certain maturity, and we just decide which is the most economical credit line available."

Software packages also help improve treasury's ability to analyze and report borrowing and investment information. In the experi-

| Unit/company and country _____ | | | Date: _____ | | | |
|---|---|---|---|---|---|---|
| Investment or borrowing | Amount and currency | Instrument | Date Initiated | Date matures | Rate | Comments |
| | | | | | | |

**Figure 5–4: Sample Spreadsheet Layout for Investments/Borrowings Outstanding**

ence of one United States treasury manager, "When you start dealing with parent company borrowing, then you need sensitivities. The Chairman of the Board wants to know what happens if prime goes down $x$%—what is the cross-over point where commercial paper becomes more cost-effective than long-term debt. These things are endless. It helps to see it graphically. We just started to do these graphs when I came here—but we can't run a treasury function without it." Likewise, another treasurer inputs debt monitoring information by type, level, and average interest expense, and then uses a spreadsheet to show which bank debt and commercial paper are coming due. This helps the firm determine, for example, how to stagger more expensive bank debt to get more easily into the commercial paper market.

By storing this type of historical borrowing information, treasurers also have an effective tool to determine borrowing strategies and to negotiate with lenders. For instance, one treasurer of a United States manufacturer uses a spreadsheet to analyze the firm's commercial paper program. "We input 30-, 60-, and 90-day rates from the Fed composite, Telerate information service, and our dealers. We compute an average rate for the Fed composite and Telerate numbers so we can compare how we're doing. We usually borrow at 12 over Telerate. So if I call up my dealers tomorrow and they quote me 30 above Telerate, I can say 'What do you think you're doing?'" The treasurer also graphs the average daily borrowings versus the computed averages of the Fed composite and Telerate numbers. "It shows me where to borrow in a yield curve. It really kills you when you get out to 120 days. Right now, 14 to 21 day rates are the best."

Debt and investment management software is also a standard module on many treasury workstation packages. For further details, see Chapter 8.

## AUTOMATED TRACKING OF BANKING COSTS AND RELATIONS

Of all the functional areas of cash management, none offers greater potential savings than bank relations management. For one thing, banking costs constitute a heavy and highly-visible financial burden for all companies. For another, local managers are all too often unfamiliar with the latest techniques and services that can be used to reduce these costs.

For this reason, respondents to the survey predict that they will substantially increase their use of computers to monitor and manage bank relations, track and analyze banking costs, and evaluate local subsidiary performance. According to the survey results, the percentage of firms with highly automated bank relations systems will increase from 5 to 20%.

Companies are automating banking relations for the following four reasons:

1. **To track banking costs.** Information is a strong ally in negotiations with bankers, and one that is absolutely necessary. For instance, a European automaker set up an automated bank cost tracking system several years ago to get firm data. The program records all bank compensation—including fees, spreads, commissions, and value dating—and calculates the firm's level of business with each bank. It also estimates the profitability of the firm's business to each bank. "We mark every bank movement that comes through our accounting system," explained the company's treasurer. "The point of this project is to help us treat a bank exactly like any other supplier. It's very useful in negotiations, because you know what you can ask for and what you can't." And, when the firm asks for below-market rates, the banks usually give in. "This is because the firm knows precisely how much business we are giving to each of the banks we use," said the spokesperson. "We simply prove to them that they are receiving an adequate rate of return from our business. When they come to complain about the low rates we pay, I just call up the report again. Most of the time, they walk away with their heads down."

2. **To assess and minimize bank risk.** To protect itself from the threat of bank failure, a United States automaker regularly assesses the credit risks of its banks by examining balance sheet rations and using such outside agencies as IBCA and Standard & Poor's. Based on this credit analysis, the firm sets and records the limits on the amount of funds it will deposit with a bank on a worldwide basis. The firm's computer automatically notifies treasury staff when a bank's investment ceiling has been reached.

A German MNC has developed an interesting variation on this theme in response to the failures of two major German banks in the early 1980s. Its computer measures bank credit risk, and then calculates the spread the company should earn on its deposits with a particular bank, compared to an investment in risk-free government paper.

3. **To evaluate performance.** Computerized analysis of banking relations also gives headquarters the ability to assess local managers' banking practices. One consumer goods firm that uses over 1000 banks electronically tracks local account analyses "just to stay on top of things," in the words of the company's banking manager. "We don't go through every account analysis every month; though if they are atrocious enough, it pays off to do so. When we first started monitoring the divisions' banking relations, we discovered some really bizarre things. I think we've really reduced the number of those mistakes by being able to embarrass the local account officer by sending it back and asking if they really reviewed this before they sent it out."

4. **To control administrative details.** Keeping track of details is a made-to-order application for computers. For instance, an assistant treasurer for a large beverage distributor was responsible for tracking 3000 bank accounts with multiple signatures. Keeping tabs manually was a nightmare because people constantly changed positions. To solve the problem, the firm developed a simple search-and-find program on a microcomputer to look up the names.

The sheer volume of standard bank correspondence can also cause problems for a manual operation. At one services firm, the cash manager maintains bank relationship information on a word processing system. "It's just for changing signatories or opening and closing a bank account. We have a form letter that gets kicked out along with a signature page. It also generates reports on which banks we use. As we open or close accounts, it feeds a report that is the current list of banks—maintained alphabetically by bank or sorted by division." In sum, the potential applications of software for monitoring banking costs and resolving administrative relations is great. The survey shows that this potential is only starting to be tapped.

## SUMMARY

Cash management has its foundations in three functions—cash reporting and forecasting, credit and collections, and disbursements. Tangentially, it affects debt and investment management, and banking costs and relations. By automating these functions, companies can generate tremendous savings in time and expense. The study shows that most companies are following this lead of common sense, and that this is one of the most highly automated areas in global treasury. The leaders in automation tend to be centralized, North American, intermediate goods and high-tech manufacturers with annual sales over $2 billion. However, the survey indicates that this profile will be challenged by the growth of cash management computerization among smaller firms and in Asia.

In terms of the business cycle, the primary cash management functions are being affected by automation in the following ways:

**Cash Reporting and Forecasting:** Timely and accurate data are the key to effectiveness in this field. Treasurers need this information to assess performance, monitor cash positions, and maximize profit making. Delays and inaccuracies in the data often proved costly in the past, but the survey shows that era to be over, as 25% of surveyed companies have already largely automated their systems, and 91% plan to introduce automation to at least some part of their operation in the next few years.

**Credit and Collections:** Receivables management is a field ripe for computerization. Systems that can identify, track, and dun slow-paying customers; that can evaluate the credit risk and limits of each client; that can process order-to-invoice procedures — these are the systems of today that are generating enough interest so that 54% of survey respondents will have some type installed in their firms in the next few years. As testimony to their usefulness, 37% have actually automated this function to a high degree at this point in time.

**Disbursement Management:** Controlling how accounts payable are managed has never been a paramount goal for most companies, but automation has its uses in standardizing disbursement schedules, float, and procedures. The goal of maximizing the amount of time before payment, estimating and taking advantage of funds during float, and automating the rote processes of check processing is appealing enough that 39% of respondents have already largely automated payables management and 56% plan to be in that position within three years.

The secondary, noncyclical parts of cash management—debt and investment management, and banking costs and relations—are also warranting attention. Through wise use of microcomputers and spreadsheets, analysts have taken great advantage of short-term investment and borrowing activities. Likewise, by tracking bank operations, costs, and reports, firms can realize tremendous savings. In both cases, the key is information-tailored to a firm's needs; by monitoring market positions and matching those with funds a firm has available to invest (or that it needs to borrow), gains can be realized. And, by evaluating banks that service a firm's account in exactly the same manner as if the bank were a customer, a firm can gain the upper hand in fee and interest negotiations.

# CHAPTER 6

# Automating Foreign Exchange Management

## INTRODUCTION

Of all the areas targeted for automation within the global finance function, none has received less attention than currency management. As shown in Table 6–1, the survey reveals that only a handful of companies have computerized any aspect of their exposure management. This serves as stark contrast to the time and effort these same respondents have lavished on their cash management systems.

Why do companies prefer to automate cash rather than currency management? For one thing, the cost savings from forex automation are more difficult to quantify, making senior management approval a tough battle to win. As one treasurer in the United States put it, "There is a payoff on the cash management side in terms of identifying excess cash. If someone says I've got a million dollars in extra cash, you know exactly what you're going to do and how much you're going to make doing it. But if a system tells you you've got a million dollars in French franc exposure, that's only half the battle. Doing the right

**TABLE 6-1**

**Computerizing the Currency Function (in %)**

|  | At time of survey | Three-year projection |
|---|---|---|
| Reporting exposures | 13 | 33 |
| Tracking historical rates | 11 | 31 |
| Tracking contracts | 15 | 30 |
| Forecasting exposures | 5 | 25 |
| Hedging balance sheet exposure | 2 | 14 |
| Hedging specific transactions | 4 | 13 |

thing with the exposure, either covering it or leaving it open, is another thing altogether."

Making matters worse, companies cannot turn to their banks—as in the case of cash management—to get electronic currency management information. Explained a treasury management consultant, "The data needed for currency management can only be generated by the corporation itself, specifically by its foreign subsidiaries. And, they aren't as computerized as the banks. So automating currency management means that the company has to do a lot more work on its own."

Finally, because exposure management styles and definitions vary widely from company to company, corporate software requirements are more personalized and therefore more expensive than in the case of cash management. Some companies focus on translation exposure, others on transactions, and still others on economic exposure. Given the limited budgets of foreign exchange departments, such software is often hard to find. As one forex manager complained, "It has been difficult for software manufacturers to come up with computer packages flexible enough to serve many companies. Since the software is not available outside at a reasonable cost, you have to develop it in house. But few firms have the necessary resources, and many that do don't give it priority."

But times are changing. Companies are discovering that a lackadaisical attitude toward currency management, including the potential for automation, can have drastic consequences. An example is the experience of a Canadian petrochemicals firm that saw its financial statements battered by the currency markets in the early 1980s. With 75% of its sales denominated in foreign currencies and a small, overburdened forex, the company watched foreign exchange losses lop 17 million Canadian dollars off its income in 1981.

The company took immediate action. It brought in a treasury planning manager who instituted a sophisticated hedging program that used computers for reporting and analyzing exposures, as well as an on-line technical model for forecasting. The payback was swift: In 1982, forex losses were cut to C$4 million, and in 1983 they were halved to C$2 million. The company generated a C$300,000 gain in 1984, and last year, in the first quarter alone, it picked up C$6 million on its balance sheet and C$600,000 in income.

This savvy company is not alone in its drive for better currency management through automation. As can also be seen in the previous table, respondents to the survey will increase their use of computers markedly in some aspects of currency management over the next few years. This growing group of firms are automating for the following reasons:

- **Increased currency market volume and volatility.** With the liberalization of international capital and currency markets, a tremendous amount of hard currency now moves quickly across national borders, which, in turn causes tremendous volatility. Daily market tremors also force many firms to pay more attention to currency management automation. As one manager who recently automated the currency function put it, "We have just purchased a foreign exchange management system because we perceived a need to be more formalized in exposure management. What we were doing was crisis management. There was no forethought or plan. So we needed a vehicle to process the information. I think the benefits of the system will be tremendous. We'll be able to manage our exposure, and I think the bottom line results will show up very quickly."

- **Small treasury staffs.** Faced with the increasing demands of today's currency markets, traditionally small corporate forex departments need computers to do their jobs. According to a treasurer of a United States services firm, "For three to four years, the forex staff has not expanded, although the company has doubled in size. We couldn't handle the increased volume of trading without computers."

- **Improved software.** Fortunately, as companies have become more preoccupied with foreign exchange management, more advanced software and improved computer systems have also come out on the market.

Flexibility in fine-tuning systems to unique company needs has enabled companies to overcome one of the major impediments to computerized currency management—differing definitions of exposure. Explained one forex manager, "In the past, if you weren't using an accounting-based exposure definition, the system was really not very good for you. The beauty of the system we purchased is that it is not highly preset in the sense of exposure definition. You can plug in an accounting-based system or a pure cash flow system. It's completely wide open in the way you want to structure your exposure definition. You could even do two different kinds of exposure definitions if you wanted to. This system looks like it would allow people to do it any way they wanted."

This chapter explains how companies are taking advantage of these recent developments to protect themselves from currency market swings. It shows how computers can facilitate subsidiary-to-parent reporting and ease the task of headquarters staff by consolidating and identifying corporate-wide exposures and outstanding hedges. The chapter will also examine the latest decision support software used by firms to develop hedging strategies and currency forecasts.

## Case Example: The Evolution of an Automated Currency Management System

A United States chemicals concern with extensive overseas operations and enormous currency exposures illustrates both the dramatic transformation many multinational companies are now undergoing in their approach to automated forex management, as well as the numerous functions a sophisticated computer system can perform. From elementary beginnings, the firm's exposure management evolved over the last ten years into a highly sophisticated computer system.

A decade ago, the company began to operate in the foreign exchange markets "in a modest way," according to a spokesperson. "We may not have thought so at the time, but compared to what's happened in the markets since then, and with the growth of our business, it looks like kindergarten."

Given the low level of currency trading activity, the firm had "just the beginnings of automation. Prior to that time, the very few forward contracts we had were just kept on a big spreadsheet. Somebody would copy it and pull off information when they needed it. But then we began to use what we referred to as automation, but it was no more than a sorted computer list. It was just a listing of our forwards that you could sort by maturity, or date, or bank, or currency, or which company held them, and so forth."

But that degree of automation soon proved too primitive. "About four years ago, we were growing like crazy. For a while, we were growing at 10% a year. Then we acquired a major petroleum producer. All of a sudden, our foreign exchange transaction volume tripled and then it went up again by 25%, and we recognized that we had to do something because we could not manually carry on an operation of that size."

To find the answer to its automation problems, the firm tapped its own internal resources. "We started ourselves, with four or five people, with a PC tied into a mainframe—no programmer, writing our own programs, setting up things like a listing of the forwards, what our limitations on bank exposures were, and certain dates. So we put that on and we did it all ourselves, and that helped us to sort of keep going through this rapid growth period."

The company quickly discovered, however, that this was only a stopgap solution. According to the forex manager, "We realized that we couldn't keep writing separate, individual programs every time something came up. And the accounting and cash disbursement people had to use our information. We couldn't just be on our own, insulated from the others, running kind of efficiently in our own shop, but with everybody else taking a printout and punching it into their own systems."

Two years ago, therefore, the company set out to prepare a multi-purpose system that served not only forex, but also the people who used the results of those transactions. The company considered a number of outside packages, but ruled them out because they didn't suit their accounting needs. Consequently, the firm decided to write its own software.

The company called in programmers from its MIS department as well as professionals from other relevant departments, and then hired an outside consultant. "A great deal of [the consultant's] help was in systems design and flow charting rather than the actual programming," explained the spokesperson. The system runs on a mainframe, and "We are very pleased with it," he added. "It tracks all of the data we need internally, it automatically generates all the paperwork required for a foreign exchange transaction, and it handles the accounting and cash disbursement chores. It's allowed us to really increase our volume significantly with fewer people, and we have much better control, and an audit trail." Believing that other companies would realize the same benefits, the outside consultant asked and received permission to license and market the package.

### Which Companies Are Automating Currency Management—and Why

When making the decision to automate currency management, treasury staffs should bear in mind that their computer requirements are largely determined by the nature and extent of their firms' multinational operations. According to the survey, the factors of size, industry type, domicile, and type of organization play a major role in shaping corporate currency systems and strategies.

As pertains to size, the survey revealed the same pattern in currency management automation as in treasury management automation in general. Size is a key determinant in a company's decision to computerize the function, as shown in Table 6–2.

The reason for these sharp variations is simple: Large companies, especially those with multiple overseas operations, have much greater needs than smaller firms for automated systems that monitor their heavy forex trading activities and identify and forecast global currency exposures. But as with treasury management, the future will again see sharp growth in computerized systems among small and medium-sized companies positioned to expand their international operations.

The second factor evaluated in the survey was industry type. And, as can be seen in Table 6–3, high technology firms and intermediate goods companies, as usual, are at the top of the survey. But producers of consumer goods are nearly as automated.

**TABLE 6–2**

**Automation in Currency Management**
(In percent of survey respondents)

| | Reporting currency exposures | | Tracking terms of currency contracts | | Making decisions on hedging balance sheet exposure | |
|---|---|---|---|---|---|---|
| Annual Sales | Auto-mated | Will automate in next few years | Auto-mated | Will automate in next few years | Auto-mated | Will automate in next few years |
| Over $2 billion | 24 | 47 | 29 | 47 | 5 | 14 |
| $500 million–$2 billion | 15 | 38 | 15 | 31 | 2 | 2 |
| $200 million–$499 million | 4 | 26 | 4 | 18 | 0 | 18 |
| Under $200 million | 4 | 16 | 5 | 15 | 0 | 14 |
| **Number of Foreign Operating Units** | | | | | | |
| Over 40 | 28 | 57 | 40 | 56 | 9 | 18 |
| 21–40 | 21 | 51 | 26 | 50 | 8 | 24 |
| 11–20 | 15 | 37 | 15 | 32 | 0 | 18 |
| 6–10 | 8 | 29 | 4 | 14 | 0 | 9 |
| 1–5 | 7 | 17 | 8 | 19 | 0 | 9 |

**TABLE 6–3**

**Industry Type and Automation in Currency Management**
(In percent of survey respondents)

| | Reporting currency exposures | | Tracking terms of currency contracts | | Making decisions on hedging balance sheet exposure | |
|---|---|---|---|---|---|---|
| | Auto-mated | Will automate in next few years | Auto-mated | Will automate in next few years | Auto-mated | Will automate in next few years |
| High-Tech | 19 | 33 | 17 | 32 | 6 | 21 |
| Consumer Goods | 14 | 39 | 16 | 35 | 2 | 12 |
| Intermediate Goods | 13 | 33 | 19 | 33 | 4 | 14 |
| Capital Goods | 11 | 29 | 12 | 19 | 0 | 16 |
| Services | 8 | 29 | 10 | 28 | 0 | 10 |

210

The explanation for these trends goes to the heart of a company's cross-border trade and currency flows. For example, consumer goods producers rank high in currency management automation because they generally manufacture and market their products locally in a variety of countries and currencies. Such action generates heavy forex exposures. On the low end of the scale for automating currency management are the services companies. In this case, the lack of automation may be attributed partly to the fact that such concerns often bill only in the currency of the parent and are not highly internationalized.

Third, the survey analyzed the location of the parent company. Unlike the statistics for overall treasury management, the survey shows that European and Asian companies will place greater emphasis on most aspects of currency automation than their North American counterparts over the course of the next few years, as shown in Table 6–4.

The reason behind these findings is that European and Asian companies generally are much more heavily export-oriented than North American firms, and thus deal in a broader range of currencies. According to the survey, 31% of companies headquartered in North America logged more than a quarter of their consolidated worldwide sales overseas as did 53% of Asian, and a staggering 80% of European respondents. As a result, companies domiciled outside North America have a greater percentage of their revenues exposed and are forced to manage a larger number of foreign currencies.

Lastly, the survey looked at organization. As with other aspects of treasury management, the survey clearly shows that companies with centralized treasury management operations—whether at parent or regional headquarters—are more likely to automate the currency function than decentralized firms, as illustrated by Table 6–5.

Companies that manage currency exposures from parent or regional headquarters have found that computers greatly assist in the centralization process. "We don't have staff locally who are capable of managing their currency exposure," remarked an executive at a United States manufacturing MNC. "We had to develop a system to do it from headquarters."

**TABLE 6-4**

**Parent Company Location and Automation in Currency Management**
**(in percent of survey respondents)**

| Location | Reporting currency exposures | | Tracking terms of currency contracts | | Making decisions on hedging balance sheet exposure | |
|---|---|---|---|---|---|---|
| | Auto-mated | Will automate in next few years | Auto-mated | Will automate in next few years | Auto-mated | Will automate in next few years |
| North America | 12 | 29 | 15 | 27 | 3 | 14 |
| Europe | 16 | 41 | 17 | 34 | 1 | 15 |
| Asia | 7 | 39 | 7 | 36 | 0 | 11 |

212

**TABLE 6-5**

**Organization Type and Automation of Currency Management**
**(in percent of survey respondents)**

| Organization Type | Reporting currency exposures | | Tracking terms of currency contracts | | Making decisions on hedging balance sheet exposure | |
|---|---|---|---|---|---|---|
| | Auto-mated | Will automate in next few years | Auto-mated | Will automate in next few years | Auto-mated | Will automate in next few years |
| Centralized | 13 | 34 | 15 | 31 | 2 | 17 |
| Regionalized | 20 | 55 | 16 | 41 | 5 | 15 |
| Decentralized | 11 | 25 | 13 | 24 | 1 | 7 |

## AUTOMATING CURRENCY EXPOSURE REPORTING AND FORECASTING SYSTEMS

Before treasurers can manage their companies' exposures, they must be able to identify corporate currency positions accurately and quickly. As the treasurer of a United States MNC put it, "The main push in currency management automation is just getting the information as fast as you can. First get your information automated, then you can automate the analysis. What you want is to cut down on the time it takes to get to your analysis." Therefore, it comes as no surprise that survey respondents made automating the reporting of exposures their top priority: 13% have already automated this aspect of the forex management function, a figure that will rise to 33% over the next few years.

Computerized currency reporting involves two basic elements. First, computers can provide the foundation for effective management by enabling subsidiaries to electronically transmit exposure reports from the field. Second, they can provide parent and regional headquarters with a variety of reports on the overall corporate foreign currency position, giving forex managers a concise picture of exposures and outstanding hedges. This section will discuss both these aspects of the automated currency reporting process.

### Electronic Subsidiary-to-Parent Reporting Systems

As shown in Table 6–6, the survey reveals that over the next few years companies will rapidly move away from traditional methods of

**TABLE 6–6**

**How Foreign Subsidiaries Report Currency Positions to Parent (in percent of survey respondents)**

|  | At time of survey | Three-year projection |
|---|---|---|
| Computer link | 7 | 26 |
| Computer tape/disk | 1 | 7 |
| Mail | 34 | 19 |
| Telex | 32 | 21 |
| Facsimile | 18 | 15 |
| Telephone | 12 | 6 |

intracompany currency reporting methods—mail, telex, and facsimile—to using computer disks and computer-to-computer links.

This trend can be explained simply by the fact that the extreme volatility of international currency markets is forcing companies to demand up-to-the-minute reporting from foreign subsidiaries. That is, asked the spokesperson for a leading capital goods manufacturing company: "How do you manage a Deutschemark exposure that was committed at Dm2.10:$1 if it's at Dm1.80:$1 by the time headquarters gets the information?"

Fortunately, much of the subsidiary data required for effective currency management can be gleaned from standard balance sheet information, that is, intracompany and third-party receivables and payables, inventories, cash balances, credit facilities, investments, and the like, broken out by currency. Thus, companies that have already automated the accounting function often need not ask hard-pressed subsidiary managers for special forex reports. They already have the information, probably stored in their accounting database.

But some vitally needed information, especially as regards exposure forecasting, must be reported separately, and this can cause problems. For example, an American plastics producer recently installed a regional European treasury center and now requires its European subsidiaries to submit rolling three-month exposure forecasts via computer. According to a manager at the center, "Getting these people to do a forecast is not easy. They're not familiar with it because they're accustomed to monthly balance sheets and income statements. And it's just more work. You have to be very diplomatic to get it kicked off. We gave them a lot of time to provide input and give us feedback. We made personal visits. The European treasurer visited all the local controllers. It's a delicate issue."

To avoid this obstacle, firms are beginning to install currency forecasting software at both the local and headquarters levels. According to the survey, only 5% of respondents are currently using computers to forecast exposures, but that figure is projected to rise to 25% over the next few years. For example, a small United States MNC developed a forecasting model used by each subsidiary on its own personal computer. According to the firm's international finance director, "The subs forecast what their anticipated positions might be through the balance of the current year and we monitor those positions. The forecasts are revised throughout the year. It's mostly forecasted balance sheet items that go into the model—they'll forecast their receivables, their payables, their inventory and input that. The model has the ability to then plug in the proper numbers to get the balance sheet to balance, and break all the numbers down into our anticipated exposures by currency. [The data is relayed to headquarters, where] we consolidate and run an overall forecast here in treasury. If appropriate, we can then hedge from a corporate perspective."

Companies should also track and request reports on any forward contracts taken out by subs. This effort enables parent or regional headquarters to keep tabs on the local hedging programs to ensure that they jibe with overall corporate policy. A United States communications firm, for example, requires its overseas operations to submit a quarterly "currency cash budget," which details receipts and disbursements by type and by currency, and which includes any forward contracts entered into by the units. This report shows total exposures in that country and can include one or more of the firm's divisions in that country. Overseas entities also send in a balance sheet report that breaks down accounts receivables and payables by currency.

### Case Example: Automating Subsidiary-to-Parent Reporting

A good illustration of a highly automated internal forex reporting system is provided by a United States electronics firm. Under the system, subsidiaries report the details of their exposures and their hedging actions directly into the parent's computer, which consolidates the information, stores the history of the company's exposures, and monitors the cover the firm takes.

Subsidiaries primarily telecommunicate their data through leased data lines to headquarters. The manager of foreign exchange at the company noted that many subs have terminals that are hooked into the mainframe: "Subs that are not hooked up to the mainframe have the possibility of preparing the report locally and transmitting it using a modem. There has been a program written for them to give them the ability to zap their report into headquarters. And, in certain remote locations, we have a manual system where they telex the report in and we enter it for them."

The subsidiaries send reports on a monthly basis. "Our reporting system is based on reporting the prior month's end balance sheet, broken down into all currencies. They take the reported balance sheet in dollars and spread the items into the various currencies that they're really denominated in." In addition, any forward contracts the subsidiaries enter into get reported through the system. "There's a separate line item on the exposure report for forwards," added the manager.

The reports also include short-term exposure forecasts. "We take an outlook of the next one to two months. We ask for the details, so we know the big shipments that are coming in, if the receivables are going to go up or down, payables up or down. Basically all the forecast contains is 'what are the major activities that are going to take place that would impact the exposure in the particular country?'"

The firm does hedge some individual transactions, but only "the big-ticket items," according to the manager. And computers are not involved in these transactions at all. "It's just a slug of phone calls back and forth when there's a big overseas transaction and we'll agree on the proper strategy."

The company's hedging policy is aimed at maintaining neutrality in the currency markets, which means 100% cover on forecasted exposures. That policy, along with the sheer volume of paper that would accumulate in administering such a system manually, led the firm to automate the reporting process. "We need to know our exposures precisely if we are to remain neutral," said the manager. "And we'd spend all our time inputting telexes and consolidating reports if they didn't feed directly into the database. Additionally, we've saved at least two people, in terms of not having to add them to the staff."

## Analyzing Exposures at Headquarters

Once an internal reporting system is in place and is working correctly, a company can turn its attention to automating the currency management function at the parent or regional level. The most basic use of computers in this role is to consolidate subsidiary and corporate reports, enabling forex managers to pinpoint worldwide exposures quickly and easily. As the treasurer of one high-technology firm put it, "We have 50 subsidiaries. If we didn't have a computerized system to crunch these numbers we wouldn't know what was going on until months after the fact unless we hired a huge staff of clerks. As it is, we run a good treasury function with a small staff."

Such a system can be integrated into a company's operations smoothly. For example, a United States personal care products MNC has leased a sophisticated software package to help digest exposure reports from its subsidiaries. The biggest overseas units transmit a two-part currency report to headquarters each month, and the smaller entities each quarter. The first part of the report is a balance sheet statement, including cash, receivables, inventory (if the sub is in a hyperinflationary country), payables, short-term liabilities, debt, and equity. The second part details remittances to the parent. Raw materials purchases are also included if they are not in local currency. This data feed directly into the corporate computer system, which also contains a database of exchange and tax rates.

The software package then consolidates the information, permitting the forex manager to break down the data in any number of ways. For instance, the firm can call up an exposure report for each subsidiary. The system then can calculate after-tax exposures and divide them into four categories: transaction exposure (cash flow-related balance sheet items), remittances, off-balance sheet items, and translation exposure. The analyst can see all exposures over specified time periods, such as 30 days or 12 months.

This report allows the firm to classify each subsidiary's exposures by currency and category. By looking at the breakdown, explained a spokesperson, "It's much easier to identify which transaction exposures we should be hedging. I can say the total against the Belgian franc is this much, but if you consider dividends, royalties, and raw materials purchases, it's this. You can pull out a similar schedule for the whole European bloc, or worldwide, or whatever. It's very easy to identify the various elements of risk."

The system also analyzes cross-rate exposures. "Our Danish sub periodically receives payment in Norwegian krona," said the forex manager. "That means the sub is long in Norwegian krona and short in Danish krone. Someone unfamiliar with the report might make the mistake of hedging that exposure against the dollar. However, the system generates a cross-rate matrix that lets me determine which exposures are not against the dollar. This is especially important in European and Far Eastern regions."

In addition, the system produces a report for all operating units located in one country and shows exposures in all currencies by country. Still another report calculates foreign exchange gains and losses—both income statement and balance sheet—based on current exchange rates and exchange rates forecast one year out.

In sum, the treasury manager can know what the receipts and disbursements are for every currency important to the company. Observed the international treasury manager, "These flows are netted out, with the flows already hedged by the divisions factored in. At that point, a decision can be made whether or not to hedge the remaining exposure on a corporate level. We might say we are comfortable with our exposure. Or we might say, 'This has gotten out of control; we have to do something about it.'" The choice is theirs because the information is at hand.

## Keeping Tabs on Currency Contracts

Besides providing a variety of consolidated subsidiary reports, computers can greatly assist headquarters staff in the critical task of monitoring foreign exchange transactions. According to the survey, 15% of companies are heavily dependent on computers for tracking currency contracts, and that number will double over the next few years. The treasurer of a United States capital goods manufacturer explained the trend this way: "For us, tracking foreign exchange contracts is perhaps the most important use of the computer in exposure management. We have many different short- and long-term contracts and we cover them with individual hedges because of their unique exposures. The computer gives us information on where our exposure is and where it's going. We couldn't do this manually without having an incredibly large staff."

A number of banks and software companies now offer computerized monitoring systems that vary widely in sophistication and price. In general, though, these software packages streamline one or more of the following four aspects of currency management: monitoring hedges and exposures, generating internal and bank documentation, evaluating internal performance, and evaluating bank performance. The sections that follow analyze each of these functions in turn.

### Monitoring Hedges and Exposures

This is the most obvious application of a contract monitoring system. For example, a small United States manufacturer has set up a simple system to perform this task. "I use a PC with a spreadsheet to monitor the history of outstanding contracts," said the parent's treasury analyst. "We deal primarily in Deutschemarks and I just input into the cells of the spreadsheet the amount of the receivable, the month of the invoice and the total amount, the due date on the contract and the rate, and the dollar equivalent. And that's it. It doesn't produce any confirmation statements or generate multiple reports on the various aspects of the contracts." Basically, this system is a record-keeping function.

The relative simplicity and ease of use of this program has led other corporations to develop similar tracking applications. "We have a PC, and we've written our own programs for tracking," said an assistant treasurer of a fleet management organization. "We deal in only two currencies—pound sterling and the Canadian dollar. Our Canadian exposures are quite complex. Because we are actively funding our Canadian sub, we do up to 15 contracts a month with maturities out to four years. These are entered into a simple program, which constantly tracks them and can sort them any way you like—by currency, by original maturity, by remaining maturity, by date done." In sum, the system keeps the firm constantly updated on outstanding contracts.

The spokesperson added that "our Canadian funding operation must be automated; we couldn't do it without automation. The loans are longer term, so we have to take out a series of forward contracts to cover the interest rate payments. If you had to analyze the situation with 15 different forward rates by hand, by the time you got your analysis done, the market would have moved on you. We got a microcomputer just to handle the Canadian transactions. And the savings on our first long-term loan to Canada paid for the PC." Before the firm purchased the PC, this type of long-term funding simply was not done.

## Generating Internal and Bank Documentation

An active hedging operation requires a lot of paperwork, both internally and between the company and its banks. In the words of a foreign exchange manager at a capital goods company, "On the administrative side of foreign exchange management, writing out all the tickets to go to the bank and advising the internal audit people—the controller's department and the cash disbursement people—there are just lots of little steps that are time consuming. We're automating those steps because while you're doing those things, the market is moving. You've got to be able to spend your time watching your positions, devising your strategy, thinking."

Likewise, greater control and automation of the details of bank correspondence and internal reporting goes hand in hand at a European subsidiary of a United States MNC. The foreign exchange management program at the company's in-house factoring center automatically confirms foreign exchange contracts. After a deal is consummated, an operator calls up a foreign exchange contract form on the screen (see Figure 6–1), and inputs the appropriate fields. As soon as the relevant data have been entered, the operator can request validation. The system will check the data for errors due to the dealer or the key entry operator, generate a confirmation sheet for the bank, and adjust the accounting transaction and foreign exchange contract file.

---

**Export Factoring Co, BV**
**Foreign Exchange Contract**

Date: _____

To: _____    A/C No.: _____    Status: _____

Profit Center: _____    Trans. No.: _____    Spot Date: _____

| PURCHASE | | Contract | SALE | | | | |
|---|---|---|---|---|---|---|---|
| Currency | Amount | Rate | Currency | Amount | Maturity | Type | Days |
| XXX | X.XX | XX.XX | XXX | X.XX | XX/XX/XX | X | XXX |
| Spot: XX.XX | | Premium: XX.XX | | | | | |
| | | Discount: XX.XX | | | | | |

---

**Figure 6–1: Sample Forex Contract Form Screen**

| | | | | **Forex Register by Maturity** | | | |
|---|---|---|---|---|---|---|---|
| Maturity | Profit Center | Currency/ Amount Bought | Currency/ Amount Sold | Contract Rate | Spot Rate |
| 11/19 | 1 | Dm1,097,400 | US$500,000 | 2.1948 | 2.19630 |
| 11/25 | 2 | US$184,800 | £100,000 | 1.8480 | 1.84400 |
| 11/25 | 3 | £100,000 | US$188,300 | 1.8830 | 1.88350 |
| 11/27 | 1 | US$1,782,213.51 | Ffr10,000,000 | 5.6110 | 5.54300 |
| 11/27 | 1 | Ffr11,639,250 | US$2,100,000 | 5.5425 | 5.42750 |
| 11/27 | 1 | US$2,100,000 | Ffr11,605,650 | 5.5265 | 5.41900 |
| 12/10 | 1 | US$997,008.97 | Bfr40,000,000 | 40.1200 | 40.1200 |
| 12/10 | 2 | Bfr40,000,000 | US$928,720.69 | 43.0070 | 43.4000 |
| 12/10 | 2 | US$818,778.89 | Bfr33,660,000 | 41.1100 | 41.1500 |

**Figure 6–2: Sample Forex Register Screen**

The system also generates a foreign exchange register by maturity, detailing each contract and currency as shown in Figure 6–2. The cash manager then accesses this report to find out when to clear each contract.

### Evaluating Internal Performance

Sophisticated firms use contract monitoring systems to calculate the effects of their hedging actions. For example, according to an executive at a high-tech company, "Our system allows us to know where we stand on a treasury basis by having taken out a hedging contract. It's useful to know, because at the end of every month, the controller's office reports a variance on the cost of sales due to the foreign procured material account. So when they say there is an unfavorable variance due to currency fluctuations, we can hit a button and show how we've compensated for that loss in the forward market."

Depending on a firm's attitude toward currency management, such an automated system can range from being fairly simple to exceedingly complex. At one small United States producer, for example, the treasury analyst uses a spreadsheet to evaluate the gains or losses on the firm's forward contracts. "It's a simple calculation. We judge hedging actions based on the amount we're receiving in dollars versus the dollar equivalent of the foreign currency receivable converted at the book transfer price established at the end of the year. We also enter the spot rate on the day the contract matures, to see if it would have been wiser not to enter into the forward."

One United States computer company with a more active stance toward currency management adopted a rigorous evaluation system to help guide its hedging strategy. The firm's computer analyzes the cost of cover by averaging the premium or discount for a number of forward contracts in a given currency. "We know we're incurring some premium or discount when we buy forward cover," commented the company's currency manager. "We try to keep that cost to a minimum by buying or selling the maturities that seem to offer the best rates. However, we also keep enough in short-term forwards to ensure that we don't end up buying and selling a currency forward when exposures change."

The system reports also contribute to the regular monthly analysis of how effective the hedging operation has been. "We compare the forex gains and losses with the effects of our forward cover, identifying the effects of tax gross-up and the cost of cover." Any major deviation must be flagged quickly to ensure that the level of cover is not out of line with the company's hedging policy.

### Evaluating Bank Performance

One of the largest benefits of contract monitoring systems is their ability to keep a record of the banks called on a specific transaction and their respective currency bids. Such an application can yield substantial cost and time savings to companies that actively trade foreign currencies. For example, the foreign exchange manager of a United States computer manufacturer has developed a bank evaluation program that lists each bank in rank order of its bidding performance in a given currency and tells treasury staff how close each bank is to the winning bid. In addition, the computer program indicates how many bids were won (or tied) out of the total number of bids, and the dollar amounts involved. When trading activity becomes especially heavy, the system can be simultaneously accessed by two or more users.

The system helps forex staff quickly identify the best banks for bids on particular currencies. "When deciding whom to call," stated the foreign exchange manager, "I look at the list of banks ranked in order of performance for that currency. I know right away who has performed the best for us."

## CALCULATING THE REWARDS OF LOCAL CURRENCY FUNDING

Many automated systems track foreign exchange gains and losses on forward cover contracts. But in hyperinflationary countries, the best (and sometimes only) hedging option is local currency borrowing. One manager found a way to track the gains from local currency funding and record the profits made for the company by using a computerized spreadsheet on a microcomputer that documents the tradeoff between interest expense and foreign exchange gains and losses.

The spreadsheet contains nine columns. Five are input; four are calculated. All figures are rounded to the nearest whole numbers. The data in the nine columns are as follows:

- **Month:** the month of the fiscal year.
- **Currency rates:** the month-end exchange rate in units of local currency per United States dollar.
- **Debt levels:** the amounts of local currency debt in units of local currency.
- **Foreign exchange saved:** the savings realized from financing locally rather than in dollars, stated in dollars. This is calculated from the previous two columns. The current month-end debt level is divided by the current month-end exchange rate, and the result is subtracted from the result of the current month-end debt level divided by the previous month-end exchange rate.
- **Interest expense:** the pretax interest expense of carrying the local currency debt, stated in dollars.
- **Interest income:** local interest income, stated in dollars.
- **Net effect on management profit:** the pretax profit or loss for the parent in dollar terms. It is equal to the foreign exchange

savings plus any local interest income minus interest expense.

- **Tax effect:** if interest is tax-deductible but foreign exchange losses are not, this column equals 1 minus the local tax rate multiplied by the interest expense. If both items are tax-deductible, the column is not used because both items would be adjusted by the same number, resulting in a wash.

- **Aftertax net:** the final aftertax gain or loss in dollar terms on the local currency borrowing calculated by adding the net profit and the tax effect.

The spreadsheet does three things: First, it shows the precise tradeoff, month by month, between interest rates and currency devaluation. Second, it tax-adjusts interest expense to show the true cash benefits of local currency borrowing. Third, it enables the manager to record the benefits of the funding decision and document the company's savings.

The bottom line is that, "The first year we used the schedule, there was a difference of over a million dollars between the winning bids and the losing bids," claimed the forex manager. "That number has come down, because now we're able to be more selective in calling good banks."

According to the spokesperson, several banks are usually within a basis point of one another in the major currencies. This means that if the best banks are called, the manager can be fairly confident of getting a quotation very close to the best rate. "But with currencies like the Australian dollar or the Mexican peso," the manager continued, "a bank's quote can be way off. With many of the minor currencies, banks can easily vary by 20 to 40 basis points. Keeping track of this is where our schedule really helps us out. Sometimes we call up the banks and point out that if they could shave a few pips, they'd get our business. I've found that about half the time, banks respond to that." Consequently, this firm has benefited not only from their knowledge gained by experience and stored in the computer, but also from the banks' knowledge that the firm tracks their performance.

### Tracking Currency Rates

Computers can access outside sources of exchange rate information or store rates input from within the company to give managers an historical perspective on the market. According to the survey, 11% of companies are largely automated for this function, and that figure is expected to grow to 31% over the next few years.

A number of banks and on-line service vendors provide access to such currency data. The database supplied by one electronic services vendor provides a good taste of the type of information available to companies. The system provides New York closing rates—spot rates, and one-, three-, six-, and 12-month forward rates (bid and offer)— for the past 90 working days for 34 leading currencies. Opening New York rates are provided for the past 10 working days. Closing and average monthly rates are provided for the the past 120 months, and closing and average yearly rates for the past 28 years are provided for the same 34, in addition to 12 more exotic, currencies. The trading room of a New York money center bank provides the daily rates, and the statistical office of the International Monetary Fund and the United Nations supplies the historical rates.

Corporations can use this information in several ways. First, it can be used to forecast currencies. Due to the fact that currencies can fluctuate wildly throughout the day, a forex manager has to use his or her knowledge of the market to predict whether the shift is permanent or temporary. Historical databases can give the manager the facts about past fluctuations so that an informed judgment can be made. Moreover, with the advent of microcomputers, this information can be downloaded into a PC, enabling off-site treasury staff to perform in-depth analysis.

For instance, at a United States minerals MNC, the micro-based system automatically downloads historical rate information into a spreadsheet. The data can be plotted in many ways, and the system can perform a variety of statistical analyses such as moving averages and percentage changes. It saves the company time and money because they don't have to staff a research group or pay a clerk to key data into the system.

Next, computers can help currency managers translate subsidiary reports. This manager is all too often responsible for establishing an internal translation rate for accounting purposes. Subsidiary balance sheets and profit and loss statements are converted at this corporate-wide exchange rate, usually the closing spot rate on a particular day near the end of the month.

According to the foreign exchange manager of a electronics MNC, "We have our own internal system for maintaining exchange rates. We input it here out of corporate treasury each month, and feed it into our internal system. All the worldwide organizations have access to those rates. The rate is used for translating this month's end balance sheet and next month's P&L. That is the rate to be used by all the subs for that particular currency. The same system feeds some of the automated accounting systems."

Lastly, automated systems help managers evaluate performance. The ability to use historical data to assess the performance of treasury staff is a valuable part of any automated forex system. On a periodic basis, key currency exchange rates can be input into a computer program, which can then generate a management report summarizing foreign exchange gains and losses.

For instance, a chemicals manufacturer has its foreign exchange traders input the forward rate and the spot rate into its contract monitoring system. According to a currency trader at the company, "Our performance is judged here based on the spot rate of the day we are notified of the transaction, the forward rate for the day the contract matures, and the future spot rate for that day, which is unknown. We input the rates ourselves based on numbers that come from a computer service. It's all maintained in a database and we generate management reports off of it, to show how good or bad we did."

## Case Example: An Advanced Exposure Reporting System

The task confronting the director of international money management at a decentralized firm with sales exceeding $10 billion was to deal effectively with risks spread over 50 currencies while making the most efficient use of his staff's time. To that end, four years ago the company developed a computerized currency management information system to help meet this challenge. "It's a system that allows us to log in our currency flows or exposures, and then, subsequently, the contracts on the exposures," explained a foreign exchange trader at the company. "This particular system generates confirmation letters to the banks as well as tallies up our positions. In other words, it nets our exposures in the various currencies."

In addition, continued the trader, "We can link the contracts with the exposures. Let's say our battery division comes to us and advises that they have a series of rand payables over the next six months. We'll put that data into the system—the company that we have to pay the rand to, and the date we have to pay it on."

The firm also puts in currency rates for performance evaluation purposes. There are four benchmark rates resident on the system: the forward rate when the foreign exchange department was first notified of the exposure (the hedge-everything decision), the closing spot rate (the hedge-nothing decision), the forward rate at which the exposure is hedged if it is hedged, and a "final responsibility rate" that is the average of the first two rates. Currency managers at the firm must therefore concern themselves not only with the hedge rate, but with the unknown future spot rate.

Explained the trader: "Say the rand was at 35 cents yesterday and we bought forward today and got 33 cents. If the rand never dips below 33 cents for the entire life of the exposure, then we have done the best we could have done."

Once all this information is input, it can be sorted any number of ways. The computer can print out, or display on a screen, all the company's exposures, according to the following variables:

- Hedging entity (as part of the parent company, a domestic division or an overseas affiliate)
- Currency
- Amount
- Inception date
- Forward rate
- Hedging history (at what forward rate, the amount, and with which bank)
- Definition of exposure (cash payable or receivable, translation or nonconfirmed commitment)
- Accounting treatment

Aside from storing all the details of the firm's exposures, the system can also combine the information into a number of useful reports. Any mix of the variables is possible. For example, the system could be programmed to provide:

- All Deutschemark exposures incurred by a specific division
- All Deutschemark hedging transactions with a specific bank
- All exposures in EMS currencies maturing in the fourth quarter
- All transactional exposures (payables and receivables) in a specific currency

The director of international money management estimated that this mainframe system is saving the company two foreign exchange professionals and two clerks. Even though the company is spending $1500 to $2000 per month on time-sharing costs, there is no question that the savings outweigh the costs. Commented the trader, "It's a tool we need, to keep our heads above water here because our positions are changing so fast." Convinced that many other companies will realize the same benefits, a money center bank has licensed the system.

## USING COMPUTERS FOR HEDGING DECISIONS

After a company has automated its systems for reporting and analyzing its currency positions, the next logical step is to use computers as a decision-support tool in evaluating alternatives for hedging transaction and translation exposures. But this is an area in which the promise of automation remains largely unfulfilled: Currently, only four percent of companies rely on computers to support decisions on hedging transaction exposure, and just two percent are largely automated for hedging balance sheet exposure. The survey also shows, however, that over the next few years these percentages will grow fourfold.

Thus, the treasurer of a United States capital goods producer that has already put its currency reporting on line, spoke for the minority of his colleagues when he stated that "the next major phase for us will be to use our computer to examine hedging alternatives, to calculate their costs, and to simulate the effects of different hedging scenarios. It will give us more insight into making the best hedging decisions."

This section will examine the three basic applications of decision-support technology for currency management: determining whether to hedge a position, selecting the best hedging techniques, and forecasting currency movements.

## Making the Hedging Decision

Several software packages are available that can assist forex managers in determining the effects of hedging all, part, or none of their exposed currency positions. For example, the treasurer of one computer manufacturer described the simple program his firm uses: "Our system can be used for what-ifs to see what would happen if we hedged. It tells us what our currency positions would be before we hedge anything, or after we hedged everything, and before and after any proposed hedges. It shows our balance sheet position, income statement, and expected remittance from overseas. It doesn't calculate the foreign exchange gain or loss, but only the amount exposed."

A more sophisticated computer program, known as an optimal hedging model, has been developed by a United States software house. According to the firm's president, the model is not for use in a vacuum, but is "an additional tool for making decisions on what exposures to hedge, and for finding the best strategy for reducing your risk at the lowest possible cost." To arrive at an optimal strategy, the model examines five major variables: the actual exposure, the period the exposure is to be hedged, the historical correlation between the currency and other major currencies, the elasticity relative to other currencies, and the current forward rate.

The first two variables are straightforward. For the third, the software firm researched correlations and built them in to the program. Over the last seven years, according to the research, 22 of the most widely traded currencies have demonstrated a significant level of correlation: 0.75 or better. The fourth variable, the elasticity of a cross-rate, measures the magnitude of response to a change in another currency's value. Currencies may be more or less reactive depending on the direction of change. For instance, a 1% rise in currency $A$ might cause a 1.2% rise in currency $B$. But a 1% fall in $A$ might trigger a more significant 1.3% fall in $B$. The model attempts to capture this elasticity.

From the user-supplied exposures and durations, and built-in functions, the model identifies potentially offsetting exposures. Then, incorporating the relative costs of forward cover in each currency (implied by the forward rate), the model seeks to develop an optimal hedge. That is, according to the president of the software company, "the hedge that will cost you the least, as well as reduce your risk to zero if past market trends continue." The program, therefore, attempts to define the residual exposure (the sum of the exposures not naturally offset) in terms of the currencies that are the least expensive to hedge. According to the firm's spokesperson, companies using the model can cut their hedging costs "by a factor of three to four."

### Evaluating Hedging Techniques

Once a forex manager decides to hedge an exposure, computers can be used to refine the use of a variety of techniques. For example, some firms have purchased software packages that assess the cost-effectiveness of hedging via *forward contracts*. One module on the foreign exchange software in use at a consumer goods MNC calculates the break-even spot rates for forward contracts—the rate at which the cash gain exactly equals the cash loss on the contract. For instance, if the break-even spot rate is Dm3.11:$1 and the daily spot rate falls to Dm3.05:$1, the foreign exchange manager at the firm might strongly consider closing out his or her long-dollar position. Notes a firm spokesperson, "No other system offered us the capability to quickly ascertain the spot rate at which each contract goes from gain to loss. Given the number of contracts we have outstanding at any time at different forward rates and different maturities, this feature is crucial."

In addition, if a forward contract covers a bundle of exposures, the currency manager has the option of identifying which underlying commitments are covered by the contract. Thus, when he or she closes out a contract, which exposures it covered and whether they should be rehedged immediately is known.

Other computer models aid firms in deciding whether to hedge by *borrowing* in the exposed currency. "One of the benefits of the micro-based software package we just purchased is that it compares interest rates with forward points," declared the foreign exchange manager at a United States equipment firm. "It evaluates whether it's more appropriate to borrow a currency or to sell a currency forward."

The manager pointed out, though, that the entire procedure is not automated. "You can't just generally ask it a question. It's specific to data that you're picking up somewhere. It does not maintain a database of interest rates. You have to know something about a specific market, a specific type of instrument. You put those rates in and it has a preset analytical format that it follows. That specific set of transactions would represent the options you are considering."

One firm that did automate the whole procedure is an Italian automaker. The company purchased a bank-developed software package for use on a personal computer. After combining the exposure forecasts furnished by the subsidiaries with exchange rate forecasts gleaned from technical models (explained in the next section of this chapter), the system produces a forecasted gains and losses report by currency and by country. Explained a company executive; "We use this report for what-if analysis. Our main borrowing is done on the Euromarkets and the bank's information system tells us what borrowing lire or Deutschemarks would cost on the Euromarket, in Italy, or in Germany. Our policy is to hedge as much as possible. We have the capability of inputting the forward contract rate, and feeding in the interest rates in Italy and in the foreign currency to get an analysis that reveals the cheapest hedging technique we can use. The computer gives us the costs and then we execute."

Companies also turn to computers to evaluate a third hedging alternative: *raising local prices*. Explained the treasurer of a high-tech firm, "Our computerized system has a decision algorithm that asks how quickly the subsidiaries can change their prices to recover devaluation losses. For example, if we feel that we are locked into our local currency prices in a country for 12 months, then our ability to react and cover our exposure changes dramatically.

"When we developed this program, we tried to create a model of each of our countries because each country operates on different terms. From that modeling process we tried to determine for each country how many months on average it would take our subsidiaries to raise prices. Then we try to cover that position forward, based on their forecasted exposures. The number of months forward differs by country."

Finally, a growing number of companies are using software packages to hedge with *currency options,* an innovative instrument that gives forex managers the right, but not the obligation, to buy or sell foreign currency on or before an expiration date at an agreed-upon strike price. Although many firms still shy away from options because senior management tends to view them as risky or speculative, a beverage-manufacturing firm feels differently. On any given day, its director of foreign exchange is responsible for several thousand outstanding options contracts. "Because the number and volume of options contracts have grown so much in the past few years, we scrapped our manual system and purchased software," he said. "The computer allows a level of sophistication in structuring and adjusting our options positions that you just don't get with a manual system."

The firm purchased its options software system from a New York-based computer services company. The software runs on micros or mainframes. The company uses the system primarily for two activities: determining the optimal level of hedging, and stimulating the effects of currency movements. For the first purpose, unlike a forward contract, the change in the value of an option premium does not always mirror the change in the spot rate precisely. Instead, the change in the value is always less than or equal to the change in the spot rate. For this reason, a foreign exchange manager who wants to cover 100% of a foreign-currency receivable always buys at least as many put options as the number of underlying receivables.

To account for this characteristic, the software calculates a hedge ratio that the manager needs to adjust the initial position. The hedge ratio is a number between zero and one that indicates how much the premium changes for a given change in the spot rate. It gives the manager an "equivalent dealing position," that is, how many contracts he or she should sell or buy given the day's spot rate movement. Suppose, for example, that the foreign exchange manager wants to cover a £10 million receivable by buying puts. If the hedge ratio is 0.4, the manager's equivalent dealing position is £25 million (10 million divided by 0.4). Dividing 25 million by the lot size of 12,500 yields 2,000—the number of puts that should be purchased to protect the £10 million position. If the hedge ratio goes to 0.5 the next day, for example, the manager needs only 1,600 contracts (£10 million divided by 0.5, divided by 12,500), so 400 should be sold. When the option goes into the money, the hedge ratio goes to one and the manager reduces the position to 800 put contracts. "The hedge ratio is a valuable tool we use every day," says the manager. "It gives us an idea of how effectively we are hedging our underlying currency position."

Turning to the second primary use of the software, the what-if function shows how currency movements will affect both the foreign exchange manager's equivalent dealing position and the profit or loss if he or she trades in the options held. "The system gives me an upside and a downside for my positions, and a profitability band to work with," explains the manager. "If I'm considering a particular trade, I can run it and see how profitable a choice it is."

In a recent position analysis, the manager had two outstanding Deutschemark options: He bought a put that expired the following August, and he sold a put to expire in March. He wanted to see how a range of Deutschemark movements would affect his equivalent position and the trade-in price of the contracts. To do this, he specified the change in spot movement, a time period, and a volatility factor. He chose his own volatility factor, and he could have used the system's calculation based on data already in the system (premium, strike price, and maturity of outstanding contracts).

The system tells the foreign exchange manager, for example, that if the Deutschemark depreciates by 0.97% overnight, his equivalent position will be a positive Dm23,073. To offset that equivalent position he should sell Dm23,073 worth of put options.

The system also calculates how spot movements affect option premiums. In the example, if the Deutschemark appreciates 1.97%, the manager will make a profit of $896 by trading in his contracts. (The system converts Deutschemarks to dollars, using the forecast spot rate.) That is, he will sell back the put he bought and buy back the put he sold.

Aside from these decision support services, the system also can account for currency gains and losses, and monitor exposures. After a clerical staff inputs spot exchange rates, for example, the system automatically "marks to market" each contract for general ledger purposes. "After the daily updates are made, each morning I can call up my positions on the screen and know exactly where I stand," commented the manager. To do so, as efficiently, with a manual system would be nigh to impossible.

## Forecasting Currencies

Increased uncertainty in global currency markets is causing a significant minority of firms to rely on computerized foreign exchange forecasting models when making hedging decisions. In fact, according to the survey, the number of companies using bank currency forecasting models alone will grow from 10 to 35% over the next few years. Such models can also be developed in house or purchased from computer software vendors.

Two types of forecasting models currently dominate the market. Fundamental models predict currency values by analyzing economic factors. Proponents of these models claim that inflation, interest rates, balance of payments, and foreign reserves determine a currency's value. Technical (or momentum) models, on the other hand, take moving averages of a currency's trading level in a given period and extrapolate the trend.

Naturally, financial executives have differing viewpoints on what type of model works best. Commented one treasury manager, "At one time, we used a momentum model, but it was discontinued because it didn't work. We now use fundamental analysis and try to gauge a four-to-eight-week dollar outlook based on things happening both in the United States economy and the local economies, and we examine political and social considerations." Opposing this evaluation, an assistant treasurer of a MNC derided fundamental models as "inconclusively, inconsistently accurate" and said that "momentum models have built a good record over the past six years. In spite of being from the University of Chicago, where I was taught that no one beats the market, I think technical models conclusively have."

A consumer goods manufacturer has come up with a possible solution to this dilemma. It uses both. To manage its currency position, the firm hired a bank that has a momentum model and a private company that uses a model analyzing economic fundamentals to forecast exchange rates. The firm lets the two forex services trade with a free hand, but wisely tracks their moves carefully. The advisors calculate portfolio gains and losses on a daily basis and notify the company's assistant treasurer. They also keep him informed about their strategies so that he can understand their actions.

To remedy the traditional complaints against both momentum and fundamental models, some forecasters are now taking advantage of a new area in computer science by developing artificial intelligence programs that can learn from the way the market moves and adjust forecasts accordingly. For example, one currency forecaster has a very primitive version—the "Model T of artificial intelligence," in his words—that provides a glimpse of what's to come. The system contains a simple set of algorithms assigning weights to various trading factors. For instance, if a currency devalues slightly near Christmas, the computer's forecast takes the holiday into account and knows that it is not necessarily a sign of weakening. The difference between regular forecasting models and this system is that the computer notices when the influence of holidays wanes, as it has in recent years. The computer then adjusts the weight given to holidays and changes the forecast accordingly.

Seasonal changes are taken into account, too. For example, the pound sterling traditionally rose in value in March during tax season. Lately, though, that influence has declined. The computer noticed the change, comparing the recent rates to the ten-year currency history in its database, and adjusted the forecast. In a regular model, the change in weighting would have to be done by the programmer. The forecaster's system also writes out the weightings into a file so that he has a record of which factors have a greater impact on the currency. The system contains a number of modules that can be selected at the discretion of the individual firm. The available modules are listed on pages 239–242.

## CHOOSING A TECHNICAL MODEL

### Can Your Advisor Pass This 15-Point Test?

According to one advocate of technical models, the treasury planning manager at a Canadian company, "We have gone from being a net loser in the foreign currency markets to a net gainer in recent years. I attribute a large portion of the change to our using a quality technical advisory service." And, because the firm's treasury staff manages significant foreign exchange exposures each year, choosing a good technical service was essential. The planning manager offers the following advice for deciding on a technical service:

1. **Insist on an audited track record.** "When we looked at the records in depth, we found a lot of problems," says the manager. "It's important to see a track record that is certified correct by an outside accounting firm."

2. **Look for longevity.** Firms come and go in the advisory field. Companies that have been in business only a short time cannot show a long-term performance record. But, says the manager, "A number of advisory companies have been in the business for much of the floating-rate period. That says a lot for firms that have stuck with it."

3. **Don't correlate quality and price.** The planning manager found fees ranging from a few thousand to half a million dollars. Some firms charge a percentage of profits on top of that. "There doesn't seem to be a direct link between performance and cost," he says. Some of the better performers are cheaper, and some of the worst are the most expensive."

4. **Examine the quality of the hardware.** It's a good idea to see the facilities and computer equipment for yourself. According to the planning manager, "Some firms use a small personal computer. Others are very sophisticated in terms of mainframe computers and back-up systems."

5. **Examine the quality of the software.** The software is an important criterion, according to the manager. Some firms offer what-if and special research capabilities, while others are very rigid in terms of what they can offer. "Software flexibility is important," he says.

6. **Examine the quality of the database.** Some firms store historical floating rates dating from the early 1970s, with minute-by-minute quotations on a 24-hour basis. Others have more limited databases. "This was a key criterion for us," concludes the manager. "Technical analysis, by its nature, depends on prior price history."

7. **Look for substantial research and development budgets.** Staying on top of volatile foreign exchange markets requires dedication to ongoing R&D. Many firms spend more money

marketing their product than they spend on top equipment or improvements. "And that's exactly the reverse of what they should do," says the manager.

8. **Find out if the firm trades for its own account.** Companies that believe in their own models often put their own capital on the line. "One firm really impressed us because over a period of years their own portfolio grew exponentially," the planning manager states. "And that was a completely audited track record."

9. **Check the objectivity of signals.** The treasury planning manager stresses the importance of an unambiguous, objective signal. Subjective human input is undesirable. "We looked for a system that clearly tells you whether you should buy or sell a particular currency," he explains.

10. **Talk to other customers.** "It's important to ask longstanding customers hard questions about a system," says the manager.

11. **Look at the firm's reputation in the marketplace.** A high profile in the press is a plus. As the treasurer notes, "It shows that their advice is valuable to their peers."

12. **Remember that bigger does not necessarily mean better.** The manager believes that smaller firms that specialize in technical systems outperform big operations. "We found that the best firms are small and owner-operated," he reports. "We weren't impressed with the service and performance of large institutions like banks and brokerage firms."

13. **Be wary of one-man shows.** On the other hand, "We didn't want a one-man operation," the manager says. "What happens if he gets hit by a truck?" Support staff is absolutely critical.

14. **Insist on confidentiality.** Foreign exchange managers should be convinced that the advisory firms keep all information confidential. Data and results should be absolutely proprietary.

15. **Check for past or pending lawsuits.** Surprisingly, the treasury planning manager found some firms in the midst of litigation. One Dutch company absconded with the money

of several large clients. "You can find out about these irregularities by word of mouth," he says. Alternately, a legal search is a worthwhile investment.

1. **Exposure reporting and forecasting.** The system consolidates the monthly exposure reports that subsidiaries telex to the parent. "The reports are basically the balance sheet broken down into the various currencies," explains a consultant who helped develop the model. "Each sub also submits a three-month forecast for each currency. These are entered into the system at the parent, and the system then consolidates all the currencies and produces reports that show the currencies by asset and liability field. It also produces a summary report for each subsidiary so you get a full detailed background on your exposure in German marks, for example. In some European countries, a subsidiary may have assets and liabilities that are measured in as many as 12 different currencies." Therefore, the system helps the foreign exchange manager establish the corporate-wide exposure in each currency.

2. **Bank performance evaluation.** After reviewing the consolidated exposure report, the parent decides what to hedge. If it decides to cover some portion of the exposure, notes the consultant, "The traders will go to the system to determine those banks that have historically provided the best performance—that is, the cheapest rate—for that particular currency for forward contracts. They then select the top two banks."

   The bank performance information is entered whenever a trader enters into a deal. According to the consultant, "The traders call the two banks they have selected. They get the two bids and enter them both in the system, with an indication of which bid won." The history of the "last dozen or so" trades with each bank in each particular currency is maintained so that the traders can judge how that bank performed in similar circumstances.

3. **Forward contract monitoring.** Besides the bank performance information, the traders also input the amount of the contract, the currency it's in, the dollar equivalent, the maturity date, the

traders' names, the names of the bank representatives and, if desired, an interim date at which the status of the contract should be reviewed. "The system creates a forward contract record," describes the consultant. "It also indicates in a calendar file when that contract needs to be reviewed. And there may be several dates. They may want to review it in six months to see if they want to assign the contract to another bank. There will also be a date when the contract comes to maturity and has to be settled."

As a result of that information, the system can produce several useful reports, "such as information on contracts by currency, contracts by bank, contracts by bank within currency, contracts by date done, and contracts by maturity date, among others. The system also updates the exposure report to reflect the hedging actions taken.

4.  **Bank confirmations.** "Once the computer files have been up-dated," the consultant notes, "the system will generate a letter of confirmation for the bank that the contract was made with, which is the formal document that solidifies the contract. The firm signs off on it and mails it to the bank."

5.  **Bank exposure monitoring.** According to the consultant, most companies want to limit their exposure with any given bank. To that end, "The system automatically logs the amount of the contract and keeps the company aware of how close it is to the established exposure limits. And there are two sets of bank limits the system monitors. The first is if the company says that it will have a $100 million limit on the number of contracts it has with a bank in New York in a net posture. The second limit is called a three-day limit. That says the company doesn't want any more than $x$ dollars in contracts that are in the process of being confirmed, that are in transit between the time the deal is made and the formalization of the deal, because if the bank goes under in those three days, the company is vulnerable."

6.  **Tax analysis.** By inputting various tax rates on foreign exchange gains and losses from the countries in which the firm operates, the company can keep track of the tax implications of hedging in those countries. "They have to sit down and understand the tax situation in each of the given countries and determine what the gain or loss posture may be as a result of contracting in that

country's currency. Because the contracts can be for billions of dollars, there can be substantive tax effects," says the consultant. For example, suppose the firm had $100 million in net assets in Deutschemarks representing all the subsidiaries that deal in German currencies. "If I know that three of the countries represented in that combined exposure are going to take some of those assets in taxes, I don't want to protect that proportion of the assets."

7. **Accounting reports.** The foreign exchange manager at the firm wanted to lighten the burden of his reporting responsibilities to the accounting department. So, according to the consultant, "The system automatically goes through the process of amortizing the cost of exchange protection on each contract on a monthly basis. It then automatically distributes the cost of exchange protection across the divisions that are involved in a specific contract. The company may have seven or eight divisions that the contract is protecting against exposure, and the cost of that protection is allocated to those companies according to a predetermined allocation formula. As a result, the system produces at month-end a dozen or so journal entries that fit in to the main general ledger system. It is not an automated interface, because the company wanted the ability to error-check the report before it was posted."

8. **Cash vouchers.** The cash disbursement side of the company must also know of the foreign exchange manager's actions so that the money is available to cover the cost of a maturing contract. Says the consultant, "Fourteen days before the contract comes due, it appears on a daily listing of the things the company has to deal with. The foreign exchange manager then makes the decision of whether he or she wants to roll the contract over or settle it. If it is settled, he or she needs a cash voucher for the cash disbursement people. The manager keys in that the contract is to be settled and the voucher is produced automatically."

9. **Exchange rate tracking.** At the company, the closing spot rate is keyed into the system on a certain workday near the end of the month for internal accounting purposes. "It's an ITR—internal translation rate," declares the consultant, "for translating balance sheets and P&L statements. The system provides the capa-

bility to enter those rates daily if you wanted to do that. It could also be tied into Reuters, which would give the company minute-by-minute reports on exchange rates." Based on the exchange rate information in its database, the system also produces monthly reports on foreign exchange gains and losses.

## SUMMARY

Foreign exchange management is not only a difficult function to control, but its automation is thought of as nearly impossible. Indeed, for certain operations, less than five percent of the surveyed population is attempting computerization and, for the field as a whole, the results are almost as unencouraging. While there are tentative promises made to improve on this lot, the qualitative nature of the business and the problems associated with quantifying exposure and hedging practices points to little enthusiasm for the subject. Only the twin issues of increased currency market volume and volatility will put more pressure on treasury staffs to find automated tools to assist them in trading decisions.

Today's leaders in currency management automation are larger firms with multiple overseas operations in the high-tech or intermediate goods industries. That is, the greater the volume and complexity of a company's trading and exposures, the more likely it is to automate the function. However, small and medium-sized companies who will expand their international positions will soon be faced with the automation issues. The top firms in automation today tend to be European and Asian, due to their large percentage of export revenues, and firms with centralized currency management. All of them have to deal in the following areas of currency management.

**Currency Exposure Reporting and Forecasting Systems:** The first step in automation is creating a mechanism to collect and identify the data necessary to identify the corporate currency position. A fair minority do so already—13%—and three times that plan to automate in the near future. Most subs use traditional methods to relay the data, but computer transmission should barely overtake the mail as the favored medium of the future. Parent firms also want their subs to start forecasting, as part of an information package that is critical for the MNCs who need accurate local data for planning and tracking currency contracts. Of assistance in that area is the growing number of service companies who can provide historical data as well as store current information.

**Making Hedging Decisions:** When compared to using software for business-decision support, the automation of reporting and forecasting currency management is child's work. For this area is very grey and qualitative—a statement supported by the fact that almost none of the surveyed companies have even attempted its automation. The hesitancy to move into this field is based in three primary problems: First, the art of hedging is best practiced by those who can calculate residual exposures in terms of currencies that are the least expensive to hedge. Risk and potential costs are high. Second, when hedging exposures, managers must use more knowledge than that available at the touch of a button. They must choose from hedging by forward contracts, by borrowing in the exposed currency, by raising local prices, or through the use of currency options. It is hardly a straightforward game, and one that is terribly exhorbitant to program. Finally, managers are divided as to use fundamental or technical models to forecast currencies. Both methods have avid proponents as well as opponents; many companies have tried both in sequence and at least one uses them in tandem. Neither has a clear record of success, but an AI-based system is starting to show promising results in the field.

# CHAPTER 7

# Automating Cross-Border Treasury Management Systems

## INTRODUCTION

Once companies have developed sound systems for cash and currency management at the subsidiary and parent levels, a process explained in Chapters 5 and 6, the next step is to integrate overseas operations into a cohesive cross-border treasury system. Such cross-border systems are critical because they can improve a company's bottom line by thousands, or millions, of dollars by cutting borrowing needs, reducing currency risks and costs, minimizing float and fund transfers, increasing investment yield, minimizing taxes, and paring other financial expenses.

Many firms can ensure that their cross-border cash and currency flows operate at peak efficiency by applying relatively simple techniques, such as cash pooling, hold accounts, leading/lagging, and netting. However, for multinational corporations with very large and complex trade flows in Europe, these steps may not be sufficient. These companies may need to establish full-fledged treasury management centers—reinvoicing, in-house factoring, or finance companies—to coordinate their global treasury activities from one central point.

Given their myriad financial advantages, it is no surprise that cross-border treasury management systems are growing in popularity among companies with multinational operations. Tangentially, a rapidly growing number of these MNCs are turning to automation to help manage these techniques and vehicles. According to the survey, the percentage of respondents that are largely automated for managing cash cross-border will grow from 8 to 23% over the next few years. And, over that same time frame, nearly 60% of respondents will have automated at least some aspects of the function.

The reason? While a rudimentary treasury vehicle can be managed without computer support, treasury staffs at most MNCs would be quickly overwhelmed by the sheer volume of number crunching and administrative work required. "There are so many transactions involved," said one treasury management consultant, "that it would be impossible to manage such sophisticated systems without extensive computer processing and analysis."

This chapter will show treasurers how they can determine whether their firms are good candidates for a cross-border vehicle and how to take advantage of computerized systems to facilitate cash pooling, multilateral netting, reinvoicing, and in-house factoring.

### Should Your Company Establish and Computerize a Treasury Vehicle?

To decide if a cross-border automated system can benefit your company, three key factors must be examined: size and forex volume, industry type, and location. Let us examine these in turn.

As regards the first factor, companies with large annual sales and forex positions are far more likely to establish and automate cross-border systems than their smaller counterparts. As can be seen in Table 7-1, the vast majority of those survey respondents that have already automated their cross-border systems are large firms. This is

**TABLE 7–1**

**Size and Location of Firms with Automated Cross-Border Treasury Systems**
**(in percent of survey respondents)**

| Sales | Automated | Will automate in next few years |
|---|---|---|
| Over $2 billion | 17 | 38 |
| $500 million–$2 billion | 11 | 23 |
| $200 million–$499 million | 0 | 15 |
| Under $200 million | 2 | 13 |
| **Number of foreign units** | | |
| Over 40 | 29 | 52 |
| 21–40 | 23 | 46 |
| 11–20 | 6 | 22 |
| 6–10 | 2 | 15 |
| 1–5 | 0 | 9 |

true whether measured by sales volume or number of foreign operating units.

However, small companies should not dismiss cross-border systems. According to the survey, the use of computers for managing treasury vehicles and techniques will soar among smaller firms over the next few years. As a $140 million United States manufacturer of materials with operations in Europe explained: "The opportunities for us are rather small right now. The concept is that in the next two to three years our volume will get bigger, and the right trade flows will develop. It's not going to be a wholesale shift in our operations; it's just the fact that business is growing, so it will be worthwhile to undertake the effort."

Turning to the influence of the second factor, the survey results supported the idea that certain industries are ideally suited for use of cross-border systems. As can be seen in Table 7–2, manufacturing firms, thanks to their complex international trade flows, are the most likely candidates.

On the other hand, service companies show little interest in computerized treasury vehicles; none of the survey respondents in this sector have automated cross-border systems, and only 13% plan to in the future. The reason is that they tend to trade less than

**TABLE 7–2**

**Industry Type of Firms with Automated Cross-Border Treasury Systems (in percent of survey respondents)**

| Industry | Automated | Will automate in next few years |
|---|---|---|
| High technology | 9 | 32 |
| Consumer goods | 13 | 27 |
| Intermediate goods | 7 | 26 |
| Capital goods | 7 | 16 |
| Services | 0 | 13 |

manufacturing firms and have less complicated cross-border cash flows. For instance, airlines have established extensive networks of local sales offices spread around the world. However, the cash flows from these operations are typically one-directional. After covering local expenses, proceeds from the sales are remitted to the parent. There are few, if any, flows from the parent back to the local offices, or among the local offices themselves.

Location is the third factor evaluated for these systems. The survey findings indicate that companies headquartered in North America are the most likely users of automated cross-border systems, as shown in Table 7–3. Furthermore, over the next few years the gap between North American respondents and those based outside the region is predicted to widen significantly.

The main reason for the lower popularity of automated treasury management systems among Asian- and European-owned firms is their strong ideological commitment to decentralization. Because of their organizational approach, they are therefore reluctant to introduce techniques and vehicles that may impinge upon the autonomy of local financial managers. Indeed, as displayed in Table 7–4, the

**TABLE 7–3**

**Location of Firms with Cross-Border Treasury Systems (in percent of survey respondents)**

| Location | Automated | Will automate in next few years |
|---|---|---|
| North America | 9 | 26 |
| Europe | 10 | 19 |
| Asia | 0 | 14 |

**TABLE 7-4**

**Organization Type of Firms with Automated Cross-Border Treasury Systems**
**(in percent of respondents)**

| Organization | Automated | Will automate in next few years |
|---|---|---|
| Centralized | 9 | 26 |
| Regionalized | 9 | 19 |
| Decentralized | 5 | 16 |

survey shows that centralized companies are nearly twice as likely to automate cross-border treasury management than their decentralized counterparts.

## Automating Cross-Border Cash Pooling Procedures

Cash pooling arrangements help firms move surplus funds from cash-rich subsidiaries to parent or regional headquarters, where the cash can either be invested or lent to cash-poor subsidiaries. Cash pooling provides the following benefits to a parent company: control and rationalization of liquid assets of subsidiaries, greater flexibility in shifting funds from cash-rich to cash-poor subsidiaries, a higher rate of return on short-term investments because larger investments often earn higher interest rates than smaller investments, reduced borrowing needs and associated costs, and better knowledge of cash needs and surpluses.

Automation can assist companies in pooling in many ways. First, it can help in monitoring subsidiaries' cash positions to identify potential sources and uses of funds. To operate a cash pooling center, treasurers need to actively track and consolidate cash and currency data from home-country and overseas subsidiaries. For MNCs, this task is difficult to do on a timely and efficient basis without advanced computer and telecommunications systems. For instance, a company may require electronic bank reporting systems to identify cash balances, a software model to calculate internal borrowing and investment rates, and a databank to record the allocation of funds.

Second, computers can be used to initiate funds transfers. Based on the subsidiaries' reports, a pooling center must decide from where to draw funds, in what quantity, and where to invest or lend its accumulated cash. Because time is of the essence, computers can help the center issue instructions and maintain an audit trail. The alternatives, phone calls and other traditional methods, are expensive, prone to error and impossible to standardize.

Third, a computerized system can provide solid information for making investing and borrowing decisions. Treasurers can use decision-support software programs to analyze such alternatives as whether it is cheaper to borrow from a bank or use internal funds.

An interesting case in point is that of an Italian company with a central-bank approach that relies heavily on computer processing and decision support. This multibillion-dollar firm, with manufacturing and sales units across Europe, uses a computer system that allows cash-poor subs to borrow from rich ones by tapping funds on deposit with the company's internal bank or by drawing on a bank line of credit. Details on each operating unit's lines of credit, including currency of denomination and amount, are lodged in a computer database.

The cash-pooling center offers an intragroup interest rate to its borrowers and lenders. If Subsidiary A needs funds, for example, it borrows at 17%. If Subsidiary B has excess funds, it invests with the center at 17%. These are actual, not merely bookkeeping, charges, with the borrower paying 17% to the center and the lender credited with 17%. "We are a pool of funds—we collect and distribute the money," confirms the money manager of the firm.

Armed with this information, the money managers at the company can compare the costs of drawing upon a commercial bank's credit line or borrowing from a fellow subsidiary. "We look at the available credit lines and financial markets in Italy," says the money manager. "We do the same thing for the Euromarkets at different exchange rates. All the information is plugged into our centralized information system. The computer presents an analysis of available funds and credit lines. When the need arises, we use the available credit line with the lowest margin of cost, interest, and exchange rate. The computer will show that sometimes it's better for Subsidiary A to utilize the credit line of Subsidiary B. So when a domestic or foreign sub needs money, we give it to them according to the computerized priority listing."

### Case Example: A Computerized Cash Pooling System

Using what its treasurer calls "cascading cash pooling," an oil services company has established a daily cycle for pooling cash flows of its operations worldwide. Because the firm has assets of over $6 billion, its operations are managed from three regional headquarters in Houston, Tokyo, and Paris. A total of 235 operating units—subsidiaries and branches—report into these headquarters sites. The regional headquarters are, in turn, governed by two main offices in New York and in Paris. The system pools the cash from these local operating units and concentrates liquidity into the accounts of seven regional holding companies, where the monies can be most effectively managed.

The cash pooling arrangement is supported by an electronic bank reporting system and a worldwide system of networked PCs. Computers are used not only to generate and receive reports, but also for analysis. "Without computers, we would spend our whole day just figuring out where our money is," the treasurer said, "and most of that time would be spent on the phone."

The pooling system works as follows. Cash from all of the operating units is pooled upwards to individual country holding companies. Then, the cash is funneled to one of seven regional holding companies, depending on the location of the country. Each of the holding companies maintains its own bank account. These seven balances, ultimately maintained in New York, are then invested by an Amsterdam subsidiary, which was established expressly for the purpose. The treasurer claims his company operates with so little cash outside the pool that "the subs are expected to operate with absolute zero in their accounts, and in most cases they do."

To facilitate funds concentration and reporting, all operating units deposit into local branches of a major American money-center institution, which also provides a global electronic bank reporting system. In the opinion of the firm's spokesperson, using only one bank sidesteps potential reporting problems other companies have experienced when using several banks to pool cash. These problems range from incompatible report formats to different reporting schedules.

The company taps into the bank reporting system through its proprietary computer network. Each operating unit has a PC connected by modem to its local bank branch, allowing access to balance information at the local level. Receipts (credits in the form of wire transfers and lockbox remittances) and disbursements (checks, payroll, wire and forex transfers) are tracked by the bank, which generates reports for the subs. "Local managers can call their accounts and learn all the movements of the previous day to find out whether collections came in, whether checks they've issued had cleared, and so forth. Our field units are responsible for monitoring all the activity in their individual accounts, and that's where we really need the PCs."

Actual funds movement—the upwards pooling from local to concentration accounts—is done automatically by the bank, so the firm does not need to use computers for transaction initiation until the funds reach the investment (or holding) account levels. "From the zero-balancing aspect, that is really a cash management activity done by the bank," noted the treasurer. "The bank is offsetting all of the debits and credits and moving excess cash up into the concentration accounts. The accounts that are in a negative position are being funded by the concentration accounts, so at the end of the day we look at the concentration accounts in a net position. If it's excess cash, it is automatically zeroed out of the concentration account and credited into the investment account. Again, this is all done by the bank. If it's in a negative position, then what happens is that it creates an overdraft and the next day's activity is used to pick up any overdraft position. We pay interest on the overdraft."

The Amsterdam investment group accesses the balance information on the seven regional holding company accounts electronically through a terminal. The reports are matched against investment information maintained on a separate computer system, using a calendar module that flags maturing investments or regularly recurring disbursements. These are added to or subtracted from the daily balance reports to calculate a net cash position; this step is done manually.

Computers are not yet used to support investment decisions, either. "These are still made using phone calls and Telerate. We're still basically in our infancy on the manipulation side of the system," said the spokesperson. "We are using the PCs and mainframes just to access the balances and the daily activity."

The firm intends to upgrade its automation in two areas: cash reporting and data analysis. "For our investment team, all of our operating units' accounts, not just the holding company accounts, will be hooked up to a system which our investment company would access," said the cash manager. Thus, the Amsterdam group would get full details of all the operating units' cash inflows and outflows, enabling it to make investment decisions more accurately and quickly than currently possible.

At the same time, the firm plans to develop decision-support software that would download rate information from an electronic service into a computer program that contains all internal corporate restrictions on investment alternatives. The computer would then automatically compare the various options, indicating the best available rates and maturities.

## USING A COMPUTERIZED NETTING PROGRAM

Perhaps nowhere in treasury management is there as ready-made an opportunity for computerization as with multilateral netting. Firms have realized they can sharply reduce their foreign exchange transactions and funds transfers by netting payments among subsidiaries within the corporate group (see the box on p. 254 for more details on netting). Furthermore, netting systems are readily available through banks or other third-party vendors. Alternatively, companies are developing netting systems internally.

Because netting systems routinely have 20 to 30 participants, although some may have more than 100, the calculations required to put together a sizable netting operation are ideally suited to computerization. Programs vary considerably in their flexibility and optional applications. Some are written to calculate only the current period's netting requirements. Indeed, most programs began in this simple form. Today, however, most have expanded to include other features such as:

- Remote input capability, which allows subsidiaries to report payables directly into the netting system
- Detailed information on intracompany accounts with reconciliation capabilities
- Aging of payables/receivables over user-specified time periods

- Automatic generation of telexes to participants informing them of their positions and giving remittance instructions to net payers
- Simulation of lead/lag strategies
- Inclusion of forward foreign exchange contracts, bank loans and deposits, and third-party obligations
- Calculation of foreign exchange gains and losses (pretax or aftertax) for an individual subsidiary or on a consolidated basis

### Linking Netting to Automated Reporting Systems

Netting can save a company substantial transaction costs, as well as help firms improve their reporting systems. For example, a high-technology MNC found its reporting system was greatly improved as a direct result of setting up a multilateral netting system. Prior to netting, the company had an inefficient intercompany reporting system. But, because the individual business units were not consistent in their reporting, the company developed a computer system to consolidate the intercompany accounts and to standardize intercompany invoicing. Now, for all intercompany transactions, each unit must complete a transfer advice form that details current intercompany sales and the corresponding currencies of transaction. These transfer advices are then fed into a database designed specifically for this purpose, which then provides a detailed map of the intercompany cash flows.

---

## NETTING MECHANICS AND BENEFITS

Simply defined, netting is a technique for settling intracompany, and sometimes third-party, obligations. Under a netting arrangement, creditor and debtor positions are offset within a corporate group, with the net amount transferred from the net debtors to the net creditors. Over the years, the technique has evolved into a complex process that can assume different shapes to adapt to a company's needs and operating conditions. The variety of approaches can be classified into two basic categories—bilateral and multilateral netting.

The simplest form of cross-border netting is bilateral offsetting of payables and receivables between operations in two countries, usually between a parent and a subsidiary, but sometimes affiliate-to-affiliate. Multilateral netting is more complex and involves offsetting intragroup debit and credit positions across a variety of currencies and countries. With this latter technique, each corporate participant pays or receives a net amount, usually on a regular cycle. Because multilateral netting may include many participants with complex trade flows, it usually requires a group coordinator to consolidate information on group receivables and payables, as well as to make final settlement of trade accounts.

Three types of netting packages are available to companies: systems they design and operate themselves, packages designed by banks but company-operated, and packages both designed and operated by banks.

The main benefits of netting are:

1. **Reduced currency conversion costs because of fewer forex transactions.** For example, one United States computer company slashed the number of currency deals from approximately 75 a month to less than 30. According to the firm's treasurer: "We have generated $500,000 in annual savings by more than halving the number of forex transactions."

2. **Finer forex spreads due to centralized foreign exchange trading.** The treasury manager of a United States company states: "We get an enormous amount of efficiency and savings because of the more competitive bidding."

3. **Lower funds transfer costs because of fewer transactions.**

4. **Minimal float by obtaining same-day value on transfers.** "A vital part of the system is the fact that all funds are transferred with same-day value, eliminating float," commented one company's assistant treasurer.

5. **Better and more consistent banking transfer channels.** One United States multinational established a worldwide netting program that channels all funds transfers through the global branch network of one bank. "We find the transfers go easier having each subsidiary transfer or receive its funds at a branch of Bank X or one of its correspondent banks," said the firm's treasurer.

This reporting system yields benefits that go far beyond netting. It has resulted in strict control over cash management, which in turn facilitates leading and lagging (see box on p. 257). The system also allows the company to retrieve and classify worldwide company information on the basis of business unit, country, and transaction type. Finally, it enables the firm to identify account discrepancies between business units and promptly resolve unmatched items among subsidiaries. These item discrepancies occur approximately 15% of the time, and create a sizable problem that must be rectified swiftly to operate an efficient cash and exposure management system.

To meet corporate needs for better computerized reporting, some banks are now designing second-generation netting systems that include information useful for managing other treasury functions. First-generation netting has been geared to large, centralized companies and simply uses one-way information flows between the subsidiaries and the center. This second generation of netting systems offers more—and more detailed—information that can support numerous treasury functions. In most cases, the subsidiary enters its data into the system directly, thereby making the information available at both the local level as well as at the netting center level.

A software package from a European bank provides an example of this new generation of netting software. The system is designed to store and manipulate a broad range of data. For example, it permits companies to enter data regarding their debts or claims in any currency, including nonconvertible ones. The package also accommodates data on, and analyses of, foreign exchange regulations, transfer costs, exposure management, liquidity allocation, and leading and lagging. Because the netting system does not stipulate a particular currency for settlements or for reporting, the user can convert amounts into any currency or combination of currencies.

To eliminate any rekeying efforts at the central facility, information is reported on-line via a telecommunications network, rather than by telex. By using appropriate security codes, subsidiaries can also access this central database. The data can also be run through what-if simulations to improve formulation of strategies. For example, the user can make calculations based on predictions of future exchange rates; this information can help refine leading and lagging policies.

## AUTOMATING LEADING AND LAGGING

Computerized netting systems can help international companies take full advantage of one treasury technique unique to their multinational status: adjustment of intracompany accounts through leading (prepaying) and lagging (delaying). The key benefit of leading and lagging is that it enables companies to shift liquidity among subsidiaries, thereby reducing financing costs.

For example, a firm can instruct cash-rich subsidiaries to lead payments to cash-poor ones so that the latter need not take on further bank debt. Cash-poor subsidiaries may be told to lag intracompany payments. Leading and lagging also facilitates exposure management by enabling companies to direct funds away from depreciating currencies and toward appreciating currencies when interest rate differentials justify this course of action. However, governments facing pressure on their currencies will frequently restrict the use of this technique.

Computers can facilitate leading and lagging by helping treasury staff evaluate pertinent data, such as short-term interest rates, currency market trends, local tax rates, and subsidiary cash positions. By feeding this information into a computer model, a treasurer can assess avenues and amounts of savings. Unfortunately, many companies still take a seat-of-the-pants approach. That is, when they find that a subsidiary is cash-poor, they tell it to defer payments on trade accounts or have subsidiaries with weak currencies lead payments. But effective leading and lagging is not that simple; companies should examine all the variables involved.

To make correct leading and lagging decisions, treasurers must determine the effective aftertax interest rate, adjusted for anticipated currency movements, pertaining to each possible approach. Because of the complexity of this calculation, which contains several changing variables specific to each subsidiary, it is best handled on a computer spreadsheet or through a model. In brief, the calculation is performed as follows:

The local aftertax interest rate of the subsidiary bearing the exchange risk is determined first. Then, the expected aftertax change in the exchange rate is added or subtracted. The resulting number should then be subtracted from the local aftertax interest rate of the country not bearing the exchange risk. If the interest rate differential is positive, the corporation as a whole will either pay less on borrowing or earn more on interest through investing if transfers are made. If the differential is negative, the corporation will pay higher rates for money borrowed or earn less on money it invests. Therefore, a positive differential means payments should be led to a receiving country; a negative differential, that payments should be lagged to a paying country.

## Multilateral Netting: Two Case Examples

A French consumer goods firm had been interested in a multilateral netting system for some years, but was confronted with two obstacles: its decentralized structure across Europe; and difficulty in obtaining permission to net in regulated countries, such as its home country. Faced with nearly half of its sales outside France and nearly Ffr 1 billion in intracompany sales among 60 subsidiaries, failure to net was becoming a costly affair.

The firm decided to ask one of its major banks to conduct a feasibility study. The bank was already thinking about offering a netting system of its own as a cash management service, so the process was a joint learning experience. However, while the bank assisted by working out its requirements to support the system—foreign exchange, funds transfers, and information flow—the firm designed the netting scheme itself, including all software programming.

The netting system now in place encompasses all the company's European subsidiaries except Spain, where government exchange controls proved insurmountable. Because of the low volume of interregional trade, non-European subsidiaries do not participate in the system.

On the fifth working day of each month, all netting participants telex the company's headquarters with information about their intragroup receivables outstanding at the previous month-end, denominated in their local currencies. This data is fed into the firm's central computer, which on the tenth day generates a verification telex back to the subsidiaries specifying the amount to be paid.

Three days before the settlement date—the fifteenth working day of the month—the subsidiaries telex back payment data on the amounts to be paid. That same day's foreign exchange rates are fed into the central computer, which then generates a matrix of net receivables and payables for all the subsidiaries. On the next business day, the company's finance subsidiary in Luxembourg buys and sells the foreign exchange required for the netting operation, trying to obtain rates as close as possible to those used in generating the matrix. Any exchange gains or losses between the thirteenth working day, when the foreign currencies are purchased, and the settlement date's spot rates are absorbed by the finance company.

On the night before settlement date, the firm's head office receives final notification on the exchange rates from the finance company and transmits the data to the local branches of its bank electronically. The local branches then make specific debit and credit entries to the accounts of the local subsidiary operations.

"A vital part of the system is that all funds are transferred with same-day value, eliminating float," the company's assistant treasurer commented. "All the netting participants must use the local branches of the same bank to make the transfers, however, to obtain same-day value." Although there is no commitment to buy foreign currencies through the same bank, in practice the company's regular bank is used most often. According to a company spokesperson, "Our bank has no official role, but it has the branches in all locations where we have subsidiaries. We may choose any bank we want. It's just a matter of convenience to use our main bank."

The firm's netting efforts have paid off handsomely, both for the company and its bank. Although the firm is unable to pinpoint the cost savings of its netting system, it claims to have completely eliminated intracompany float within Europe. Moreover, the value of funds transferred has been reduced by over 40%. These cutbacks have greatly minimized charges for foreign exchange, conversions, and funds transfers.

Switching to another scenario, a United States electronics firm recently set up an elaborate netting operation in Europe and North America with the help of a major United States money center bank. It was necessary because the company's previously decentralized organizational style, under which corporate treasury had no authority over local business units, had extremely inconsistent reporting techniques and methods of monthly settling of intracompany accounts. Observed the director of international finance, "When I first came on board we had five different intracompany invoicing systems. Each business unit had a unique system with different forms, procedures and the like."

Decentralization proved costly. Discrepancies that often appeared between subsidiaries on intracompany accounts made centralized cash and exposure management—including hedging, leading and lagging, and netting—difficult, if not impossible.

To review existing intracompany procedures and set up the information infrastructure for a multilateral netting system, the company called in the United States money center bank. Based on the consulting study provided by the bank, the firm constructed a standardized, computerized reporting system to collect and analyze data on intracompany trade flows. The company opted for its own reporting system, rather than the bank's, because it wanted a format tailored to its intracompany operations that would have the flexibility to tighten internal controls and solve accounting problems.

The bank engineered a novel financial arrangement, integrating the firm's reporting system with the bank's multilateral netting program. Specifically, the bank generates a netting matrix that draws on the account information the company puts together by consolidating transfer advices received from local units. The bank then tells each of the company's participants the net amount it owes or is due from the netting center in its local currency. This is done by telex every month, two weeks before the final settlement date. In the two-week period before final settlement, differences and discrepancies are resolved. "We go back and forth with our subsidiaries," explains the treasurer. "We initially propose an amount due, and they may disagree or have special circumstances, such as excess cash or a cash shortage. Each go-around is called an *APROX.* Sometimes we go all the way to APROX 8 before we actually settle."

Under the netting system, each of the participating countries is considered one unit for local tax and reporting purposes, even though there may be more than one business unit in that country. All amounts owed to or due from business units within one country are consolidated for the purposes of netting.

Under the setup designed by the bank, the firm has a series of multicurrency concentration accounts in London, through which all netting payments pass. Subsidiaries send the net amounts they owe in their local currency to the United Kingdom netting center; the funds are credited to the appropriate currency account and are used to settle spot forex transactions.

Currency trading is handled at the firm's United Kingdom netting center and is conducted mostly through its bank. Subsidiaries that are net cash receivers then get paid from the same accounts. These funds transactions are facilitated by the fact that each subsidiary transfers or receives its funds at a branch of that same bank, or with a correspondent bank in its home country.

So far, the system includes Austria, Belgium, Canada, Denmark, Finland, France, Germany, the Netherlands, Italy, Norway, Spain, Sweden, Switzerland, the United Kingdom and the United States. The firm estimates that the system has generated $500,000 in annual cash savings by cutting the number of forex transactions it handles by more than half.

## AUTOMATING REINVOICING VEHICLES

In addition to cross-border pooling and netting, some companies have developed sophisticated reinvoicing operations that can centralize the management of many international treasury functions, including cash management, borrowing, leading and lagging, and export financing. The box on page 262 explains the operations of a reinvoicing center.

Given the number of transactions an active reinvoicing center must monitor, as well as the variety of its activities, companies would find it impossible to run such a facility without extensive computer support.

Computers can be used to facilitate reinvoicing in any number of manners. First, they can keep track of a multiplicity of trade transactions. That is, intracompany and third-party trade transactions can be keyed directly into the computer by the exporting subsidiaries or the reinvoicing center. This operation greatly improves a company's control over its trade flows and increasing efficiency. Next, automation can be used to easily change the currency of billing. Computers can handle this critical process swiftly. For instance, they can automatically convert an export bill from the currency of the exporting subsidiary to that of the importing company. Furthermore, managing currency exposures is an easy task for computers. They can support one of the principal functions of most reinvoicing units—centralizing exposure management. All exposures arising from trade transactions can be captured by the reinvoicing center's computer, netted and managed centrally.

Issuing invoices and setting transfer prices are two other primary uses for computers. In the former case, for example, an exporting subsidiary can use a computer to issue both invoices—the invoice to the reinvoicing center and the invoice the reinvoicing center sends to the importing subsidiary. Firms may want to draw up service contracts that compensate operating units for this support. In the latter case, computers can help companies determine transfer prices by any of the three primary methods. Under the *cost-plus formula*, which is preferred by manufacturing-oriented companies, the firm adds a profit margin to the cost of producing the item. Under the *resale-minus method*, the company takes a preset discount from its local selling price. This approach is frequently used by a marketing-driven company whose prices are determined by local market conditions. The third alternative, *setting a free market price*, is generally chosen by companies selling commodities or goods with a known market value. No matter which formula is chosen, a computer can automatically apply the appropriate mark-up or discount on a consistent basis.

---

## WHAT A REINVOICING CENTER DOES

A typical reinvoicing company works as follows:

- **Takes the title and rebills purchaser.** A reinvoicing company purchases and takes the title, although not physical possession, to finished goods or raw materials produced by the parent company, subsidiaries or third parties. The center then rebills the goods either to other subsidiaries or directly to third-party customers.

- **Changes the billing currency.** The reinvoicing company is usually billed in the currency of the selling company and, in turn, reinvoices in the local currency of the purchasing company. In this way, foreign exchange exposure is centralized at the reinvoicing center and removed from the selling and purchasing companies.

- **Sets the exchange rate.** To avoid accusations of profit shifting, reinvoicing centers must develop a method for setting a rate of exchange that is acceptable to tax authorities. Some companies use the spot rate, others the forward rate.

- **Charges a commission.** Most reinvoicing centers charge a commission for the service they perform. "This commission should be relatively small to avoid accusations of profit-shifting," advises a financial executive. The relationship between the reinvoicing center and the subsidiaries must be at arm's length.

  Reinvoicing offers MNCs many advantages:

1. **Centralizes currency exposure and removes risks from subsidiaries.** Typically, the reinvoicing center is billed in the exporter's local currency, and reinvoices in the importer's local currency, thereby assuming the exposure risk. If staffed with experienced currency specialists, a reinvoicing center is well equipped to manage a company's exposure through advanced techniques such as options and swaps.

2. **Upgrades monitoring and control of cash and trade flows.** Because they handle billing centrally, reinvoicing companies simplify the tracking and analysis of intracompany payables and receivables. Just as important, they impose discipline on intracompany billing practices and observance of credit terms. Reinvoicing centers also encourage subs to provide thorough and timely reports.

3. **Facilitates liquidity management.** Reinvoicing gives a company greater flexibility in shifting liquidity between subsidiaries by leading and lagging intracompany payments.

4. **Cuts borrowing costs and increases investment yields.** By handling bank borrowings through a reinvoicing center, a company has more financial leverage than if each subsidiary financed on its own.

5. **Improves export trading, financing, and collection.** Reinvoicing enables firms to concentrate the needed expertise to trade successfully with low-volume, highly complex markets.

6. **Acts as a central purchasing agent on behalf of a company's**

**subsidiaries.** Reinvoicing companies can centralize group purchases, thereby achieving greater market potential and lower prices.

7. **Reduces bank transaction costs.** By handling banking transactions from a central point, the reinvoicing center may negotiate same-day value on funds transfers, obtain preferential forex rates, and reduce other banking fees. In addition, it reduces the number of funds transfers and currency conversions, further cutting transaction costs.

## Case Example: A Fully Computerized Reinvoicing Center

A communications manufacturer manages an American-based reinvoicing center to consolidate currency exposures and cut costs. To help administer the massive number of foreign currency transactions that pass through the center daily, the firm uses a computer system to gather and process the information flows. According to the manager of the center, "You could do it manually if you didn't have a lot of transactions. But if you didn't have a lot of transactions, why would you set up a reinvoicing center? We need a computer to make this work."

The reinvoicing center handles all the cross-border intracompany trade transactions for the firm's domestic divisions and 27 foreign subsidiaries. If a United States division is selling equipment to the French subsidiary, for example, the division bills the clearing center in dollars and the center bills the subsidiary in French francs. Similarly, if the German subsidiary sells a piece of equipment to the French subsidiary, Germany bills the clearing center in Deutschemarks and the center bills France in francs. In all, the center now bills in 18 currencies.

An examination of the firm's automated system reveals that the firm has computerized virtually all aspects of currency management. Specifically, the system enhances currency management in the following areas: communicating to and from subsidiaries, exposure reports, contract tracking and administrative issues, exposure forecasts, and decision support. These areas will be discussed in turn.

## Communication To and From Subsidiaries

The information cycle starts when a subsidiary enters into a transaction. "They are online with the clearing center," explained the manager. "Each sub has a terminal and they can dial up the system on which the clearing center runs. We lease a portion of a communications satellite that beams the transmission here. Once the subs gain access to the system, they can input any invoices they have, pull off any invoices sent to them by the clearing center, and input any remittances they are making to the clearing center. They do all that locally."

Suppose a United States division enters an invoice for a transaction with an overseas subsidiary. According to the manager, "The key is, that out the other side of that invoice statement comes an invoice in local currency to be transmitted to the subsidiary automatically. There's also an invoice printed out here that can be used as a shipping document."

## Exposure Reports

The transmitted information updates the transaction file. "We collect the exposure information here," explained the manager, "and because it's all computer-driven, with some minor program writing, we are able to get a daily exposure report. It's just a summary by subsidiary and by country. It starts out with our beginning monthly exposure, that is, the month-end balance sheet. Then it summarizes the changes—any additions in invoices for that sub that the clearing center sent out, any hedges that are in there. And, it takes out any cash payments the subs have made. They input remittance advices when they make payments to the reinvoicing center and that reduces the exposure."

"We look at the exposures day by day," continued the manager. "If we see something that we think is getting out of line, we'll go back and find out why. If there's a major shipment going out, we may see a $5 million blip in the exposure, and we have lists of all the shipments going out. If a sub doesn't have the ability to borrow because it just changed its bank, that can affect the report. There's a lot of things that might affect it."

After finding the cause of the fluctuation, said the manager, "if we determine that it will correct itself, we leave it alone. If it's something that looks like it will keep going in that direction, then we will make the decision to hedge or not to hedge."

### Contract Tracking and Administrative Issues

If the firm decides to hedge, according to the manager, "We bid on a competitive basis, using Reuters to keep us up on market rates. We fill out our own trade tickets for spot and forward transactions. (The manager also enters bank names and bids on the tickets to maintain bank performance data.) That information is entered into a separate database, and the system generates confirmation tickets that we send to the bank. It also keeps a list that can be sorted several different ways and we can pick out whatever sort we want of our forward positions." The contract data is used to adjust the exposure report as well.

To handle funds remitted from the subs to the clearing center, the company has a concentration account in London. If the subsidiary has remitted funds to the clearing center, it must advise the clearing center by Monday of the week it plans to send the remittance. "On Tuesday morning, I will go to market and sell, say, five million Deutschemarks spot to a bank for value Thursday. The subs are on a weekly remittance cycle, so they wire the funds to our London account on Thursday. We'll go in and make a transfer back out of the account to the New York bank's branch in Frankfurt. Meanwhile, the bank in New York will transfer dollars to our New York accounts. No money stays in that London account. We have electronic balance reporting and we monitor it very closely."

Once the remittance is received, the exposure report is updated for that subsidiary and an advice is generated, notifying the unit that the remittance was received.

### Exposure Forecasts

The company needs to forecast two kinds of exposures. First, the remittances that come from the subsidiaries to the reinvoicing center are forecast four weeks out. "It's a very simple system," commented the manager. "The subsidiaries get on the system and put in the anticipated transfers to us. We know the day the remittance is coming, the bank that's sending it, all the information. On Monday of that week, they have to go in and indicate on a particular line in the forecast if that's a firm remittance or not. If it was just a forecast, we don't do anything with it. If it becomes firm, then I will make the necessary currency trades on Tuesday morning."

The second type of exposure arises from commercial transactions. The company wants to automate this aspect, but has had little success so far. "That's a very difficult thing to do in the kind of business we have, because you have different segments of the business. For example, our engineering services business is shipping parts worldwide daily, and their forecasts by country are almost impossible because of constant flow."

However, continued the manager, "The one big area we could forecast exposures in is large systems. We do get reports on that and we can identify the $5 million, $10 million, $15 million blips in exposures, but that's not automated. Unless you've got highly centralized order processing for all of your businesses, for everything, it would be very hard to pull off that type of information. We're looking at a number of different packages and we haven't found one that meets our needs yet."

### Decision Support

Although the manager maintains that the hedging decisions are made "manually, through brain power," the firm uses some of the computer's analytical capabilities to aid decision making. "We have done some pooling of currencies. We've done correlation analysis on what we call the *Germanic pool*—Germany, Holland, Denmark, and Austria. We found there's a very high correlation in the movement of those currencies. So we would take our exposures in those four currencies and net them together and find that our exposure was a push without going out and doing a hedge. We've done that in Scandinavia as well, and it's worked very well for us. It cuts down on costs because you're not buying forward contracts."

Another decision-support service the firm is considering is a currency forecasting model. "We have the authority to go out and purchase models, but because we are currently restructuring the loan agreements with our banks, we haven't done it. We have the authority to go ahead and use them and see what would happen if we introduced them."

## AUTOMATING IN-HOUSE FACTORING

In-house factoring is yet another type of sophisticated treasury vehicle that relies heavily on computer support, and many companies have set up such centers to accomplish many of the same goals as reinvoicing centers. A factoring operation purchases receivables from various operating subsidiaries and discounts them to centralize cash and exposure management. The factoring unit normally pays the exporting sub in its local currency and, in turn, receives payment in the importer's currency. Thus, foreign exchange risk and liquidity management can be centralized at the factoring center, which creates a similar effect to reinvoicing. Furthermore, the savings generated by a factoring vehicle can be enormous. For instance, the European-based factoring operation of one United States MNC adds $2 million per year in profits and cost savings to the company's P&L statement. (See the box on page 269 for more about the mechanics of in-house factoring.)

Computers are used to support in-house factoring units in several ways. First, they can help track invoices. This is necessary because the volume of trade transactions handled by a sophisticated factoring company requires substantial computer time. All bills and payment instructions can be entered on the computer, which then keeps track of the status of all transactions. In addition, data from the invoices can be used to develop reports that can be used for cash management, exposure management, and accounting. Second, computers can swiftly and accurately calculate the discount on factored exports and issuing contracts. They can automatically calculate the discount rate to be applied to each contract, pay the exporter, and bill the importer. Third, computers can assist in shifting currency exposure. They can automatically pay the exporter in its local currency and invoice the importer in its local currency, thus removing exchange risk from both. Fourth, effective automation can improve foreign currency management. A computer can generate reports identifying a company's exposures and existing forward contracts by currency and maturity. Automated systems can also confirm foreign exchange contracts. Next, computers can be used to monitor cash flows and perform other cash management tasks. In one factoring company, for example, the cash manager uses a computer to check maturities, availability of cash, bank balances, and funds transfers.

Finally, computers are of great assistance in issuing reports. A computer can provide all the reports needed for accounting purposes. In one company, for example, a computer report provides the accounting staff with the interest accrued, broken down by currency. The system also allows them to evaluate the profit or loss on all outstanding forex contracts, which is done by comparing the rates of exchange used in the contract with current market conditions (according to spot or swap rates). This difference is then written into the accounts, and a provision is made at the close. The system generates all relevant financial reports, including management reports, the general ledger, journal entries, and trial balances.

---

### THE MECHANICS AND BENEFITS OF IN-HOUSE FACTORING

In-house factoring can be complicated, but it typically involves the following key steps:

1.  The exporter invoices the importer directly and then sells the receivables to the in-house factoring unit. The fact that the exporting subsidiary sells its products directly to the importer, not through a rebilling center, is the key difference between factoring and reinvoicing.

2.  The factoring unit normally pays the exporter in its local currency and receives payment in the importers' currencies.

3.  The factoring unit sets a discount rate reflecting the prevailing interest rate and invoice term.

4.  The factoring unit normally includes the cost of covering exposure in the discount.

5.  The factoring unit usually charges a fee for the services it performs. These can range from 0.1% to over 2%, calculated on the face value of the receivable, depending on the collection risks assumed by the factoring center and the services it provides.

In-house factoring units offer companies eight major benefits:

1. Can be done from a manufacturing unit or regional headquarters, thus avoiding the legal costs and problems of incorporating a new corporate entity.

2. Is usually simpler and less expensive to establish and operate than a reinvoicing center. Because only one invoice is needed for factoring, rather than two with reinvoicing, administrative work and costs are reduced.

3. Avoids transfer-pricing problems. Because factoring merely involves the discounting of trade receivables, not the transfer of title from subsidiaries, it avoids the tax and legal problems associated with transfer pricing.

4. Removes currency exposure from operating units and centralizes it at the factoring center. By paying the exporting sub in its own currency and receiving payment in the currency of the importing sub, the factoring unit can assume and centrally hedge foreign exchange risks.

5. Reduces funds-transfer and currency-conversion costs. Due to the fact that factoring units handle financial transactions centrally, they often gain increased leverage with their banks and can negotiate low funds-transfer costs and narrow forex spreads.

6. Shifts liquidity through a variety of techniques. The most common methods are providing discounted payments immediately or at maturity, leading and lagging import payments, and altering credit terms on exports.

7. Cuts borrowing costs and increases investment yields. One factoring company, for example, estimates that it saves about $1.75 million in borrowing costs thanks to its presence in the marketplace, and improved handling of internal funds.

8. Delivers important services to exporters. For example, factoring operations can provide export financing by discounting receivables, conduct credit investigations of importers, and provide bookkeeping services to the exporting subsidiaries.

### Case Example: A Highly Computerized Factoring Vehicle

The following extended case example illustrates how a United Kingdom tobacco company used computer technology to develop an in-house factoring company that also does a form of reinvoicing. In addition to $17 million in savings on forex rates annually, the treasurer believes the center saves at least $2 million a year in reduced borrowing costs through better rates and tighter management.

The company found that its expansion and diversification program had led it into a labyrinth of repetitive and redundant treasury functions. It had nearly 500 separate subsidiaries and no clear centralized control. The company's treasurer determined that this dilemma could be solved by establishing a highly automated hybrid factoring/reinvoicing vehicle.

The center was set up to factor all intracompany and third-party sales, netting wherever possible, and it now serves as a central purchasing agent for imports from third-party suppliers, conducting what the company refers to as reinvoicing. And, while the factoring company is located in the United Kingdom, the entire factoring operation is run off an on-line database maintained in Antwerp. It factors all intracompany and third-party sales, and nets whenever possible.

It works as follows: If a German manufacturing plant wishes to ship Dm1.5 million worth of products to a subsidiary in the Middle East, it enters the sale to the Middle East as a document on the database. This document indicates the Dm1.5 million contracted Deutschemark price and the payment terms, 30 days net. The factoring program then puts the Middle East company's dollar price into the system based on the forward rate coinciding with the payment terms, that is, the 30-day forward rate. If, on the day the document is entered, the 30-day Deutschemark-to-dollar forward rate is Dm2.99:$1, the Middle East importer would owe the factoring company $501,672 (Dm1.5 million divided by 2.99), due in 30 days. The factoring center runs a monthly netting system that would then automatically match the Middle East importer's payment against other intracompany trade flows.

The system automatically calculates currency equivalents based on appropriate forward rates. Said the treasurer: "The program goes out to whenever the due or payable date is. So, if we're talking about a contract 35 days hence, it will confirm based on the forward rate, weighted to reflect the same period." The system computes rates for transactions with terms of up to 190 days, but terms are usually under 45 days. Currency conversions are made weekly, using each Thursday's New York closing spot and forward rates for 15 currencies. To cover administrative and data processing costs, the factoring unit levies a percentage charge on all transactions, depending on the method used for processing the transaction, whether interactively or by batch (which can save as much as 30% of telecommunications costs).

"What we have now are *cold* and *hot* jobs," the treasurer went on to explain. "If we desperately need a report, or if an invoice suddenly comes in for a lot of money to be paid out tomorrow, it will come through on a hot job." Such rush jobs are performed interactively during the day, while the computer center is fully staffed. Three full-time staffers are in Antwerp handling the workload. To eliminate unnecessary hot jobs, the center bills them at the maximum rate of 0.05% of the invoice price. "We're gradually getting the operators to put all their transactions in on a cold job basis," said the treasurer, "which means they're run overnight on automatic [in the batch mode]. These cold jobs are the least expensive, as low as 0.01%." As the users have gained experience with this process, the treasurer reports, "costs for this process are coming down and can pass those savings on to the subsidiaries by reducing our handling charges."

For purchases from third parties, the factoring company performs a version of reinvoicing that works like this: After receiving instructions from the ship delivering the tobacco, the United Kingdom subsidiary will make a document on the database instructing the factoring company to pay the supplier in his billing currency on the due date. At any time, the subsidiary can access the supplier's account, which is recorded on the database, to determine if the supplier has been paid.

This sophisticated treasury management system allows the company to use many other cost-saving techniques. For example, the factoring center nets payments on a monthly basis. The treasurer estimates that the center successfully nets 70% of all company-wide foreign exchange. The netting process is run through the database in Antwerp, which receives all account information, including invoices, payment instructions, and third-party transactions. The netting system currently includes the major European operating subsidiaries; and subsidiaries in the Far East, Canada, and Australia will soon be added. Each week, the system reconciles intracompany trades and then inputs confirmations. The subs are able to access their accounts and request whatever status reports they require.

The system settles the accounts once a month. "It settles in the sense that the system records whatever is being factored through, subtracts what's being reinvoiced, and produces a net balance," explained the treasurer. "Then we can match things up." The center conducts as many matches as the system can identify.

The company's system enables subsidiaries to lead and lag by adjusting payment terms. If the importing sub elects not to pay an invoice, the factoring company will still credit the supplier's account on the contracted due date. "If we don't receive payment, that flags the system to hang on a minute—we've paid out to the supplier ahead of our receipt," said the treasurer. "Therefore, we begin a settlement with interest. That is, we begin charging interest." Because the factoring company gives value on the due date, the database is alerted to charge the exporting unit when a third-party customer doesn't pay on time.

The factoring company has an excellent record on hedging. The company follows a policy that all transaction exposure over a total of £50 million must be covered. To determine overall corporate currency exposure, the company uses a 12-month rolling forecast. Each month, the subsidiaries submit a detailed "best guess" of their commodities requirements, along with expected sales. These are combined at the operating-company level, and sent to the factoring company. Once a month, the company incorporates these estimates into a rolling, 12-month forecast.

The company inputs the information into a computer program that "throws out the oldest and adds the latest month's forecasts," according to the treasurer. "We've found there's a basic pool. That is, we tend to need the same amounts of board [paper products] and leaf [tobacco] in any given one-year period. If there's a major change, it's because of a change in marketing strategy or sales, and we're kept informed of that." The net economic exposure is determined, and then is combined with transaction exposure for a detailed exposure portrait.

To support its factoring company and other global treasury operations, the company has also created a fully automated internal reporting system to track its subsidiaries' cash flows and positions throughout Europe, North America, Latin America, and the Middle East. Originally, the firm considered using a program designed by bank consultants. "We used them as far as the initial overall design concept," the treasurer reports. "But when it came to operational detail, we parted company."

What was wrong with the bank system? According to the treasurer, "Nobody had a package tailor-made. We discovered that if we bought the bank's program, we'd end up paying consultants vast sums of money to doctor a specific package. It so happened we had a very knowledgeable data processing manager in our Belgian subsidiary. He had some spare capacity and put in a contract tender, literally to develop what we needed in house. It was accepted, and he was put in charge of rewriting the bank's programs."

The system operates with three separate modules, all linked to support the centralized treasury. The three perform synergistic functions, as shown in the descriptions that follow.

### Module One

The first module contains all invoices, payment instructions, and third-party transactions, which are transmitted electronically by the subsidiaries to a central computer in Belgium. According to the spokesperson, "The companies either input data off their computerized export sales ledger and invoices into the reporting system through an interface, or they enter it manually, especially if the transfer is for purchasing or capital expenditures. Due dates are attached, based on customer credit terms, payment schedules, and so on."

Corporate finance staff can tap into the Belgium computer to retrieve a wide range of information. Says a manager, "On this module, we can pull out 50 different reports—all kinds of reports on the customer, the region, or an entire reporting cycle. You can apply it to anything you want." The information is reported monthly by foreign subs and daily by local subs. This module is also equipped with an exchange rate package, purchased from a computer service company, which is updated weekly for 15 currencies and includes both spot and forward rates.

The company uses the data stored in this module to run its factoring operation. The factoring center's staff uses the system to monitor each operating unit's export transactions. Once a week, the firm factors all receivables, paying manufacturing subsidiaries in their own currencies at rates taken from the exchange software package.

The operating companies can also access the data. "The operating companies working through the factoring company have no need to keep ledgers of their own," said the treasurer. The database, for instance, maintains over 800 specific customer ledgers for the United Kingdom alone. According to the treasurer, this cuts down on costs. "They can access, at any time, their complete ledger, or any subsets of that ledger for which they can devise a code." The operating companies can then break down any information by settlement, country, quantity, or any combination of these variables.

The system consolidates all account information and prints confirmations. The subs are then able to access their accounts, and can extract the status reports they require. (The European operating companies can access and updates their accounts daily; systems that interface with foreign divisions are still under development.)

The module also helps the factoring center calculate its total exposure and forecast forex positions. This particular capability was a key selling point to top management. "This is a tremendous aid to our planning processes—especially hedging and forex," the treasurer pointed out. Based on the information that can be retrieved from the document files, the system can create detailed reports of anticipated cash flows and signal potential surpluses and shortages of specific currencies. This system is also used to provide 12-month exposure forecasts.

### Module Two

The second module stores all data on the firm's investment and banking activities. Said the treasurer, "It reports on our various accounts, instruments we've entered into, maturity schedules of these instruments, and the rates." Data on United Kingdom domestic accounts and the parent's foreign currency hold accounts are received electronically via automated balance sheet reporting services, provided by major United States and United Kingdom banks. Information on the balances of foreign subsidiaries can be retrieved through the internal on-line reporting system.

In conjunction with the accounts receivable and payable information stored in the first module, the firm can calculate its overall cash position. The treasurer depends on this module to identify excess cash, which can be used for investments or intracompany loans.

The system provides what the company calls a *Tactical Transition Forecast,* which lets the treasurer see forecasts of the firm's cash position for each day of the next six months. This is a particularly valuable tool for liquidity management. In the treasurer's words, "It provides us with a total company account balance position."

### Module Three

The third module is an administrative internal bookkeeping system, which taps into the central database to create a complete accounting record of the company's transactions. This module functions as a bridge, able to assimilate data from the other subsystems into necessary internal and external accounting reports. This has allowed the company to cut down enormously on administrative costs, paper, and head count.

"We really couldn't run our cash management system without this reporting package," he continued. "It does a little bit of everything—exposure management, keeping our factoring operations straight, managing our overall liquidity, keeping our books." Indeed, the reporting system has enabled the firm to centralize its foreign exchange exposure safely, reduce its bank borrowings and slash its cross border funds transfers by an estimated 65 to 70%. In addition, the automated program has reduced personnel costs by minimizing the need for large treasury and accounting staffs at the subsidiary level.

## SUMMARY

After a company has developed, tested, and emplaced sound cash and currency management systems in its operations, it is ready to take the next step in automation—to create a cross-border treasury management system. Because of the volume of transactions associated with this function, especially in MNCs, the need for such computerized systems is obvious, as is the population that now actively endorses them. Firms with such systems tend to have sales over $2 billion, own at least 20 subsidiaries, be in manufacturing, have a centralized organizational outlook, and be headquartered in North America.

There are essentially two levels of sophistication involved in such systems: The first includes using traditional techniques such as cash pooling—in which surplus funds are moved among subsidiaries to maximize profit, netting—in which intracompany and third-party obligations are offset within a corporate group, and leading and lagging—in which intracompany accounts are adjusted by prepayment and delaying strategies. The second level operates on a different degree of magnitude in both complexity and volume. It includes two techniques, the first of which entails establishing reinvoicing centers. In such centers, title of goods (but not the goods themselves) are processed and rebilled to subsidiaries or third parties. The major thrust of centers is to centralize currency exposure and remove risk from subsidiaries. The second technique is to create in-house factoring centers. In this operation, a factoring house purchases receivables from operating subsidiaries and discounts them to centralize cash and exposure management. Both types of systems require tremendous integration of reporting and accounting data.

FERF research shows that the development of cross-border automated treasury systems is proceeding rapidly. By automating the techniques just described, many companies are now enjoying the fruits of improved reporting systems, the consolidation of intercompany accounts, and better planning of short-term investments. Computers are also assisting companies by providing a locus for storing and using data on short-term interest rates, currency market trends, and tax rates. In addition, automated systems have facilitated the reinvoicing process by keeping track of multiple trade transactions, changing the currency of billing automatically, and managing currency exposures. Likewise, in-house factoring operations have been supported by the ability of computers to keep track of invoices, shift currency exposures, and issue accounting reports. In sum, the benefits are three-fold: these systems 1) increase the amount of information a company can compile and use for accounting and analysis, 2) maximize profit through their speed, accuracy, and real-time applications, and 3) save staff costs and time.

## AUTOMATING A FULL TREASURY VEHICLE—AN INFORMATION CHECKLIST

Sophisticated companies may want to set up a full-fledged treasury center to integrate the various systems and techniques discussed throughout this section. But to do so they will need adequate information and computer support. Here is a checklist identifying the necessary accounting information and computer capabilities:

**Raw Data**

1. **Get information on purchases to determine cash and currency outflows and status of payments:**

   Selling company name (usually a manufacturing site)

   Invoice number (or description), date, and due date

   Currency and amount

   Special terms (e.g., discount for prompt/early payment, interest charges on late payments)

   Ultimate purchaser (i.e., company actually receiving goods)

2. **Get information on sales to determine cash and currency inflows and status of receivables:**

   Purchasing company name, country, paying bank if known

   Invoice number (or description), date, and due date

   Currency and amount

   Special terms

3. **Enter information on exchange rates and interest rates:**

   Book rates

   Market spot rates (actual)

   Market forward rates (and forecast spot rate)

   Interest rates

   Standardized 360- or 365-day basis

4. **Keep track of other pertinent accounting data:**

   Nontrade receipts

Nontrade payables

Borrowings

Investments

Forward contracts

Operating expenses and taxes

Capital infusions

Dividends

### Computer Requirements

The above information can be processed using one of the following:

* The on-site computer(s) of the finance center
* A sister company's computer(s), with each export having a subledger that is managed on behalf of the center
* An outside vendor's computer

The choice will be determined by what is available at the sister company level, how it can be adapted, and how information can be communicated to/from the computer center for the vehicle. Alternatively, use of on-site accounting and management information systems will depend on the funds available and the time that can be spent on start-up. Figure 7–1 is a list of typical reports that can be generated.

### Computer Calculations

The calculations that produce the data used in this report are as follows:

1. Sales equivalent of purchases—determined by multiplying purchases by the exchange rate applicable to ultimate purchases
2. Accounts receivable by currency and company—determined by adding sales and deducting receipts
3. Accounts payable by currency and company—determined by adding purchases and deducting payments
4. Inventory or stock in hand—determined by adding purchases and deducting sales after converting to base-currency equivalents

# REPORTS

- **Detailed list of purchases—month to date**
  Date   Seller   Invoice No.   Due Date   Currency   Amount

- **Summary list of purchases—month to date and year to date**
  Seller   Currency   Amount   Exchange Rate   Base Currency Equiv.

- **Detailed list of sales—month to date**
  Date   Purchaser   Invoice No.   Due Date   Currency   Amount

- **Summary of sales—month to date and year to date**
  Purchaser   Currency   Amount   Exchange Rates   Base Currency Equiv.

- **Summary list of Inventory**
  Seller   Currency   Amount   Exchange Rate   Base Currency Equiv.

- **Calculations of sales price of purchases and sales**

  | Purchases | | | | Sales | | |
  |---|---|---|---|---|---|---|
  | Invoice No. | Currency | Amount | Ex. Rate | Currency | Amount | Invoice No. |

- **Accounts receivable by company**
  Company   Currency   Amount   Exchange Rate   Base Currency Equiv.

- **Accounts receivable aging (in days)**
  Company   0–30   31–60   61–90   91–180   No Days

- **Accounts receivable by currency**
  Currency   Amount   Exchange Rate   Base Currency Equiv.

- **Accounts payable by company**
  Company   Currency   Amount   Exchange Rate   Base Currency Equiv.

- **Accounts payable aging (in days)**

| Company | 0–30 | 31–60 | 61–90 | 91–180 | No Days |
|---|---|---|---|---|---|

- **Accounts payable by currency**

| Currency | Amount | Exchange Rate | Base Currency Equiv. |
|---|---|---|---|

- **Accounts receivable by currency and due date**

| Currency | Current | 1 Month | 3 Months | 6 Months |
|---|---|---|---|---|

- **Accounts payable by currency and due date**

| Currency | Current | 1 Month | 3 Months | 6 Months |
|---|---|---|---|---|

- **Detailed list of borrowings**

| Currency | Amount | Date | Maturity | Interest | | Bank |
|---|---|---|---|---|---|---|
| | | | | Rate | Owed | |

- **Detailed list of investments**

| Currency | Amount | Date | Maturity | Interest | | Bank |
|---|---|---|---|---|---|---|
| | | | | Rate | Due | |

- **Detailed list of FX contracts**

| Currency Bought | Currency Sold | Amount | Date | Maturity | Bank |
|---|---|---|---|---|---|

- **Currency exposure statement**

| Period | 1 | 2 | 3 | 4 | 5 | 6 |
|---|---|---|---|---|---|---|
| + Receivables | | | | | | Total |
| – Payables | | | | | | |
| = Trading exposure | | | | | | |

**Figure 7–1: Typical Reports**

**Figure 7-1 (continued)**

+ Investment and cash
− Borrowings
+ FX purchases
−FX sales

= Total exposure

Base currency equiv.

- **Currency exposure statement summary (by currency or base equiv.)**

| Currency | | | | Period | | | |
|---|---|---|---|---|---|---|---|
| | 1 | 2 | 3 | 4 | 5 | 6 | Total |
| US$ | | | | | | | |
| £ | | | | | | | |
| Dm | | | | | | | |
| Ffr | | | | | | | |
| L | | | | | | | |
| etc. | | | | | | | |

- **Hedging tactics analysis**

| Currency | Amount | Spot Rate | Hedged Rate | Earnings (Costs) |
|---|---|---|---|---|

- **Summary of hedging earnings (costs)**

| Currency | Earnings | Base Currency Equiv. |
|---|---|---|

5. Borrowings outstanding by currency—determined by adding borrowings and deducting repayments

6. Investments outstanding by currency—determined by adding investments bought and deducting investments sold or matured

7. Forward-purchase contracts by currency—determined by adding forward-purchase contracts and deducting contracts matured

8. Forward sales contracts by currency—determined by adding forward sales contracts and deducting contracts matured

9. Aggregate exposure by currency—determined by adding items 2, 6, and 7; and deducting items 3, 5, and 8

10. Exposure by currency and date—determined by adding items 2, 6, and 7; and deducting items 3, 5, and 8 that bear the same due date or maturity range of due dates and maturities

11. Base currency or currency of domicile—determined by multiplying any of the above by the appropriate exchange rates.

12. Revenue
   a. by currency—determined by adding sales, exchange gains and interest income
   b. by base currency or currency of domicile—determined by multiplying revenue by exchange rate

13. Expenses
   a. by currency—determined by adding cost of goods sold (purchases have been reinvoiced), interest expense, exchange losses, and operating expenses
   b. by base currency or currency of domicile—determined by multiplying expense by exchange rate

14. Profit (loss) by currency, base currency or currency of domicile—determined by subtracting expense (item 12a or 12b) from revenue (item 13a or 13b)

15. Net finance cost/earnings of hedging transactions—determined by converting the forward exchange premium or

discount profits into an annual percentage, by dividing points by the spot rate and annualizing

16. Earnings (costs) of hedging tactics—determined by multiplying aggregate exposure (item 9) or exposure by date (item 10), by net finance cost/earnings

17. Accounts receivable aging by currency and company—determined at user's option from invoice date or due date, applying gross amounts to time periods

18. Accounts payable aging—determined as in item 17

19. Balance sheet—determined by converting assets and liabilities to base currency or currency of domicile

# CHAPTER 8

# Electronic Banking: The New Frontier

## INTRODUCTION

No area of financial automation has received as much attention and publicity in recent years as the field of electronic banking. Thanks to the seemingly endless array of electronic services now offered by commercial banks, companies can use desktop computer terminals to gain access to a full range of financial information—from bank balances and money transfers to currency rates and financial news. They can also initiate funds transfers, short-term investments, and other day-to-day bank transactions, such as direct debiting and automatic investment. Firms can even use bank-designed software packages and full treasury workstations to make critical cash and currency management decisions. In short, electronic banking has given financial managers the tools to automate their international treasury operations.

As can be seen in Table 8–1, companies are moving quickly to take advantage of these services, pushing their banks for state-of-the

**TABLE 8–1**

**Corporate Use of Electronic Banking Services
(in percent of survey respondents)**

| Type of service | In use at time of survey | Three-year projection |
|---|---|---|
| Electronic balance reporting | 56 | 80 |
| Direct debiting/depositing | 47 | 67 |
| Automatic reconciliation | 36 | 59 |
| Automated clearinghouses | 34 | 49 |
| Treasury workstations | 23 | 47 |
| Automatic investment (or sweep arrangements) | 11 | 28 |

| Electronic transaction initiation | In use at time of survey | Three-year projection |
|---|---|---|
| Transferring funds | 33 | 69 |
| Making inquiries | 15 | 41 |
| Investing excess cash | 10 | 47 |
| Issuing commercial paper | 8 | 24 |
| Borrowing short-term funds | 7 | 36 |
| Trading foreign currencies | 4 | 34 |
| Opening letters of credit | 3 | 27 |

art systems that assist them in every area of treasury management. In the process, firms are reaping the benefits of improved decision making, more timely information, lower internal administrative costs, and speedier execution of transactions.

Despite these positive developments, there is still a gap between corporate expectations and the reality of electronic banking. In the words of one international treasurer, "The millennium has not yet arrived." Specifically, financial executives have the following concerns about electronic banking services:

- **High banking costs.** According to the treasurer of a United States oil firm, the company is "paying in a total of approximately $200,000 a year to seven major banks for computer-related services." And, the fees keep going up: "We used to pay one bank, up until last year, about $300 per month, per account for balance reporting. Now they have changed their algorithm so that we pay on a usage basis. We are paying much more now, maybe double or triple."

- **Pricing confusion.** In many countries, companies face a bewildering array of prices and payment methods for electronic banking products. The assistant treasurer of a United States conglomerate, for example, has found that "European bankers don't like pulling out a price list; in fact, they're distinctly uncomfortable talking about prices at all. In Italy, if there was a fixed price schedule, they didn't communicate it to me." Instead, banks may ask for payment in compensating balances, increased business, or other hard-to-monitor methods.

- **Lack of standardization among electronic banking products.** Many corporate spokespersons express frustration over the absence of commonly accepted standards within the international banking community. Even in the United States, one treasurer complained, "The lack of standards creates tremendous obstacles for companies. There is no standard on electronic funds transfers, transactions, balance reporting, and so forth." Outside of North America, the situation is even worse. In the opinion of one assistant treasurer, "Internationally you can't get banks to cooperate on anything. That's the biggest drawback to electronic banking today."

- **Overselling**. Too often, companies find that electronic banking systems fail to live up to their claims. As one corporate spokesperson put it, "There's a world of difference between the brochures and what the service actually does." Indeed, intense bank marketing efforts may have backfired in some cases, resulting in corporate demands that cannot yet be met. The treasurer of a highly automated United States firm, for example, stated that, "We just cannot get what we want. The banks don't have systems they can give you that will totally automate your back office processing. We want to achieve total integration with the banks from a system's point of view, and that's just not possible now."

To help companies overcome these obstacles, this chapter will analyze three broad areas of electronic banking: information reporting, transaction initiation, and decision support. The chapter will identify what specific services are available both in North America and abroad, focusing not only on the benefits, but also the drawbacks of the various systems. Most importantly, it will show how companies have met their needs successfully by devising interim solutions suited to the current capabilities of the banking community.

## Which Companies Use Electronic Banking—and Why

Although there is an overwhelming trend toward corporate use of electronic banking services, the survey reveals significant differences by size, organizational style, industry, and domicile of respondent, as shown in Table 8–2. For example, large firms, because of their greater resources, earlier commitment to automation, and higher potential for cost savings, are far ahead of small ones in the use of key electronic bank systems.

The same pattern holds true when size is measured by the number of foreign operating units owned by a respondent, as illustrated in Table 8–3.

However, smaller firms are taking major strides to catch up. For instance, while large firms will increase use of electronic balance reporting nearly 90% over the next few years, respondents with sales of less than $500 million will leap to around 75% over the same time frame—a growth rate of about 66%, almost double that of larger companies.

When viewed from the perspective of organizational structure (see Table 8–4), centralized firms are by far the heaviest users of electronic services.

The group treasurer of a United Kingdom consumer products firm that has centralized global treasury management through a sophisticated reinvoicing and factoring center explained the trend: "When you're trying to run an operation as complex as ours, you can't do without automation and all the electronic banking systems you can find. We're in and out of the markets all day long, moving funds around and trading currencies. We couldn't live without electronic services."

High technology firms are entrenched in every aspect of electronic banking as shown in Table 8–5.

In electronic balance reporting, for example, the survey shows that 73% of respondents manufacturing high technology products use the service; 10 percentage points higher than capital goods producers, and about 20 points higher than firms engaged in inter-

**TABLE 8–2**

**Size of Firms with Electronic Banking Services**
**(in percent of survey respondents)**

| | Electronic Balance Reporting | | Electronic Funds Transfer | | Treasury Workstations | |
|---|---|---|---|---|---|---|
| | In use at time of survey | Three-year projection | In use at time of survey | Three-year projection | In use at time of survey | Three-year projection |
| Over $2 billion | 66 | 79 | 47 | 75 | 41 | 61 |
| $500 million–$2 billion | 63 | 88 | 39 | 71 | 28 | 54 |
| $200 million–$499 million | 44 | 73 | 23 | 71 | 8 | 29 |
| Under $200 million | 46 | 77 | 17 | 57 | 7 | 38 |

**TABLE 8-3**

**Number of Subsidiaries Associated with Firms with Electronic Banking Services**
(In percent of survey respondents)

| | Electronic Balance Reporting | | Electronic Funds Transfer | | Treasury Workstations | |
|---|---|---|---|---|---|---|
| | In use at time of survey | Three-year projection | In use at time of survey | Three-year projection | In use at time of survey | Three-year projection |
| Over 40 | 71 | 87 | 50 | 87 | 47 | 69 |
| 21–40 | 65 | 90 | 35 | 78 | 28 | 58 |
| 11–20 | 61 | 79 | 43 | 75 | 34 | 52 |
| 6–10 | 49 | 77 | 23 | 60 | 11 | 40 |
| 1–5 | 52 | 76 | 30 | 61 | 13 | 37 |

**TABLE 8–4**

**Type of Organizational Structure of Firms with Electronic Banking Services**
**(In percent of survey respondents)**

| | Electronic Balance Reporting | | Electronic Funds Transfer | | Treasury Workstations | |
|---|---|---|---|---|---|---|
| | In use at time of survey | Three-year projection | In use at time of survey | Three-year projection | In use at time of survey | Three-year projection |
| Centralized | 62 | 85 | 36 | 75 | 26 | 54 |
| Regionalized | 36 | 72 | 28 | 64 | 20 | 48 |
| Decentralized | 49 | 72 | 27 | 55 | 15 | 31 |

**TABLE 8–5**

**Type of Industry of Firms that Use Electronic Banking Services (in percent of survey respondents)**

| | Electronic Balance Reporting | | Electronic Funds Transfer | | Treasury Workstations | |
|---|---|---|---|---|---|---|
| | In use at time of survey | Three-year projection | In use at time of survey | Three-year projection | In use at time of survey | Three-year projection |
| High Technology | 73 | 95 | 49 | 76 | 27 | 51 |
| Capital Goods | 63 | 82 | 26 | 60 | 23 | 55 |
| Services | 54 | 81 | 38 | 80 | 23 | 50 |
| Intermediate Goods | 54 | 74 | 37 | 82 | 21 | 46 |
| Consumer Goods | 48 | 75 | 26 | 57 | 21 | 40 |

mediate goods, consumer goods, and services. Over the next few years, an astonishing 95% of high-tech firms will have electronic bank reporting—the highest rating for any individual market segment.

Finally, Table 8–6 shows that the location of parent headquarters of respondents has a profound impact on service use.

The North American corporate fascination with electronic banking reporting began in earnest in the 1970s, as companies sought relief from rapidly escalating banking costs. The intensely competitive nature of the North American banking industry—especially in the United States, where a great many financial institutions vie for corporate business—made the conversion of banks to the cause of automated services swift and pervasive. In fact, aggressive United States banks are spearheading the drive for electronic banking abroad.


## ELECTRONIC BALANCE REPORTING SERVICES

Of all the automated financial services currently offered by banks, none has been so widely embraced by multinational corporations as electronic information reporting. Over half of the survey respondents have already purchased electronic balance reporting systems, and another quarter plan to purchase them within the next few years. Thus, by the end of the 1980s, about 80% of all companies will be using the service. This trend is graphically illustrated in Table 8–7, which shows that as electronic methods of transmitting bank information grows, use of traditional balance reporting methods will decline.

The corporate appetite for electronic balance reporting is not hard to explain. Up-to-the-minute balance data is essential for daily funds management and forecasting, for tracking inflows and outflows, for confirmation that payments have been executed, and for account analysis and bank relations management. This is especially true for firms that have highly automated internal systems. According to a manager of banking and finance at a firm with a fully integrated and computerized treasury management system, "The key thing, of course, is the daily reporting of your bank balances. And that *has* to be done electronically. The modules that we have for reporting and forecasting, investing, and so on are all helpful and necessary. But

**TABLE 8-6**

**Location of Firms that Use Electronic Banking Services**
**(in percent of survey respondents)**

| | Electronic Balance Reporting | | Electronic Funds Transfer | | Treasury Workstations | |
|---|---|---|---|---|---|---|
| | In use at time of survey | Three-year projection | In use at time of survey | Three-year projection | In use at time of survey | Three-year projection |
| North America | 71 | 88 | 44 | 73 | 29 | 55 |
| Europe | 34 | 66 | 15 | 57 | 17 | 29 |
| Asia | 29 | 72 | 14 | 74 | 11 | 46 |

**TABLE 8–7**

**How Parent Companies Receive Bank Balance Information
(in percent of survey respondents)**

|  | In use at time of survey | Three-year projection |
|---|---|---|
| Mail | 84 | 63 |
| Telephone | 77 | 54 |
| Telex | 33 | 24 |
| Messenger | 24 | 15 |
| Computer link | 45 | 65 |
| Computer disk | 8 | 12 |

without the balance reporting, you can't do much with all the rest of it."

Specifically, electronic bank information offers companies three key advantages over other reporting methods. First, it offers the promise of improved quality and timeliness of information. Electronic bank reporting provides sound data on which cash managers can base swift, informed decisions. As the treasurer of a Swiss manufacturer put it, "Electronic bank reporting provides me with better information more rapidly from the banks. And that translates into better cash management." Second, these services can provide cost savings. Companies look to electronic banking services for immediate information and increased control to help them reduce idle balances and bank charges. According to the treasurer of a United States firm that slashed its balances by 80% with electronic reporting, "The main benefit is getting rid of all those idle funds you never knew anything about before." Third, these services can reduce administrative workloads. Electronic bank reporting services can cut a company's staff needs and boost efficiency. "Writing telexes, sending letters, and reconciling manually are time-consuming and error-prone procedures," says one senior financial officer. "We're looking for less staff and more time at this office. Bank reporting will give it to us."

For these reasons, companies have put great pressure on their banks to develop sophisticated balance reporting systems. North American firms, in particular, have made the availability of electronic information services a top priority when evaluating banks. The treasurer of a major United States chemicals company, for example, now considers automated balance reporting to be "one of our three main criteria in picking a bank. We look at financing capabilities, especially for exports, global presence, and good electronic information systems."

As a result of rising corporate demand and intense competition from foreign financial institutions, banks in most countries are increasingly regarding electronic reporting as part of their core business, along with functions such as loans, foreign exchange trading, and funds transfers. Indeed, companies can now find some version of the service in nearly every part of the world.

## The State of the Art: North American Balance Reporting

The combination of a highly competitive and technologically innovative banking community and an extremely sophisticated corporate financial world has made North America the world's leader in developing and using the full range of balance reporting services. The questions that surround the availability of balance reporting services elsewhere in the world—questions of system quality, pricing mechanisms, multibank reporting, and compatible formats—have all been resolved to a greater degree in North America than in any other region. For that reason, a review of North American services reveals the state of the art in methods of delivery, frequency of update, and level of detail of electronic bank information.

### System Features: Modes of Delivery

Currently, North American companies can choose from the following three delivery methods, depending on their particular needs:

1. **Dumb terminals.** The dumb terminal is a printer or terminal that acts only as an information receiver and transmitter; for example, the data as received from a bank's computer over a telephone line after that computer has verified that the user on the dumb terminal has entered the proper codes and passwords. Banks usually charge on the basis of lines of data transmitted; consequently, the extent of the detail requested is proportional to the expense of the report.

Many companies find that this type of data transmission has serious disadvantages. First, dumb terminals require a high degree of manual supervision. To obtain multiple bank reports, for example, a staff member must sequentially request them. That is, one must finish printing before the next can be queued. Second, because the user can not manipulate data on the terminal, the data in the report must be printed and then rekeyed into a spreadsheet or other workspace before analysis begins. Finally, the service cannot be integrated with a company's internal systems.

2. **Smart terminals.** Banks are now offering services through smart terminals—desktop or personal computers in which bank data can be received and then manipulated through software. This development is in sync with the trend toward increased use of personal computers in corporate treasury departments (see Table 4–7 on page 143), enabling companies to integrate their internal automated processes with balance reports from the banks.

   Companies that use microcomputers to receive bank balance reports are able to store and manipulate bank data in house, thus cutting clerical time. PCs can also significantly reduce service costs by accessing bank data directly and storing it for off-line use and analysis, thereby reducing time-sharing and bank fees. Finally, microcomputers can, through clever programs, consolidate data from multiple banks. Because this consolidation is done in house, no cooperation is required among banks, companies do not have to favor one bank by choosing its system, and the corporate treasurer gains greater control over the format and the scheme of presentation of the information.

3. **Mainframe-to-mainframe links.** Some large firms are now discovering the limits of the microcomputer's processing power and are seeking services to deliver balance reports directly to mainframe computers. The mainframe-to-mainframe link allows data from a bank's mainframe to feed directly to that of a company's, resulting in high-speed transmission with minimal potential for human error. This highly sophisticated technique enables a firm to automatically reconcile masses of data on receivables, payables, and the full range of banking activities.

   A direct link with the bank's mainframe can help companies

resolve one of their biggest problems in the area of automation: integration of systems. According to the treasurer of a firm that recently conducted a systems study, "Our criticism of ourselves has been that we have too many different systems that don't talk to each other. We have bank systems, internal systems, outside contract systems—and none of these communicate with each other." In some cases in this company, a single transaction must be entered in up to four different systems. For these reasons, the study recommended a $400,000 investment to move as many functions as possible, including bank reporting, to the mainframe.

### Case Example: Mainframe-to-Mainframe Balance Reporting

One consumer goods retailing company is moving toward a true mainframe-to-mainframe link, albeit by an extremely circuitous route. The company uses its computer and telecommunications network to capture balance reports from its more than 1500 banks in the following manner: The firm has 2000 stores nationwide, and each one deposits its receipts daily in a local bank. The stores, depending on location, then make a report to either a time-sharing vendor in Portland, Oregon, or to a bank in Pittsburgh. "If it's a small unit," commented a corporate manager, "the report will be made over the phone. The operator at the bank or balance reporting service will have a master file. You give the operator your unit code, your company, and the amount. The operator then verifies that you exist and keys the entry into the bank system, which causes an electronic debit to be made at the local bank for credit at the regional concentration bank."

Stores outfitted with automated systems report through a computer terminal. "We're working right now to improve our ability to relay the information at the store level," noted the manager. "I think we're going to get about half the stores, representing more than 80% of the dollars, into a system that will be much more automated than what we have now. The other 20% of the dollars will still be reported over the phone."

Once the bank or the time-sharing service processes a local store's report, he continued, "There will be a credit to our account, detailing unit number so-and-so and the amount. The bank transmits that information directly onto the mainframe at one of two regional computer centers in Columbus, Ohio, or Reno, Nevada, giving them details of all the credits to that account on that particular day." After

the computers receive the data, they automatically generate preformatted reports to an electronic message center located in Dallas,
where the data can be accessed through the terminal by the treasury
department.

The company plans to refine the system in two ways. First, notes
the manager, "We are instituting a point-of-sale system at the larger
stores that will capture yesterday's sales data and we will know what
size of deposit those sales will generate. Then we won't need them to
report it to an outside agency or bank reporting system." Second, "I
will get the specifics of receivables and payables from the computer
center—those things that are now being put into little notes and fed
to me. I will access those systems directly."

---

## THE VIDEOTEX OPTION

Despite North America's current superiority in the area of
electronic banking services, one type of delivery system for bank
balance reports is not widely available. Videotex, most common
in Europe, is an alternative means of transmission over telephone lines. The system is characterized by a menu-driven, user-
friendly format and the data is usually presented graphically.

Videotex systems are aimed at small companies with simple
cash management needs. Explained the vice president at a
Swedish bank, "Our videotex system is aimed at the smaller
companies. It's a cheap alternative to our higher-priced proprietary system. Of course, the depth and range of information
on the videotex will not be of the same quality as that of our
terminal-based system."

Videotex is inexpensive because transmissions are geared to
a broad-based audience, and the costs are spread out among all
subscribers. To attract the largest number of customers, however, only the most general aspects of balance information are
reported. As one United States cash management consultant
put it: "Once you get down to the finer levels, all the costs of
doing that, have to be absorbed by individual subscriber, and
that's not what Videotex is all about. It's just not worth it in the
United States to deliver this information over videotex when the
other systems are more highly developed, provide more detail,
and in some cases are still free of charge."

### Frequency of Update

For many companies, timeliness is the most important consideration in electronic balance reporting. An outdated balance report can cost a firm thousands of dollars in uninvested funds or overdrawn disbursement accounts. As one assistant treasurer put it: "The less frequent the reporting, the more uncertainty you have to deal with." On the other hand, some companies are wary of paying a bank extra for constantly updated information they don't need. In North America, banks offer three frequencies of update: previous day, intraday, and real-time.

Previous day is the least rigorous, but most common, update frequency. Under this arrangement, account activity is updated by batch at the close of business on Day One and is available to the user on the morning of Day Two. For many firms, previous days' data is often sufficient to run a cash management system adequately. For example, a consumer products company has established a controlled disbursement account, in combination with lockboxes and a concentration account, that reduces its need for more frequent updates. "We don't have any surprises on the disbursement side," claimed the firm's assistant treasurer. "Because I know what checks are clearing as we speak, I just want to see the total that I must fund."

On the receipts side, similarly, most companies are content with previous day updates. Most banks provide only next-day availability on funds collected through lockboxes, so the company in the example has not pressed its banks for more frequent updates. Nonetheless, the assistant treasurer admits that there are some "surprises" on the receipts side. "You can still get a check drawn on Bank A deposited to a Bank A lockbox. It's immediate availability, but there's a day's delay in reporting it." However, forecasting models can obviate this problem. Turning to the next method, many aggressive cash managers use balance reporting systems that are updated at different times during the same business day. In this way, they avoid the missed opportunity of funds sitting idle overnight. "Our banks that offer same-day lockbox reporting update twice each morning," said the cash manager at a chemicals company. "We go out and pull in the last update at about 9:30 A.M. to collect the deposits that were made in the last hour or two. Getting updates more frequently than that is not really that big of an issue because 80 to 90% of your receipts are in by that time anyway."

One oil company, however, tightened its balance management further. The firm programmed its treasury workstation package to dial up its banks and retrieve the firm's balance reports at two-hour intervals until 2:00 P.M. every afternoon. "If we get a $20 million payment in at noontime," explained the manager of treasury operations at the firm, "we want to invest that payment overnight rather than let it sit." After two o'clock, rates on investment instruments deteriorate to such an extent that the manager lets the funds sit in the bank.

The third type of update frequency is in real-time, which is the state of the art in electronic balance reporting. Real-time updates allow firms to monitor their activity throughout the business day, usually within a few minutes of the actual transaction. However, despite growing corporate interest in this type of reporting, many banks have hesitated to make the substantial investment in computer hardware required for real-time updates. Internal bank systems often do have real-time capability, but they are reluctant to tie their corporate customers into the internal system for control reasons. However, real-time updates are likely to become more common in the future because of pressure from the Federal Reserve. The Fed's recent restrictions on daylight overdrafts may affect real-time balance monitoring by forcing banks to monitor customer accounts more closely.

### Types of Data

Although many banks offer a range of data in their electronic reporting systems, few companies are taking full advantage of such service. However, over the next few years, the survey shows that computer-to-computer receipt of every type of information covered in the survey should increase sharply.

As might be expected, ledger balances and available balances head the list with 40% and 38% of respondents, respectively. Over the next few years, those figures will rise to 57% and 54%. This trend is easy to explain because balance reports are the most time-sensitive of any information supplied by banks and they provide the foundation for all the various automated services.

The components or details of these balances are also important to cash managers. Data on money transfers, deposits, and collections are essential for tracking specific payments and reconciling accounts. For these reasons, 29% of surveyed parent companies usually receive data on money transfers electronically, 28% receive data on deposits, and 25% receive data on collections over their terminals. Those numbers should grow to 48%, 44%, and 43%. As one treasurer elaborated; "We need these details electronically as an audit trail. We need early notice if an expected funds transfer from a customer doesn't arrive. We make a lot of decisions based on that information."

Of the companies polled, just 16% now use computer terminals to make account inquiries. One United States cash manager explained why: "It's easier to deal with disputes over the phone with someone you know." And, computers are not the best audiences. However, a growing number of firms with large, complex accounts and frequent need for clarification are investigating this area more closely, and the survey projects that companies planning to use terminals for account inquiries will more than double to 35% over the next few years. This subject is discussed in greater detail on page 322.

Short-term borrowings and investments get even less attention from users of electronic reporting systems (only 12% and 11% of respondents, respectively), although the number of users will, again, more than double over the same period. Many financial managers feel they can manage cash effectively without this electronic information. However, an assistant treasurer who receives borrowing data via terminal disagrees: "We use our receipts to pay down borrowings every day, so we need the information fast. We also come close to our credit limits pretty often, and borrowings are a critical part of our banking relations, so we really want to keep on top of things."

At the time of the survey, less than 10% of respondents received account analyses detailing bank charges via terminal—a figure that should more than triple over the next few years. Through this method, treasurers can more easily compare bank costs from service to service or from bank to bank, and can evaluate the cost of fees as compared to other forms of compensation. "We'd really like to receive those reports over a terminal," said the treasurer of one consumer products firm. "We could get the reports sooner and feed them into the system directly. For now, we still get them on paper and they come in two to three months late."

Most parent firms still receive data on trade transactions and currency transactions in the mail as well; just 7% of companies now receive data on currency transactions electronically, and the number is one point lower for trade transactions. As an example of this minority, however, one cash manager now receives trade transactions on disks from many of his banks to facilitate input into his computer system, which is compatible with his banks' computers. "We were manually entering numbers before. With this system, the accuracy of the input has gone way up." However, as with other types of information, the figures for this application might increase over the next few years to 23% for trade transactions and 28% for currency transactions.

### Case Example: A Sophisticated Domestic Reporting System

A United States financial services company manages its coast-to-coast network of over 750 domestic accounts with the help of a highly automated system that ties together electronic balance reporting, cash forecasting, balance targeting, and a series of concentration services and investment accounts. Every day the system automatically matches all cash receipts against balance targets, calculates the daily cash position, and funnels money in excess of target balances into two special investment accounts. Explained the firm's vice president, "It's all done without anyone touching it."

The company built this system for itself and, although it cost $2–2.5 million, the company calculated that in its first year of operation (1978), it generated $14.5 million in extra daily cash flows that could be invested for high yields. However, noted the vice president, "The more important thing to us was that at 3:30 in the afternoon, we knew what was going to be in our concentration accounts the next morning. What a feeling to know that you have that money to get into the market early in the morning! And, if there was a problem with a bank, we knew before they did."

The system works like this: The 750 local collection banks are grouped into three concentration systems. Every morning, they telecommunicate the closing balances of the previous day to the firm's computer, which is operated by a computer service company. This company, in turn, relays the balance data to one of the three concentration banks, indicating the amount of excess funds in each account and instructing how much to draw out.

Of the three concentration banks, two are money center banks that are also used for excess funds investment, and the third only concentrates funds regionally and moves them by depository transfer checks or electronic funds transfers into one of the two investment banks. Once the funds are in an investment bank, the firm's investment managers evaluate the daily cash position report to decide how to use them. The managers take quotes on rates from a variety of sources, so that nonconcentration banks can also be used for investment.

The vice president offered an example of how this might work: "Let's take a bank in Nebraska. They call in this morning with their balance and transaction information. Say they have $100 and we had deposits yesterday of $50. It goes into the computer, where it is matched against a formula we have for gauging cash flows. After all information is accumulated by the service, excess funds are transmitted to a concentration bank, which draws down funds from each bank that called in. At 4:00 P.M. the time-sharing service transmits daily printouts of what happened to the home office."

The computer tracks each target balance, transfer amount, and cash balance, and handles all day-to-day operation of the system. In the words of the vice president, "The computer is making the adjustments—we merely put the parameters in. If we want to keep $75,000 on an average daily basis and we put too much in today, the program takes it out tomorrow. If we find we have more cash flow coming into an account than we forecast, we will tell the computer to change the target."

A small treasury team known as the "cash control center" controls and monitors this massive flow of money. The center accesses the electronic reporting services of the concentration banks to obtain their cash positions. They also receive reports both from the investment banks on the previous day's invested funds and the day's opening balance and from the computer service company on what happened with each account.

At the end of the month, this data is used to generate a consolidated report on the period's cash flows and collected balances, as well as the standing of each account in relation to its balance target year-to-date and month-to-date. The cash controllers also generate daily exception reports, which show banks that are over or under their targets by five percent. "If that happens," says the vice president, "they look at their list to see what the daily cash flow is through that bank.

Is it what they estimated? If not, the cash control center will call the computer and change the target number at that bank."

## Automatic Reconciliation Services

Automatic account reconciliation is one of the most useful electronic services a company can obtain from its banks. Without it, large clerical staffs must spend hours, even days, comparing dozens of bank statements with bank debit and credit advices. After a statement is reconciled, numerous entries must be made to a subledger system and then keyed into a firm's database. This manual, multistep process is slow, costly and decidedly vulnerable to human error. For these reasons, over 36% of the survey respondents reconcile accounts automatically, and their ranks will swell to 59% over the next few years.

For the most part, companies use automatic reconciliation services for their checking account activity. Under such a system, a company provides its banks with a record of all checks issued in a given period. The bank checks this information against its own files and provides a series of reports, such as a listing of all checks, indicating amounts and items still outstanding, and a balance of the activity to a firm's bank statement. Specialized reports, such as float management analyses that highlight the time between when checks were issued and cashed, may also be available.

Another way to reconcile accounts automatically is to have the bank's computer generate tapes or transmit data directly to the corporation's computer. Then, reconciliation can be done in house. One restaurant chain has established such a direct link with its banks. The company purchased a bank reconciliation program to use on its own mainframe computer—"essentially the same package the bank uses," according to the assistant treasurer at the firm. The process works relatively simply. Data is transmitted from the banks daily and is automatically stored to be reconciled in accordance with the schedule for each account. "The software program then compares what we think happened with what the bank says happened and kicks out any discrepancies," said the treasurer. The only gap in the system is the monthly paper reports that still come in from the smaller banks and have to be entered manually.

## Overseas Balance Reporting Systems

Corporations seeking state-of-the-art electronic reporting services outside North America, face serious obstacles. Although leading commercial banks in such countries as Sweden, Japan, and the United Kingdom offer sophisticated systems, automated balance reporting services continue to lag in many parts of the world. This is especially true in the developing countries of Latin America, Asia, and Africa. However, even some European nations, including Italy and the Netherlands, have only recently developed the service. Thus, companies with operations in such countries continue to rely on the telephone or mail to get a complete picture of their country-wide cash position.

For example, the assistant treasurer of a multinational conglomerate investigated the possibilities of electronic balance reporting services in major European countries. The conclusion was that "the United States is far ahead of Europe in electronic services. They could catch up quickly, but the way things stand today, you can get so much bang for your buck in the United States." Although bankers in some nations, such as Germany, "really knew their material, from the nitty-gritty right up to the big structural issues," other countries posed major difficulties.

Based on experience, the treasurer recommends that firms shopping around for electronic reporting services for foreign operations take the following steps:

1. **Go to the source.** See the products first hand and talk to the people in person. The treasurer notes that the "big picture is easy to get. It's the details that always foul you up."

2. **Explicitly communicate what you want.** In the assistant treasurer's opinion, foreign bankers often do not promote their services aggressively because they are reluctant to promote products that reduce balances and other banking costs. "You have to tell them exactly what you need and what you're prepared to pay. They may not even want to demonstrate the service, and they usually don't want to discuss prices or value-dating conventions."

3. **Get firm commitments from both branch and head office managers.** The treasurer believes that European banks often suffer from *"profit centeritis."* As he put it, "Some branch managers

are very autonomous and powerful in Europe, and if you want to get reports on all your accounts in a country, nothing gets done without their approval. The same is true for pricing decisions. It can be a real trick to get the kind of service you want under these conditions."

## Making the Acquisition Decision

When investigating electronic information reporting services in a particular country, most firms will look first to the banks holding their most active collection and disbursement accounts. As they switch over to electronic reporting, however, treasurers may discover inefficiencies in both the structure of their banking relations and the management of their bank accounts. This may spur them to concentrate funds into fewer accounts and reduce bank business. Although competitive borrowing and investment rates, extent of branch networks, quality of services, responsiveness of calling officers, and other considerations play an important role in the choice of banks, treasurers are increasingly placing a premium on the ability of a bank to report data. To that end, the following five issues should be kept in mind when assessing the electronic reporting services of overseas banks: accuracy, timeliness, price, service, and level of detail. These will now be discussed in turn.

First, treasurers should ask about the accuracy of the reports. The basic point about bank systems is that they are only as good as the quality of their information. For companies that rely on bank reporting services to support such critical tasks as credit and collections, payables management, and bank reconciliation, using inaccurate data can have disastrous consequences. For example, according to a manager at a United Kingdom subsidiary of a United States financial services firm, "An inaccurate report can result in our crediting the wrong selling agent with a sale, or crediting the wrong amount or the wrong invoice number. There must be absolute accuracy, or else our receivables and bank reconciliation will fall apart."

Second, treasurers must know if the information is timely enough. As discussed in other sections of this book, the transmission capabilities of electronic reporting systems range from real-time data to intraday updates to previous-day information. But in most countries outside North America, real-time and even intraday reporting is extremely rare. Making matters worse, banks' definitions of system features vary; what some banks advertise as real-time access, for example, is often a series of intraday updates. It is important for a company that thinks it is buying a real-time system to make sure it is not really getting a speedy batch-processing system.

Third, treasurers should evaluate the price. Keeping down service charges is always a prime consideration because these systems can be very expensive. For most overseas operations, banks have significantly different pricing policies on electronic reporting systems: some charge companies nothing at all or only time-sharing costs; others impose monthly or per-module fees, as well as additional charges based on the frequency of data access or the number of lines of data. As a general rule, however, banks will cut rates for their important customers to prevent them from moving their business. Therefore, companies should always negotiate price, while keeping certain criteria in mind.

Companies can pay for electronic reporting services with fees, balances, or compensating business. Astute cash managers in developing countries usually pay fees. One finance director explained why: "We want to compare the benefits of bank systems to their cost. You have to see how much reporting lowers your borrowing costs and idle balances. Now, if you are being charged via compensating balances or business, it becomes more difficult to monitor, because your actual charges are going up and down with interest and other rates. With fees, I know precisely what my costs are."

Fourth, the dependability of the service should be assessed. Even the best systems can break down occasionally, so treasurers should make sure they can communicate with the electronic reporting operations staff at their banks. If the system is down, for example, a bank staff member should be able to identify the problem and estimate when the system will be up again. If data shows up on the screen or printer in a garbled state, a bank staffer should be able to identify and correct the problem. As one corporate cash manager said, "The main priority for us is that we can rely on the bank if a problem occurs. We know that we have people we can talk to who are responsive to our needs." The best way to assess support facilities is to question current users of the system. Companies must also work closely with local post, telephone, and telegraph authorities to iron out any hardware or software issues that might cause communications problems.

Finally, treasurers should evaluate the system's level of detail. Companies investigating electronic reporting systems should bear in mind the requirements of their full cash management function, as well as those of marketing and other departments. To meet these needs, companies may require a system that offers full, as well as summary, data, and stores historical information. Normally, a system should have a history feature of at least three days, although some can provide up to 60 days. Gross and available balances are also important.

Reports should also value-date individual collections and disbursements where applicable. Some non-American banks are leery about this feature. For example, companies have a hard time obtaining information on value-dated balances in Italy, even though they are the basis on which Italian banks pay or charge interest. In the Netherlands, one bank has designed a reporting service that allows the company to insert back-value days itself, because the bank is the last to know about disbursements being made today that affect yesterday's balances. (For information on value-dating practices in key countries, see Table 8–8 on page 310).

To answer these questions and prevent misunderstandings, treasurers should ask bankers for references. It is a good idea to follow up with the references by phone to find out, for example, about the frequency of system down-time or of lost and scrambled data. Also, before contracting for a system, companies should insist on having the bank conduct test runs on a portable system. These test runs should demonstrate the different screen and printout formats that are available with the reporting system (such as BAI or SWIFT). The format of the transmission is a vital feature that should be evaluated carefully. Some banks will even put in actual company information for the test, and will alter it to accommodate a company's needs. Alternatively, the bank may offer a free trial run for a month or two.

### Finding Multibank Reporting Services

Electronic bank reporting is of little use to most companies unless a method for consolidating data from different banks is available. As

**TABLE 8–8**

**Value Dating and Float Times**

| Country | Instrument | Supplier credited | Customer debited |
|---|---|---|---|
| Australia | Check (1) | Same day | Same day |
| | Check (2) | 3-4 days | Same day |
| | Wire transfer | Same day | Same day |
| | Promissory note | Same day | Varies |
| Brazil | Check (1) | 0-2 days | 0-2 days |
| | Check (2) | 9-10 days | 0-2 days |
| | Wire transfer | Same day | Same day |
| Canada | Check | Same day | Same day |
| | Automated transfer | Same day | Same day |
| | Preauthorized payment | Same day | Same day |
| | Wire transfer | Same day | Same day |
| France | Commercial bill | 4 days | 1 day |
| | Automated commercial bill | 4 days | 1 day |
| | Check | 2-5 days | 2 days |
| | Wire transfer | 1 day | 1 day |
| Germany | Check (1) | 0-2 days | 1-2 days |
| | Check (2) | 2-5 days | 1-2 days |
| | Transfer order | 2-6 days | Immediate |
| | Wire transfer | Next day | Immediate |
| | Direct debit | 2 days | 1 day |
| Italy | Ricevuta | 7-15 days | 1 day |
| | Check (1) | 2 days | Same day |
| | Check (2) | 3-8 days | Same day |
| | Wire transfer | Same day-20 days | Same day |
| Japan | Check | 1-4 days | Same day |
| | Wire transfer | Same day | Same day |
| | Intrabank transfer | Same day | Same day |
| | Promissory note | Same day | Same day |
| United Kingdom | Check (1) | Same day | Same day |
| | Check (2) | 2-4 days | Same day |
| | Wire transfer | 3-7 days | Same day |
| | BACS | Same day | Same day |
| United States | Check | 1-2 days | Same day |
| | ACH | Next day | Immediate |
| | Wire transfer | Same day | Same day |

(1) Denotes intracity. (2) Denotes intercity.

Note: Customer accounts are back-valued; suppliers receive forward value.

the treasurer of an engineering firm puts it, "We deal with about 10 or 15 banks, all of which have their own systems. But I can't have 10 or 15 terminals sitting around my office. I am not a pianist." In the United States, this problem has been largely resolved by multibank reporting services that incorporate data from a lead bank with those of other banks. Multibank reporting received a boost early on in the United States from work done by the Bank Administration Institute (BAI) on standardizing reporting formats.

A money center banker explains how the United States system works: "We are a data collector for our multibank reporting system. We transmit to and receive transactions from all major data collectors, then put it up on our mainframe here to report directly to our customers." All a spokesperson from another domestic bank has to do is comply with the other banks' password controls and formats. He still has to pay the other banks for the service. We offer it because we want it to be our terminal sitting there."

United States companies can also use time-sharing firms to provide consolidated information. These networks are similar to multibank reporting systems, except that a computer service company, rather than a bank, operates them. Participating banks report their customers' balances to the computer company, which consolidates it and reports to the corporations; the company generally pays both its banks and the service company for the service. Popular time-sharing services in the United States include GEISCO, NDC, Tymnet, and Telenet.

Finally, domestic firms may use treasury workstations, which can dial up a number of banks and consolidate the various data automatically. This approach is discussed in greater detail on page 330.

Unfortunately, the options are much more limited outside North America. A European regional treasurer of a United States producer explained why: "The banks here just aren't cooperating with one another in providing consolidated information to their customers the way they do in the United States. The problem with the European banks is that they're delaying because of competition with one another and because they do not want to make it easier for companies to reduce their own use of idle funds and the float."

Until more bank or time-sharing services become available outside of North America, companies might consider developing or purchasing their own software to consolidate electronic bank information. A United States electronics firm has successfully taken this approach. To cope with the complexities of multibank relations and multicurrency cash positions and cash flows experienced by European subsidiaries, the firm's Geneva regional headquarters created a minicomputer-based program that provides an integrated, real-time consolidated bank and internal information system.

For over a decade, the firm's European subsidiaries relied on an automated internal reporting system for treasury management. The system functioned as a pipeline for all internal systems, including sales, cash management, and accounting. Through the European regional headquarters in Geneva, every subsidiary was hooked up to the system through various telecommunications networks. Each subsidiary also had an automated system to track foreign exchange contracts and credit and collections. However, consolidated bank balance information from each unit's accounts was calculated manually.

Lacking a direct connection with their banks, the subsidiaries could not use their highly automated network for real-time assessment of their bank accounts. However, with the new package, which is already operational in the United Kingdom, Germany, and France, as well as at the Geneva regional headquarters, treasury staff can access their banks' reporting systems for detailed balance information. "We just hook up and dial into the banks' computers," commented a spokesperson. "The treasurer in a country can then take that information and quickly reinvest idle funds before the end of the day."

Each subsidiary's package consolidates reports from all of its banks; the regional headquarters then uses a special consolidation module on the same package to combine each unit's full data.

Using data from the banks and from selected internal systems (accounts payable, accounts receivable and foreign exchange), the program also prepares confirmation letters and telexes, accounting reports, decision-support data, and a series of cash position reports. These reports provide information by account, bank, currency, organizational unit, and type of funds. With these reports, the subsidiary treasurers can spot cash management opportunities at a glance. By downloading data into a PC-based spreadsheet program, users can create cash forecasts and sophisticated graphics.

In addition to on-line retrieval of daily bank data, the subsidiaries' software system generates the following reports:

- An audit report presents daily details of all transactions from all accounts. The information includes amounts, reference numbers, source of transfer, and so on.

- Value-dated balances, in both detailed and summary form, show exactly how much cash is available at any given moment. Treasurers are better able to monitor float and bank clearing times, thus preventing errors. Value dating is extremely critical for managing cash in Europe, where value dating is negotiable. This is particularly true because of its influence on real banking costs.

- Deposit, borrowing, and foreign exchange positions are presented according to maturity dates, daily position, and amounts outstanding by bank and by borrower. This information alerts staff to pending due dates on time deposits and loans, and enables them to track currency requirements for forward foreign exchange contracts. Treasurers need this information to determine their borrowing and investment needs accurately.

- Cash position reports for user-defined time periods, which present the cash position by unit and country and compare actual positions to previous forecasts, lead to better forecasting.

- Accruals, interest, and commissions are detailed to reconcile internal records with bank fees and interest payments on deposits and loans. Banks in Europe do not generally provide detailed account analyses of charges and interest payments, so it is difficult to detect errors.

- A bank activity statistics report indicates daily receipts and payments by account, bank, and total. It presents average balance and activity volume, lists interest and commissions, and gives the status of credit lines. This helps treasurers detect idle balances and unnecessary credit lines.

### Solving the Global Balance Reporting Riddle

Finding sophisticated electronic intracountry balance-reporting systems in many countries is difficult enough, but those problems pale in comparison with the obstacles companies face when attempting to secure a truly global reporting service. As one treasurer put it, "What we'd like would be an American-style system that would give us the balances of all our operations all over the world. That would be the millennium. But I don't see anyone knocking down my door offering it."

The biggest obstacle has been the lack of cooperation among local overseas banks in providing information to other banks. This resistance is being worn down slowly by the combination of companies threatening to take their business elsewhere and foreign banks growing accustomed to electronic banking. "Three years ago, we could fit a list of all banks willing to provide that information to us on one sheet of paper," said one cash management consultant. "Now it's a much more extensive list."

Third-party time-sharing services may also facilitate the move toward the sharing of information between banks. Many banks subscribe to third-party services such as Automatic Data Processing (ADP), National Data Corporation (NDC), and Chemical Bank's BankLink. Due to the fact that multiple banks use the services, companies can monitor their balances with a number of banks in different countries. Time-sharing companies also have the technical capability to exchange data with other time-sharing vendors and those banks that have in-house systems. Therefore, companies are not restricted to balance reports only from banks that subscribe to the same service.

Of course, none of this happens automatically. Firms must take the initiative and request that their overseas bank provide the information to the other bank's system. And, if the overseas bank does not have previous agreements with the domestic bank, negotiations can be troublesome and time-consuming. "These things are bank by bank," explained one time-sharing company representative. "And some are a lot more cooperative than others."

## What Companies Are Doing

Firms that cannot wait for negotiations to settle the issue can turn away from conventional bank reporting systems to find home-grown solutions. The following three examples illustrate alternative methods for obtaining overseas balance reports:

The first method is to set up multiple concentration accounts. One United States firm worked out a novel solution with its bank—a United States money center institution—to obtain consolidated reports on the company's European bank accounts. The bank discovered that if the company compensated local banks, which were unrelated to the United States bank, with target balances, the local banks would channel the funds of the company into the United States bank's branch in that country. Therefore, the United States bank acted as the master concentration account for the firm in four European nations. It now reports the balances for each country on its own balance reporting system.

"The corporate treasurer can look at the company's positions in Germany, Sweden, France, and Spain, allowing the decision of how to reapportion the money," said the bank's spokesperson. "In effect, what we have done is transferred the funds of a company that may have 12 unrelated accounts in each country to one in each country. Forty-eight accounts, and 48 balance reports, are reduced to four accounts and four reports in four countries."

A second alternative is to develop in-house software. For example, the in-house program of the electronics company discussed above, beginning on page 311, permits the firm's European regional treasury department to see subsidiaries' balances. Each local treasury operation is linked to its local bank reporting system and the reports are accessible from the center through a telecommunications network. "You have much quicker access to all the data by going right to the systems locally," said the spokesperson for the firm. "It is much quicker than depending on other reporting procedures, like monthly or weekly reports, or a telephone call. You can sit down at your desk and have immediate access."

A third alternative is to tap the SWIFT network. Banks already can monitor their cross-border accounts with other banks to a certain degree through the SWIFT system (Society for Worldwide International Financial Telecommunication). With over 1200 member banks in more than 50 countries, a SWIFT reporting system can provide firms with the depth of coverage that they require. Moreover, tapping into SWIFT directly can slash balance-reporting costs in companies with the mainframe computer capability to do it.

Gaining direct access to SWIFT is more technically difficult than using a conventional balance reporting system. The connection can be established using a regular telecommunications network, but "it's not like a time-sharing network where you just tap in and pull off the report," said one bank consultant. "You actually have to go into a mainframe computer somewhere to get the information." The information would then have to be reformatted into an understandable report.

Technical difficulty may be the least of a company's problems, however, if they adopt this strategy. Politics may intrude. Currently,

SWIFT access is restricted to the banking community. However, said a spokesperson for SWIFT: "There's no reason corporates can't use SWIFT except the banks don't want them to do it. The banks have not really seen any good reason to connect the corporates."

One innovative firm succeeded in bucking the political problems and tapped into SWIFT directly. The company, dissatisfied with conventional bank reporting systems, needed bank data to manage its in-house factoring operation. The firm had hold accounts in the United States and all major European countries, which it used to collect intracompany payments to feed to the factoring center. After shopping around, the firm concluded that no bank reporting system met its requirements. Said a spokesperson, "Electronic banking is not really working yet in Europe. They're not fast enough, and they can't give you the complete picture of all your accounts unless you use just one bank."

To solve its problem, the firm worked out an arrangement with its lead domestic bank, whereby the bank opened an account in its own name in each country where the firm had a hold account. "The accounts were officially the bank's, but they were used only for us," said the spokesperson. The participating banks sent account data through SWIFT to the firm's lead bank. The bank then consolidated and reformatted the information, and passed it on through an electronic link with the firm's mainframe computer. According to the spokesperson, "Once we programmed our computer to accept the SWIFT format, there was no need for the extra step by our bank."

The company's SWIFT system provides the firm with the following benefits:

**Speed.** Said the spokesperson, "We wanted information twice a day, on a value-dated basis. SWIFT is the only method that is fast enough to do this."

**Simplicity.** The firm wanted to avoid wading through a multitude of reports from its various banks. "It's too complicated having statements come in bank by bank," said the spokesperson, "even through our computer system. It's so much easier to have it centralized by our bank."

**Low cost.** The company found the system to be cheaper than other bank services. "SWIFT is very cheap for the banks. You don't have to pay much. That's one of the main advantages to using it." Although the company pays a fee to its lead bank, the other participating banks are rewarded with preferential treatment on foreign exchange transactions and deposits in cases when their bids are competitive.

**Stable banking relations.** By using the SWIFT system, the firm maintained its traditional banking ties, rather than shifting its business to one bank. "We wanted to stay in touch with one of the major banks in each country, so we would not be cut out of the local market. If you use only one bank's system, you can't do that."

## THE NEXT WAVE: ELECTRONIC TRANSACTION INITIATION

As automated information reporting systems continue to be refined, companies and their banks are now turning their attention to the other side of electronic banking—transaction initiation. Although only a handful of companies now use electronic initiation (generally for funds transfers), Table 8–1 shows that the number of firms using terminals to handle banking transactions will grow substantially over the next few years.

Financial managers cite three main benefits to using electronic initiation systems. First, there are respectable time and cost savings to be realized. Companies can eliminate vast amounts of internally generated paperwork, such as voucher requests, signatures, accounting verifications, and associated clerical tasks, by automating transaction initiation processes. In the mind of the treasurer of one chemical firm, "Electronic initiation will speed everything up and reduce our clerical needs. We believe that our biggest cash management savings in the future will come from reduced manpower and manhours by having an interactive terminal system." Second, electronic initiation can minimize confusion and costly mistakes. Additionally, initiation services ensure that instructions are carried out exactly when corporate customers want them to be, rather than when a bank officer gets around to it. This is especially critical when banks' manual transfer and investment systems get backed up as daily clearing deadlines approach. Lastly, electronic banking is much more secure than traditional banking. Computer systems are difficult to crack, encryption makes transactions difficult to understand, and the transmission speed is bewildering.

## Initiating Electronic Funds Transfers

Funds transfers are far and away the most popular form of electronic transaction initiation service; a third of the survey respondents now initiate transfers automatically, and in just a few years the percentage will be about two thirds. The service is particularly advanced in North America: 44% of parent companies domiciled in that region already transfer funds electronically, compared with 15% of European and 14% of Asian firms.

Not only does initiating funds transfers electronically save time and paperwork, but banks usually charge much less for the service than for checks or drafts. According to one treasury operations manager, "To do a wire transfer under the old method, we would cut a check and have a messenger take it over to the bank and they would do the wire for us. They would charge us today about $20 for that one transaction, not to count the cost of the messenger, the check typist, and all of our people that were involved. If we do it on a computer system, it only costs $6."

To initiate funds transfers electronically, companies can use a bank-provided terminal, on which they type the instructions for transmission to the bank, or they can link up a personal computer to the bank through a modem. Often, a funds transfer module will be available as part of a bank's treasury workstation package. The most common type of electronic funds transfers are predefined, or line, transfers, under which a company establishes a written set of instructions with its banks with the proper authorizations needed for transfers to go through.

If a company uses a personal computer to initiate funds transfers, the time savings of such systems are further enhanced by processing a whole day's worth of wire transfers by batch. In that arrangement, clerks input the instructions during the day, then a treasury manager accesses the system at the end of the day, approve the transactions, and release the transfers. For this expeditious reason, one manufacturer is shifting its electronic banking systems from bank-provided dumb terminals to a microcomputer. "We'll eventually tie the funds transfers into the system," noted the cash manager at the firm. "Now we have to do it manually—typing in the numbers on a terminal and sending each transfer to the bank individually. We'll batch them in the future and process a number of transactions at the same time."

## Automated Clearing Houses

A driving force behind the movement toward electronic funds transfers has been the creation of automated clearing houses in a number of countries. Such systems perform the identical functions of manual, paper-based clearing houses, only in a faster and cheaper manner, giving companies an invaluable tool for automating the payment process. According to the survey, these systems can expect ever greater volumes of business in the near future, as the percentage of companies using them increases from 34 to 49% over the next few years.

The best-known automated clearing house systems are in the United States and the United Kingdom. The United Kingdom clearing banks established the Bankers' Automated Clearing Services (BACS) as a separate company in 1971; it is now the world's largest automated clearinghouse. In 1984, another automated interbank clearing system was established in London to improve the handling of high-value transfers. Known as CHAPS (Clearing House Automated Payments System), the system clears payments between banks by computer. CHAPS has two advantages over BACS: it offers same-day settlement of interbank payments (with a minimum value of £10,000) and immediate confirmation of funds transfers to the paying and receiving parties.

The Automated Clearing House (ACH) system in the United States includes over 30 ACHs designed to handle high-speed tape transfer instructions between banks in various regions of the country. Corporate users communicate with their banks through terminals and initiate transfers; the bank, in turn, transfers funds to the recipient's bank through an ACH.

ACH promises not only reduced bank charges and next-day (and eventually same-day) value on receipts, but also dramatically quicker and cheaper procedures for internal billing and processing of payments. According to the survey, 48% of North American respondents presently use ACH, and their number will grow to 64% in three years.

The main alternatives to the ACH in the United States are checks and wire transfers. Checks are expensive to process internally, especially for low-value, high-volume transactions, and can be lost or mutilated. Checks also complicate cash forecasting for both customer and supplier, because float times on check collections vary widely. Banks charge high collection and processing fees (sometimes 50¢ per item), and assign stiff penalties if checks are returned. An ACH, on the other hand, can transfer funds directly into or out of an account electronically for greatly reduced bank and internal costs. It also enables the supplier to predict clearing time, provides a high level of security, and ensures delivery of funds by the next day.

## Corporate Use of ACHs

The ACH system is most widely used for direct debiting and depositing (see also Table 8-1, page 286). One of the first companies to use ACHs for direct debiting in the United States, in an effort to reduce transaction costs for high-volume, low-value accounts, was an insurance company. According to the firm's VP finance, when the company switched from a paper-based collection system to an electronic one that debited premiums directly from customers' bank accounts, "The motivation was to cut internal processing costs." The switch resulted in big savings in paper-handling and check-processing costs. An added bonus was the elimination of late payments, so that float on mail time was reduced by as much as two weeks.

The same firm also uses ACH for direct depositing of annuity payments. "The tough sell," said the vice president, "is how to explain the disbursement float that you lose." But the company analysis concluded that, while the firm lost over $140,000 of float annually by disbursing electronically, it nevertheless ended up with a net saving of $50,000 because of lower banking and clerical costs.

In addition to direct debits and deposits, companies use ACHs for cash concentration and disbursement (CCDs). CCDs, created in the early 1980s to replace the traditional paper depository transfer check (DTC) for cash concentration, receive next-day value. Although wire transfers guarantee same-day delivery, they are cost-effective only when the time value of the money transmitted (daily interest rate X number of days saved X value of the transfer) is greater than the cost of the transfer. At $15 to $20 per wire transfer, only transfers over $60,000 or $100,000, respectively, return more than the transfer cost of this traditional method. An ACH transfer, however, costs less than 10 cents. The system can work quite effectively. For example, explained a trucking company treasurer, "With the system we set up, our lockboxes use local depository accounts and our local depository accounts are cleaned out through ACH transfer to the subs' concentration accounts. From there, we use ACH to sweep those funds into our corporate concentration account."

Finally, companies can also use ACH to pay and receive large, one-time invoices via corporate trade payments (CTP). Companies participating in the pilot CTP program, which started in the United States in early 1984, are now initiating and settling transactions completely electronically by using in-house terminals. Through CTP, companies define an expanded invoice information format as well as a settlement system that allows a virtually unlimited amount of information to accompany each transmission.

Despite the allure of low-cost systems for collecting one-time payments, however, most United States companies have resisted the move to CTPs. This is largely because payers are concerned over loss of float. As one cash manager remarked, "There's no reason why we couldn't pay suppliers using the ACH, but we normally pay our vendors by check. You get a nice float when you pay by check."

One way for suppliers to solve the float dilemma is to offer customers later settlement dates to compensate them for the loss of their use of funds. The customer suffers no loss because the new settlement date reflects the date checks actually cleared in the past. Suppliers can also remind customers of the savings they can realize in internal processing and bank costs.

Still, maintained one cash manager, "There's too much incentive to do payments as they're done now, not just from the arguable benefits of float but also because people are kind of linked to the tradition of checks. The pilot programs in CTP have been dismal failures. And I don't really see that changing unless there is some external influence, such as the Fed deciding to commit to electronics, and to start charging ten cents to process an electronic transaction and $1 for a paper transaction. Then you would see a movement."

## THE GROWING ALLURE OF DIRECT DEPOSITING AND DEBITING

The most popular specialized bank transaction services, direct depositing and debiting, are already being used by 47% of survey respondents. This figure is projected to increase to 67% over the next few years. Direct deposits are transfer instructions prepared by the paying company for issuing funds to suppliers or employees. Direct debits, on the other hand, are transfer orders prepared by the supplier and presented to the customer's bank, which then credits the supplier's account based on standing instructions from the customer.

Direct depositing and debiting are most useful for making regularly recurring payments for such items as payroll, insurance, and utility service. Companies can issue direct debits and deposits by providing banks with magnetic tapes for input into the bank's computer or by delivering instructions through a computer link. Alternatively, companies can mail or messenger paper instructions to a bank.

There are four key advantages to direct debiting and depositing:

1. **Elimination of payment delays.** All transfers are realized the day payment is due, eliminating all bank and mail float.

2. **Administrative simplification.** Direct debiting and depositing offer tremendous savings by reducing paperwork and cutting clerical costs.

3. **Improved cash flow forecasting.** Firms can predict cash flows by pinpointing the exact amount and timing of incoming and outgoing payments.

4. **Lower bank costs.** Direct debits and deposits cut bank processing costs, because banks can debit and credit accounts by computer rather than by processing thousands of paper transfer orders or checks each month.

## Terminal-Based Inquiries and Adjustments

The survey shows that 15% of companies now take advantage of modules on their electronic balance reporting systems that permit a variety of inquiries and adjustments; within a few years that figure should nearly triple to 41%. An international treasurer explained the trend: "Automated account inquiry pretty much eliminates the account officer. That saves a lot of time and potential for confusion. We can research our account right from our terminal." For example, "If there is a transfer that was not executed, we can go back into the bank's records and first, confirm that the funds were actually released; second, determine the routing of the funds; and third, get the transfer number. We then send that information on to the payee, which starts a search from its end. The only time we have to pick up the phone is if we ask for a tracer, but in 99% of these cases, it is the receiving bank that has the problem not crediting the account rather than the sending bank. And the payee handles that."

Speed is the primary benefit of the system, the treasurer added. "It certainly speeds things up on the bank's side. Before, we either had to call in or telefax advices to the bank, and they had to have some clerk take down all this information and then turn around and process it. Now we go directly into the computer at the bank, and it does the work."

A cash management and banking director has found another good use of terminal-based inquiries and adjustments to issue stop-payment instructions on checks: "I just type in the check number, the account number, and the payee. It's much more efficient than hanging on the phone."

Many companies, however, prefer to maintain a more personal link with their account representatives for all but very standard inquiries and adjustments. Dealing with a computer can be frustrating when serious and complicated problems are involved.

## Electronic Initiation of Investments

Although only one in ten companies now initiates investments through a terminal, over 47% plan to do so over the next few years. The electronic investment initiation systems in use among companies now vary widely in sophistication, from simple funds transfer programs used to pay for investments to actual investment instructions relayed electronically to a bank.

For example, one firm has established a system that, according to the treasury manager, "sets up our investments as a repetitive transfer. We are investing with banks and brokerage houses that we deal with on a regular basis. For instance, if I buy a municipal bond from a broker, and all the broker's municipal bond settlements are at Bank A in New York, I just wire the funds to the broker's account, Bank A, $1 million, for credit to my account. But I still call the broker on the phone to tell him what instrument to invest in."

Other treasurers take advantage of systems that offer the opportunity to shop around for the best rate. One manufacturer can call up various banks' rates for different short-term investments on his terminal and then electronically choose among them. Based on those quotations, the firm's cash manager can use a terminal to notify the company's concentration bank to automatically transfer the funds to the bank offering the best rate for overnight investment. In most instances, however, the cash manager also calls the banks to personally ask for opportunities that don't appear on the screen and to bargain for better rates. Only then are funds transferred. Furthermore, the largest placements are still done manually. Because of the importance of personal negotiation for rates, most firms will prefer to use electronic initiation services for investment for small amounts, or when better rates may not be obtainable over the phone. As the spokesperson acknowledges, "It's still a person-to-person business."

### Issuing Commercial Paper Electronically

Because computer-initiated commercial paper transactions reduce turnaround time and enable managers to seize market opportunities quickly, 24% of the survey respondents plan to take advantage of this service within the next few years, as compared to the eight percent using it at the time of the survey. One company that has already made the transition, formed an "electronic triangle" with a bank and a commercial paper dealer to make it work most efficiently.

---

### AUTOMATIC INVESTMENT SERVICES

For short-term investments of excess cash, electronic initiation can slash the time required to place funds. As an alternative to actively managing the funds themselves, 11% of respondents are now turning to their banks for this automatic investment service and the number is expected to grow to 29% over the next few years. Under these special arrangements, banks invest corporate funds left in non-interest-bearing accounts automatically. Furthermore, the investment instruments are usually agreed upon in advance, with the tenure of the investment one or more days.

One large French company is currently using these services. Although it invests the bulk of its cash directly in the money markets, the company uses the automatic investment services of one of its banks to invest funds undetected by its daily reporting system (which gives only the previous day's balances). Acknowledging that the rates are probably lower than if funds were invested directly, the treasurer says, "That's the only part of the monetary flows we don't control. Usually it only comes to a couple of hundred thousand francs that we don't know about. Knowing would be nice, but it's not essential."

A United States company also has an automatic investment agreement with its bank to eliminate the chance that funds go uninvested. "It's really kind of a safety valve measure," stated the company's treasurer. "If, for some reason, we don't invest the money, our bank is required to invest it in treasury bills overnight. This is particularly helpful during the holiday season. We close down from December 23 to January 4, and every once in a while money will come in from somebody in a pipeline that has not closed down. They send it into our bank and there's nobody here monitoring it, so the bank invests it for us under predetermined investment guidelines. It can only be invested in treasury bills, and they keep rolling it over until we step in and take the money away and invest it ourselves."

Automatic investment services are also helpful for any company that has difficulty tracking and controlling its funds flows. For example, one United States oil company uses automatic investment in the United Kingdom, where it has formed an exploratory consortium in the North Sea with other oil concerns. Because of its sensitive relations with its partners, "We have a unique need for automatic investment," explains the assistant treasurer. "We have a group of unrelated firms doing business together, so it's easier to let a third party handle our short-term investment of funds. The instruction to the bank is to simply invest it in overnight instruments at money market rates. This way, our excess funds are not sitting there idle, yet at the same time there are no intragroup rivalries over investment policy. It works very well for us."

According to a company representative, the dealer provides information on trades to the bank through terminal. The firm then reviews the information on its screen and keys in instructions to release an issue of commercial paper if it so chooses. The system not only allows the firm to hit market windows, but saves it several hours of clerical time on each transaction.

The financial subsidiary of a United States retailer has also recently automated its commercial paper operation. The company is a direct issuer of commercial paper, selling its notes to investors and bypassing brokers and their fees. Of the 15 issuing banks that the firm uses, four are on line with the system, representing some 70% of the notes issued by the company. "Volume is really the key in determining how we use the system," said a company spokesperson. "It's not cost-beneficial to set up the computer connections for a bank with which I may do one issue a week."

All transactions made during the day are entered into a PC outfitted with a modem and the appropriate software. At a predetermined time each day, a member of the staff communicates the transactions to the respective issuing banks. "I sit at the PC," explained the spokesperson, "and the information on the deals actually gets printed out onto notes that the bank has in its vaults. For the other issuing banks that are not connected with the system, we have to call in the notes and someone at the bank writes it down on a piece of paper and then types out the notes. Being on line with our four major banks eliminates typographical errors. It also saves time. We've had to talk to as many as three people before we get a note typed."

The system also eases the tracking and control of outstanding notes. Declared the spokesperson, "It's amazing. When you start up the system in the morning, it knows what notes are maturing today, because it's all in the system. What we had to do during the transition to this system, unfortunately, was to sit down and key in every note that we had outstanding."

"It will also hit your bank's target balances," the spokesperson added. "It knows that it's got to debit a certain account for a specified amount because that note is maturing. It knows when I've got money coming in from a new issue, so it's crediting my account. That goes on until about 1:00 P.M., so it's keeping my cash positions up to date. Then in the afternoon, it knows not to keep any excess money in the bank. It will zero out all my accounts at the 15 issuing banks, even those that are not on line for issuances, and sweep them into my concentration account. Then it sweeps the funds right back out to cover my maturities, any investments I made, all the transactions I did that day. The excess cash in the concentration account is then loaned to the parent company to cover its funding needs."

## Electronic Initiation of Short-term Borrowing

Although few companies, only 7% of the sample, now initiate short-term borrowings through a terminal, the number should rise markedly to 40% over the next few years. A good illustration of this service is provided by the experience of a United States restaurant chain. The firm currently initiates loans by sending a telex to the lead bank of its lending syndicate.

The lead bank then telexes the member banks requesting that they forward their respective shares. By replacing the maze of telexes and approvals with a computer hookup to its lead bank, the company hopes to save two or three days per loan request.

However, most firms resist the idea of using computer hookups to negotiate loans. Said a treasury manager who has automated many other banking transactions, "There are so many different things that you have to consider and choices that you have to make on a borrowing. You may have the ability to borrow based upon a Libor rate, or based upon a Fed funds rate or something else. The borrowing corporation has to decide at the time what rate it wants to choose. I think that, for the near term, it's just too complex to rely solely on the computer."

## Trading Foreign Currency with a Computer

Survey findings show that only 4% of the respondents have automated the trading of foreign currencies, but that figure should increase over the next few years to 34%. Clearly, a small but growing group of companies wants to be able to authorize banks to buy and sell foreign currencies without spending time on the telephone themselves. These firms' currency managers want to be able to call up forex rates on their screens and, if the rates are competitive, instruct their banks to carry out the transaction.

One senior financial executive described his electronic trading approach: "We have a direct line to the trading room. We get our quotes in through the computer, through the bank's computer from their trading floor. It's the same information the trader sees. It's always a couple of trades behind. So the price we see on the screen may not be exactly the same price we get—it depends on the speed of execution." He then enters his trade into the computer for transmission to the bank.

The drawbacks to this service are similar to those for investments and borrowings. As one banker observed, "It would save us a lot of clerical work. But I don't see companies doing this unless it's for small transactions and the bank will give them a discount." At issue here is the fact that on-line foreign exchange is done almost exclusively for nominal amounts, and is used to back up a foreign remittance or to replace the purchase of a foreign draft. A corporate treasurer reinforced this point of view. "We are hooked up to our bank for foreign currency deals. We can call up rates on the screen and authorize the bank to make the purchase if the rate is good. The system is more of a convenience for small deals. Without the computer, you either have to call up a trader and or buy a foreign draft, which is troublesome because you get stuck with some heavy bank charges. If it's a big trade, obviously I won't want to do it over the computer. I'll shop around instead."

An obvious disadvantage of such a system, of course, is that often it provides rates only from one bank. However, one banker predicted that, "someone will probably come up with a service that will allow banks to list their foreign currency rates with them. Banks will be asked to put their best rates on the system and prices will be adjusted as the interbank market moves. Companies will dial into the system and select from one of the rates that shows up on the screen. The question is: Are banks really going to put their best rate on that system? Somebody may look at that screen, see that Bank A has the best rate for sterling, and then he will call them to see if he can chop that rate a little bit. They can save quite a little money through negotiations."

Because of the drawbacks to trading currencies electronically, some firms prefer to use computer technology simply to initiate confirmations of forex contracts. For example, a company can execute a spot or forward contract over the telephone with currency dealers at a bank. Information on the transaction—the currencies, amounts and, dates—can then be typed into the computer, and the system can follow up by transmitting a confirmation slip to the bank.

### Opening Letters of Credit on a Screen

The headache of manually preparing letter of credit (L/C) documentation can be partially relieved through electronic initiation. When the procedure is automated, treasurers access standard L/C format skeletons on a screen, fill them out, and transmit them to the firm's bank. Although a scant 3% of the survey respondents presently open L/Cs through terminal, 27% plan to do so in the near future.

One assistant treasurer is pleased with the service: "All we do is log on and answer the questions: 'What's the amount?' 'Who's the beneficiary?'" This is a tremendous improvement over the current system of typing and then mailing L/C applications to the bank, which takes at least two days at this firm.

Another manufacturer is taking a more reserved approach to putting its L/C operations on the computer. "We have an L/C package," explained a spokesperson, "but it's not so much for opening a letter of credit as it is for recordkeeping. The L/Cs that we've opened are entered into the system with the number, maturity, expiration date, and so on. But we're steadily moving closer to a system where you can actually open them on a terminal. That would really simplify things."

## DECISION-SUPPORT SERVICES

The success of any treasury management system depends on a financial staff's skill in using information to make the right decisions. To help these staffs make critical cash and currency management decisions, banks and other vendors now offer a variety of software programs. And, perhaps the most important, and certainly the most highly publicized, decision-support product is one that collects the various packages and automated services together in one physical entity: the treasury workstation. According to the survey, 23% of companies had already acquired a treasury workstation from a bank, and 47% expected to have one within the next few years.

Treasury workstations are generally microcomputer-based systems that, at a minimum, enable companies to automatically dial up and consolidate bank balance information from multiple banks (see below) as well as initiate transactions electronically. In addition, most workstations contain modules that permit a treasurer to input internal cash data so as to create a cash worksheet and perform other cash management functions, such as forecasting receipts and payments; managing debt and investment portfolios; monitoring bank relations and costs; and performing analyses. Treasury workstations usually permit users to call up a variety of data screens simultaneously and to access different sources of information.

## How Companies Use Treasury Workstations

In addition to balance reporting and transaction initiation modules, companies most often use four programs on their workstations: a cash worksheet, a debt and investment program, a bank relations management system, and a financial model. These will be discussed in turn in the following sections.

### Cash Worksheets

This module allows treasurers to access and manipulate bank as well as internal data. After gathering and inputting information, firms can use a workstation to produce an electronic spreadsheet that, in turn, can be used to create a cash forecast. As one treasurer put it, "Our spreadsheet has rolling forward numbers, which change every time I update information. If I add a deposit today of $200,000, it rolls my position forward for the next 45 business days and pinpoints the next spot where I really need my money. It also keeps a rolling record of real and anticipated receipts in both United States and Canadian dollars."

A growing number of companies, however, are developing in-house programs tailored to their specific needs. For example, one manager of banking and cash management described his firm's step-by-step approach toward the development of such a program: "Right now, we have a PC that will eventually be the home of the great integrated database for treasury. I get my bank reports over the PC now and have to print them out every day. Then I rekey them into a spreadsheet package to develop a worksheet. We are inputting data manually because we want to make sure we get our piece right, that what is current information today shows up tomorrow as history. When we get all that done to our satisfaction, then we will look into some of the more challenging interfaces like taking that bank report and making a file on the PC out of it so it can feed into the right place automatically on the worksheet. But we don't want to introduce that too early because we want our part to work. We don't want to lose development time worrying about why some night transmission didn't show up the way we expected it to show up."

The manager hopes to integrate other information into the system as well. "We can take our file of last year's deposit information and manipulate it to forecast next year's deposit stream by influencing it with reductions for the projected increase in the use of customer credit, increases for increased sales, a speed-up in the funds flow, or anything else I think might change. It's just a matter of gaining access to the information, and giving yourself several factors that you can multiply everything by, and courageously sticking in a number."

### Debts and Investments

With this module, treasurers can track and manage outstanding investments and borrowings more effectively, and choose the best available debt and investment instruments. One overseas company recently installed such a package on its treasury management system. The program analyzes the firm's domestic and foreign investment portfolio in terms of yields, terms, and volumes, and also searches out the best investment instruments. This latter feature, according to the treasurer, "is particularly useful from a portfolio management standpoint in countries like the United Kingdom, where the money markets are more developed than they are in Belgium, and you have a very active CD market. So this is really improving our whole investment strategy." The computer also generates reports on the borrowing positions of European subs and indicates the least expensive credit arrangements available to the firm.

On the other hand, the treasurer of a company with a portfolio of more than $2 billion has been disappointed by his module. Explained the treasury manager at the firm, "We make 25 different varieties of investments—long-term investments, investments of surplus cash, invested treasury bills, United States and European investments—and they are all monitored by this system. We can also pull different reports off: what was bought, what was sold, what we hold, anything we want to know about those investments."

The savings generated by the system depend on the time perspective adopted. According to the manager, "Ten or 15 years ago, we used to have a big spreadsheet up on the board for investment purposes. We used to have two people recording our investments on a big wall with magic markers. So over that time horizon, computerization has definitely saved effort. But right before we put in this system, our investment management system ran off the mainframe in batch mode. Our bank came in and said they were going to give us a new system that runs off the micro. We had the impression that we were going to be able to save in staffing. In actuality, we found that it has not significantly reduced the number of people."

Moreover, the move to the PC caused the firm to face a new brand of problems. "We have four modules in our workstation," stated the manager. "To get all the modules integrated, they have to run off the same PC, but our size is such that we could not get all the modules to run on one PC. So we spread them out on four different PCs. For that reason, we can't get the integration." To achieve this integration, the company recently decided to eventually move the entire treasury management system back to the corporate mainframe.

### Bank Relations Management

To manage far-flung banking relations, multinational corporations increasingly are using computer programs that help track and monitor bank activities and fees. For example, an overseas subsidiary of a United States firm recently bought a module to automate its system for analyzing bank risk. In the words of the subsidiary's treasurer, "A bank sets limits on its exposure to a corporation like ourselves based on credit analysis. Similarly, we set limits on the banks we deal with for investments. We say there is a reasonable credit risk with anybody. We evaluate each bank we deal with according to certain standard ratios, and we say $x\%$ of net worth or whatever, and we will not invest beyond a certain limit."

The company is currently trying to integrate its bank relations management system with the corporate-wide database "because the banks we deal with are multinationals as well. If our limit is $100 million worldwide with one bank and I invest $50 million, I need to know where else in the world anyone in our company is investing with that bank, so we don't run the risk as a corporation of going beyond our limit. What I'd like to have is the limit constantly updated worldwide in real time. Unfortunately, no one offers that system now."

The company also uses a module to store its bank activity, both to track costs and compare performance. In the area of foreign exchange trading, for instance, the software generates reports on every currency transaction, showing the quotes of each bank contacted and the winning rate. The treasurer noted that "every single quotation we get from every single bank is kept on file. We can see the size of the deals moving through banks, and we can see who is competitive and who is not. I mean, if they're 5 or 10 pips from the winning quote, they didn't win; but if they're 41 pips off, that's just unacceptable. We're wasting their time and they're wasting ours." The program also calculates each bank's success rate in offering acceptable quotations.

The bank relationship module in use at another company shows a different aspect of these tools. "It generates correspondence to the banks, like a word processing program, but it contains the valid signatures for a given account," according to a spokesperson. "It's the least critical of the four modules we use on the workstation, but it is convenient. It saves us from the trivialities of the day."

### Financial Models

Some firms are using software to perform what-if analyses and to evaluate scenarios. One firm, for example, purchased a bank's software to track receivables and payables patterns at various times during the year; it then uses this information with modeling software to adjust its forecasts for seasonal trends. In addition, the company inputs various currency and interest rate forecasts for what-if analysis. According to the treasurer, this enables the firm "to play with the data and see what would happen if conditions change by such an amount. It's a very useful tool."

Financial models may take a giant step forward with recent developments in the branch of artificial intelligence known as expert systems. Expert systems contain a series of if-then rules that represent an expert's decision process. Rules of thumb, called heuristics, which indicate hunches or probabilities, can also be incorporated. Major software companies and some leading commercial banks are developing micro-based expert system shells that allow the knowledge of an expert to be input into a computer program. Indeed, one bank eventually plans to market such a model for currency forecasting as part of its workstation package. The advantage would be the model's ability to furnish probabilities about certain events occurring. However, most decision-support systems currently available are binary. That is, they offer yes or no answers when asked for a decision.

## How to Select a Treasury Workstation: The Corporate Experience

Treasury workstations are expensive. Depending on the complexity of the package, initial purchase prices range from $5000 to $50,000. However, as a spokesperson from a money center bank notes, "If you read the media, it sounds like you can get everything for $10,000, but that's because the applications are just for bank reporting and a spreadsheet. And, in addition to the purchase price, treasurers must factor in maintenance fees and customizing costs. Most vendors charge companies a monthly maintenance fee to cover training, servicing and enhancements. For many firms, though, the workstation will replace existing systems and services, so all of the cost is not incremental. For example, time-sharing services for bank reporting may become redundant, or space on the mainframe may be freed up.

Thus, to ensure a worthwhile acquisition, treasurers must carefully compare their real needs with the package's range of functions. One manufacturing company just completed that necessary exercise. To improve treasury control over 15 overseas subsidiaries and rapidly expanding sales volumes, the treasury manager decided that the company needed a workstation with at least four modules: debt, investment, cash worksheet, and bank relations. "The initial purpose was not to get more information but to control existing information," he says. "The second phase would be to bring in additional information for decision-making purposes."

For political reasons, the treasury manager first turned to three of the firm's major banks. He also looked at five other banks known

for their systems. Prices ranged from $10,000 to $50,000, and the number of modules offered ran from 3 to 12. All of the systems were compatible with the microcomputer the manager planned to buy.

When looking at the different systems, the treasury manager thought about the particular needs of his company. By this reasoning, the $50,000, 12-module system was overkill. As he put it, "The system was incredible in terms of the level of detail and report generation. If you're a very large company it's probably the perfect system—you can call up to 250 banks each morning. We just don't need it." He also discovered that the more detailed systems were not user-friendly. "You have to go from one submenu to another," he explained. "They assured me that I would get more proficient. But by the time I got proficient I probably would have killed myself."

At the other end of the spectrum was a relatively inexpensive system developed by a computer vendor and marketed by a major bank. At first the manager was skeptical about a bank that did not develop its own systems: "We all know how fickle fate can be for computer companies. If the computer company sells its system to a bank and then can't make it, you've bought a product that's dead. With the major banks, you have an ongoing relationship. The next module they develop will be based on the existing system." In the end, however, swayed by the bank's guarantee that it could support the package on its own, as well as by the low cost and simplicity of the program, the manager chose this package for his treasury operations.

The experience of another company that conducted an extremely rigorous analysis is also helpful. Lacking sufficient internal expertise, the firm hired a software consultant who worked with an in-house committee composed of treasury, credit, and EDP staff. The entire review process took several months, but the firm was very confident of the end results.

The committee's first action was to compile a list of desired features and to incorporate them into a questionnaire that was to be sent to selected vendors. After researching vendor and product information advertised in various periodicals, the committee and the consultant agreed on nine target vendors. Each vendor then received a copy of the questionnaire, a detailed description of the firm's needs, existing systems, and treasury organization, and a request for copies of their annual reports and promotional literature.

The committee used an objective scoring system to narrow the field to three vendors, who were then invited to make on-site presentations. The company told the vendors that they were particularly concerned with training, data storage, and several other issues, and asked that the presentation format include an hour of discussion and two to three hours of software demonstration. The demonstrations covered all major areas of cash management for which the package would be used. They were scheduled several days apart to enable staff to absorb the information and discuss the pros and cons of each system.

To ensure an objective evaluation, the demonstrations were attended by staff from different areas who could ask the vendors a wide variety of questions, especially difficult technical ones. Finally, using a checklist format, the staff evaluated the presentations and graded each vendor in a variety of categories. After checking references, the package deemed most appropriate for the firm's treasury needs was chosen.

---

### HOW TO BUY A TREASURY WORKSTATION

Companies can use the following checklist to make sure they don't overlook any important points in their search for the best package:

**Software features**

- Is the workstation fully compatible with your hardware? Every PC is different, and software is designed specifically to operate on particular models.

- Are you paying only for modules and capabilities that you need? Are there too many *bells and whistles*?

- Are any essential modules missing? The key ones are daily bank activity report, cash position worksheet, debt and investment portfolio, cash accounting, bank relations management (records bank name, account numbers, account officers, signatories, and restrictions), transaction initiation, and data storage.

- Are there any additional modules that would be useful for your firm, such as a spreadsheet, graphics, word processing, report writer, communications with external databases, what-if analysis, or account reconciliation?

- Is the system user friendly? Can you switch easily from menu to menu? Are the menu codes easy to remember and interpret?

- How large is the data storage base? Is it too small, or even too big (and therefore an unnecessary expense)? Keep in mind that companies often underestimate the storage they currently need and, especially, what they will need in two or three years.

- Does each module provide sufficient detail?

- Are security safeguards adequate to control access to sensitive information? Are there backup facilities to protect the user in the event of computer failure or natural disaster?

- Are there links with the general ledger or other databases (i.e., a foreign exchange rate database)? Can the user download information from external databases into the workstation?

- How many banks and accounts can be accessed for balance and transaction information? How much do additions cost?

- How quickly is data processed? Can more than one operation be performed at a time?

- Does the system alert you to target balances, maturing investments and debts?

**Service and support features**

- Is the software vendor vulnerable to an industry shakeout? Has another institution (e.g., a bank) made arrangements to take over servicing commitments if the vendor goes out of business? Who controls the source code? Does the vendor have full rights to the package, or is it a licensee? If appropriate, can the source code be placed in escrow?

- How extensive is your support agreement? Could future servicing be exorbitantly expensive? How expensive is regular maintenance? Are monthly fees mandatory or optional?

- Is the vendor's support staff knowledgable, helpful, and committed?

- Is customer service available when you need it, either over the phone or through on-site visits? Does the contract limit the number of service calls? Does the vendor have a strong commitment and resources for future service?

- Are future enhancements and modifications free or available at a minimal cost? New modules and features are constantly being added, and existing features are improved in most packages over time.

- Will the vendor customize the package if necessary? How much will this cost and how long will it take?

- Is there an active user group you can join to trade ideas and solve problems?

- Is the user manual complete, detailed, and up-to-date without being voluminous and too technical?

- Are there software installation and training charges? How many days of training are offered? What are the arrangements for future training of new personnel?

**The selection process**

- Have you looked at enough packages? As a rule, it's wise to examine at least three different models before buying.

- What was the quality of the vendor's proposal and presentation? Was it sufficiently detailed? Did you receive satisfactory answers to hard questions that went beyond the buzzwords (e.g., what does *flexible* really mean)? Did you advise the vendor of your particular needs and provide it with company-specific data to use in the demonstration?

- Can you arrange special pricing, such as a discount or payment through balances if the vendor is a bank?

- What is the payback period for the system? (First, calculate the hardware and software costs, monthly fees, and other anticipated service charges. Then, subtract the savings from reduced time-sharing and dumb terminal costs, improved interest and investment earnings, and lower clerical costs.)

- Did you get input from all appropriate parties before making the purchasing decision? Relevant staff could come from treasury, cash management, EDP, accounting and credit.

- Should you use an outside consultant to help you with your purchasing decision?
- Did you construct charts or checklists to track differences between packages and record responses of staff and consultants to the vendor presentations?
- Did you check the vendors' references and compare them?

## The Mainframe Workstation: A Case Example

In conjunction with its banks, a European automaker developed a "money desk system" that runs off a mainframe. The end result is a sophisticated mainframe equivalent of a treasurer's dream workstation. The fully automated system eliminates idle balances, cuts bank float, reduces borrowing needs, minimizes currency risk and foreign exchange transaction costs, and is maintained by just four treasury staffers. "We were one of the first companies that attempted something like this," commented the manager of the money desk system. "We worked together with our bankers to find solutions to value-dating, and the bookkeeping, and other issues. We're one of the biggest companies in our country, so that was very helpful in getting the banks' cooperation."

For balance information, the firm hooked its mainframe up directly to its four lead banks' mainframes. "In the beginning," according to the manager, "the balance reports came in over four separate terminals. But we have a separate data company in the group, and they engineered a link for us so that we can see the information from all four bankers on one screen in one consolidated report. As soon as an item is booked at the bank, we can see it in our computer. It is linked together, so we can follow every single transfer and incoming payment. It is real time. It also links us with our bookkeeping department so that as we receive money and send money, it will be booked in our own books. We also use the system to send information to our bankers to tell them to transfer money between our subsidiaries."

At the heart of the money desk's cash reporting system is an effective cash pooling and concentration account operation that involves the firm's more-than-60 domestic subsidiaries and its four lead banks. Established in early 1983, the system includes the firm's domestic as well as foreign currency accounts held in the country.

All the bank transactions of the company's subs are booked directly on accounts maintained with the participating banks. Each day, the banks offset the debit and credit positions of the various subs and post the net balance to the respective division accounts. The division positions, in turn, are offset. This yields a net group-wide balance at the parent level, which is the highest point of consolidation. With the money desk, all these daily activities are monitored through the link with the banks' mainframes. The system provides available balances (including value dates) and full details of all transactions.

According to the manager, "We always know what our position is, and we never have idle balances at the subsidiary level." The pooling boosts the company's interest earnings because the banks calculate the interest based on the whole group's net excess cash position. Using the transfer capabilities of the money desk system, the firm can shift liquidity within the group and reduce external borrowing requirements and costs. Internal credit lines are available for cash-poor subs at one to two points below open market rates. The internal interest rates are supplied to the banks, which include them on the subs' account statements. Moreover, the system registers the value-dating arrangements the firm has made with the banks, enabling the treasury staff to monitor bank float on funds transfers.

The link with the banks also lets the company reconcile accounts quickly and easily. According to the manager, "We send the bank our statements electronically, and they run it against what they have in their computer and produce a list of [those transactions booked by the banks and not by the company]. We also have the opportunity to give our own identification number to each transaction in the statement, so we can follow it in our bookkeeping. The reconciliation is very fast. It took a long time to do it by hand."

The money desk system also links the treasury with the internal information it needs from other areas of the company. The firm installed a cash forecasting module that uses data generated by the sales, production, and accounting functions. The money desk system stores information on the company's borrowings, investments, all incoming and outgoing payments, projected sales, and production targets. The treasury staff taps into this database to produce four-week rolling forecasts of the company's liquidity requirements.

The money desk system also helps the firm manage its 25,000 annual foreign exchange transactions. The system cut back on the mountain of paperwork that accumulated under the old methods of manual bookkeeping entries and bank confirmation letters. With the money desk, all of the group's foreign exchange transactions are fed into the computer, which automatically generates confirmation letters on forward contracts and provides detailed listings of foreign exchange exposures by currency, subsidiary, and maturity date. The system updates the group's currency exposure throughout the day and enables the money desk to monitor exchange risks as they occur. As the manager put it, "We know right away if we have to cover or don't have to cover because the positions are offset somewhere else in the group. This reduces our need for forward contracts."

## SUMMARY

In the chapters that preceded this one on electronic banking, we have focused primarily on how computers could be used to facilitate internal corporate procedures. That is, we have evaluated how PCs, minis, and mainframes can be used to improve cash and currency management in domestic and cross-border environments, as well as how they can help companies collect, sort, and assess data for accounting measures. The focus has been on how companies can use automated tools to organize themselves internally and use their resources more efficiently. This chapter takes automation outside of the corporate park and into synergistic relationships with banks.

Aside from the standard business of processing legal tender, today commercial banks are becoming leaders in the industry of creating financial information software. As a class, they are producing inventive systems that can report on many different types of information about funds' concentrations, transfers, investment, debits, and deposits. They can store instructions from customers and initiate transactions based on those rules. They can even provide statistics, based on a company's hard data, to assist in decision making.

Although the FERF survey shows an overwhelming trend toward corporate use of such electronic banking services, the results also reveal significant differences by size, organizational style, industry, and location. For example, as with most of the services discussed in this book, large firms are far ahead of small firms in their use of electronic banking. Volume is the key, although smaller firms are projected to show a healthy involvement in the service in the near future. For instance, in the area of electronic balance reporting, in which the initial outlay for the service is minimal, at least three out of every four firms of all sizes should be taking advantage of the service soon. Other demographic variables fall out along the same lines. For example, centralized firms—those that have steady and high-volume relations with a few choice banks—are by far the heaviest users of electronic services. And, high technology firms—those whose foundations are laid in creative use of software—are more involved in these services than other types of industries. Finally, the location of the parent headquarters has a profound impact on service use, with North American companies light-years ahead of their European and Asian counterparts. This is not, however, a reflection on whether non-North American companies want these services; it only shows that there is a tremendous competitiveness and drive in the North American banking community.

Of all the services provided by banks (anywhere, for that matter), electronic balance reporting is most popular. So popular, in fact, that eight out of every ten companies will be using it in some form within the next few years. The rationale is, in turn, simple. Firms cannot do anything with their funds unless they know how much they have. A PC or dumb terminal is helpful in processing or looking at this data; but many firms have found that it's necessary to go to a mainframe to get storage and computing room they need. Because companies usually spread their business among several banks, and those banks don't often have the same systems or data format, a fair-sized system is paramount for integration purposes. A subset of balance reporting is reconciliation and, while computers cannot balance accounts, they can track checks that have been cashed. Firms can then work backward from that status to evaluate float.

Another facet of electronic banking is the fascinating new field of electronic transaction initiation. Opened by the development of ACHs, this area has expanded to the point that companies regularly use PCs to inquire about investment rates, transfer money for investments, issue commercial paper for investments, trade in foreign currency, and open letters of credit. And, as these applications grow more widespread, entire armies of clerks will be replaced by plastic boxes and tractor-fed printouts, much to the improvement of the accuracy of the instruments. For the time being, however, many firms prefer to use the computer only to process investment-related paper that has first been negotiated in person.

The third, and last, electronic banking topic discussed here is decision support services, which usually take the form of software resident in treasury workstations. This field is fairly new and software developers are now trying to modularize standard services. Currently, cash worksheets, debts and investments, bank relations management, and financial models are popular components of systems. The newest passion of information technologists, however, is artificial intelligence. However, as we saw in the chapters on foreign exchange, teaching a computer to forecast market action from historical investment data is difficult. The heuristic science can be refined only if experts agree on what causes market swings. That point seems a fair ways off. In the meanwhile, companies seem fairly content to rest with systems that can watch balances, evaluate float, pinpoint borrowing needs, cut currency risk short, and minimize exchange costs—all with few staff and short turnaround time. It seems a tall order, but is being accomplished easily today.

# The Not-So-Distant Future of Financial Automation

This study has explored the latest applications of computer and telecommunications technology to the full range of finance department activities, from accounting and control to financial planning and treasury management. But what does the future hold in store for finance and automation? What lies beyond the current state of the art?

Although forecasting is always a risky business, especially in such a fast-changing area as computer technology, interviews conducted with systems experts suggest that financial executives should prepare for four substantial changes over the next few years: the widespread acceptance of electronic banking, the drive toward integration of corporate databases, the commercial application of artificial intelligence, and the ascending of the Chief Information Officer into the executive ranks. Each of these will be considered in turn.

## ELECTRONIC BANKING WILL BECOME COMMONPLACE

As companies continue to centralize the treasury function, spurred by the volatile foreign exchange and interest rate climate, the value of electronic banking systems will increase. Over the next few years, more MNCs will create systems and buy software that enables direct connections with their banks. For example, a regional cash and investments manager says her firm has just completed an 18-country, 50-bank balance reporting system. But the firm is not stopping there. In the next 12 months, the company hopes to expand the system to include 15 banks in nine Asian countries. The firm is also planning a transaction initiation package that it calls an integrated wire-transfer system. As part of a major United States money center bank's system, the package is intended to enable the company to initiate wire transfers outside of the bank. "We'll be able to transfer funds from Bank *A* to Bank *B*—using Bank *C*'s system," she noted.

Firms are also building wire transfer initiation systems with centralized control. For example, "It is now possible for a manager in Detroit to have control over his banking in London," explained an American commercial banker. He noted an increasing number of systems in which, for instance, a United Kingdom finance subsidiary of a United States MNC operates with only a small degree of transactional autonomy. "I've seen any number of systems in which the London operator can enter in a set of foreign exchange instructions, but needs to have the second initial placed from somewhere else."

Wire transfers are not the only transactions being automated. As part of a larger system, Drexel Burnham Lambert soon plans to unveil a firmwide check-processing package. The system will put checking requests, approvals, and printing online, which will eliminate "running in the halls" for check processing. The system will also pull checking account reconciliations in house, thus significantly reducing the banks' per-check charges.

While firms build new electronic links with their banks, they will also find new ways to exploit that information. For instance, reformatting data is a priority at many firms. In general, organizations will seek to improve information presentation wherever possible. A cash manager at a major consumer goods firm said, for example, that in 1988 the firm will continue work on a package to generate reports. "We're getting the information now, but I spend a lot of time trying to format it." The goal is to have the PC-based system automate reports reflecting such items as overnight loans, cost of capital, and bank activity.

Essentially, customers use transaction data provided by the banks (often through treasury workstations) and run the information through their own internal software programs. For companies, this brings the tailoring aspect of system development a giant step closer to end users. However, firms must still find their own appropriate blend of in-house programming expertise, outside consultants, and off-the-shelf packages to solve their data processing needs.

Centralized firms also face a hardware and programming decision—PC or mainframe. As volumes grow, cost equations change. In general, firms with a high transaction volume should consider a mainframe-based treasury system. Because of improved mainframe technology, the decreased cost of more powerful hardware and its associated increased functionality may outweigh the lower cost and limited capability of a PC-based system. Firms should also not dismiss the cost of telecommunications lightly, for the more information transmitted to and from the bank from an outside data-processing source, the higher the transmission cost. More powerful hardware can bring far greater processing in house, thereby reducing telecommunications costs as well as bank fees.

As more firms' computers begin to communicate directly with banking systems, the need to standardize data formats becomes imperative. According to a senior banker at Chemical Bank, many corporations will adopt the SWIFT format. Wherever internal corporate systems interact with their banks' computers, SWIFT formatting can reduce costs dramatically. This is not to say that firms can themselves use the SWIFT system, but rather that SWIFT look-alike messages can be processed easily by a bank's back office.

## INTEGRATION OF CORPORATE DATABASES WILL BECOME A TOP PRIORITY

Traditionally, companies have used computers to emulate clerical functions, such as data collection, billing, and payments. These functions usually have been performed on stand-alone systems. But now that the basic data processing needs of many businesses have been satisfied, firms increasingly are shifting their attention toward more sophisticated applications, such as linking disparate and often far-flung corporate systems into one efficient network that boosts productivity and cuts costs.

Integrating corporate databases is not an easy task. In a typical manufacturing enterprise, there are many operational systems involved in manufacturing, accounting, treasury, and administrative activities. And within each of these areas, numerous subsystems are at work. In a typical accounting department, for example, computers consolidate and store financial statements, prepare customer invoices, and issue payment checks. The payoff of system integration is so large, however, that the extra effort required is justified easily. As one systems consultant explains it, "Multiple systems require multiple development efforts and, worse, require multiple maintenance efforts. Ideally, the wheel should be invented once and maintained once."

From a corporate perspective, the economies achieved by integration are so profound that companies can not afford a haphazard approach to systems development. In the first place, integrated systems use staff efficiently. Moreover, users receive accurate and consistent responses throughout the company. On the other hand, unintegrated systems waste expensive resources, such as staff and computer time, through redundancy.

According to a recent FERF Research Report entitled "Financial Practices in a Computerized Integrated Systems Environment,"[1] All financial executives will be affected by this trend in some way, and should become actively involved in integrated systems development for at least three reasons. First, the report argues that integrating systems is inherently a long-range goal that requires careful planning and a lengthy implementation period. The study notes that the finance function is charged with maintaining a profitable current position and providing a basis for future profitability. For this reason, financial management must play an important role in determining

---

[1]Earl D. Bennett et al., *Financial Practices in a Computer Integrated Systems Environment* (Morristown, N.J.: Financial Executives Research Foundation, 1987), 10–11.

how computer integrated systems fit into the business's strategic plans. Second, the report offers the fact that financial executives have an enviable vantage point that spans multiple departments. Through the budgeting and financial justification process, financial managers affect the production bases of their companies. With knowledge of the benefits of integration and the operational costs involved, finance managers can influence departmental managers to increase capital requests collectively to place the corporation in a better competitive position. Finally, the report notes that financial managers have the skills and financial rationale to transform strategic business plans into tactical implementation plans. Through budgets, cost reporting and control methods, and capital expenditure controls, financial executives can encourage various organizational units to spend their funds according to plan and to control costs.

For all these reasons and because finance is responsible for maintaining a timely and accurate record of corporate activities, the function would clearly benefit from a faster and more efficient data reporting network. Integrated computer systems, or the absence of such systems, will create conditions that result in proactive or reactive management. This, in turn, will affect the firm's overall competitive position.

## NEW INTELLIGENT TECHNOLOGIES WILL SPREAD RAPIDLY TO FINANCIAL PLANNING AND TREASURY MANAGEMENT

Financial executives can expect to see the proliferation of *expert systems*, a commercial use of artificial intelligence (AI), in the near future. Although as late as 1983 these applications did not exist, now several major banks, insurance companies, and large corporations have prototype or full-fledged systems in place.

An expert system does much more than retrieve information and manipulate it in a narrowly defined sequence. Rather, such systems encapsulate how an expert in a specific area thinks, as well as what knowledge this person uses in the task. An expert system provides this information to others through an extensive knowledge base comprised of rules concerning a particular subject. This stored intelligence can be used for a wide variety of activities, for example, in the treasury and planning areas.

In providing guidance or answers, an expert system acts as an interactive policy manual. It can answer questions, explain terminology, and review a chain of steps that lead to conclusions. Unlike conventional computer systems, it can evaluate information on a relative basis, incorporating degrees of probability in its reasoning. Conversely, it can propose conclusions from incomplete data.

At present, most expert systems are symbolic computers, commonly referred to as LISP machines. Computers designed to process programs written in LISP have more memory and storage space, and faster processors than micros. They are also more expensive, $20,000 to $50,000, and many analysts believe that their use will diminish as micros become more powerful.

Expert-system development takes considerable time, often as long as two years. This is not surprising, given that developing a system involves defining the problems to be solved, determining what shape and form the knowledge should take, and acquiring the knowledge. Furthermore, the last phase involves sitting down with established experts in a field and capturing the facts, rules, and thought processes they use. Only then can the builders of an expert system start to understand the decision-making process and dynamics of the field.

Several companies are currently capitalizing on the demand for software for mainframe-based expert systems. They offer programs that attempt to recreate expert reasoning processes and their customers must add the knowledge and the facts that their experts use to make decisions. Costs for such systems development runs from $25,000 to $100,000.

Two mainframe-based systems are now available to provide expert financial help. *Plan Power*, devised by Applied Expert Systems of Cambridge, Massachusetts, fashions strategies in estate and tax planning, cash management, and capital management, taking into account the client's financial situation, objectives, and attitudes. In making its suggestions, the $50,000 system can analyze more than 125 financial products, from securities to real estate to limited partnerships. With a slightly different bent, *Palladian Financial Advisor*, developed by Palladian Software in Cambridge, Massachusetts, helps corporations with their capital budgeting and is programmed to understand every aspect of resource allocation. This $95,000 system is now used by several firms, including Cigna, General Motors, and Nabisco. It can forecast a project's revenue, anticipate its costs, and assess the competition. It can also analyze the underlying assumptions of the project and point out errors and inconsistencies.

In treasury and financial planning, pioneering companies have applied expert systems to risk management and foreign exchange trading. For example, some use the systems in tandem with econometric models to help corporate forex traders spot arbitrage opportunities. One systems consultant explained how this works: "With an expert system, you just write down the rules of what you're looking for—if the Dm is in this relation to the dollar, and the dollar is in this relation to the yen, then buy—and you input this information into the computer and leave it on all the time. The system can either let you know that such a situation exists, or it can go ahead with the negotiation. The user merely keys in what conclusion he or she wants it to reach." This use of expert systems for foreign exchange trading does not mean, however, that clerks will perform the function. According to the consultant, "You'll always need someone bright to come up with the strategies, someone who knows the psychology of trading and how to read the markets."

Most of the intelligent systems today run on large mainframes. However, alternatives exist. There are plenty of PC shell packages designed to do intelligent tasks. Two of the better known packages are Texas Instrument's *Personal Consultant* and Teknowledge's *M1*. These packages are similar to spreadsheets. They test cause and effect, and give the odds of a certain outcome given certain variables. Although, according to a formal definition, this is not dyed-in-the-wool AI, it serves its purposes well. Users must, however, remember that PCs are generally still limited by the amount of storage space. Nevertheless, for financial managers who are looking for ways to tap expert knowledge for enhanced performance, these packages are attractive. Furthermore, their use is likely to grow as PCs become integrated with existing databases. One industry expert feels that "two thirds of expert systems could be developed on the next generation of IBM's PC."

Because expert systems provide assistance to managers in the decision-making process, they are considered by many to be only a type of decision-support system. However, they often also analyze text and actually make decisions that formerly were made by people.

## CFOs WILL BEGIN TO LOSE CONTROL OVER MIS AS MORE FIRMS CREATE CHIEF INFORMATION OFFICERS (CIOs)

In many companies today, CFOs control the MIS function. However, these same companies are grappling increasingly with specialized applications of computer technology in nonfinancial areas, such as automated production lines and databases. To ease the transition from MIS to information technology, a growing number of firms are creating a high-level executive management position outside of the finance function—the Chief Information Officer, or CIO—who reports directly to the CEO.

The CIO, who should have a broader technological perspective than the CFO, is expected to coordinate the flow of data from computer to computer, through communications equipment. All too frequently today, corporations are tied to a confusing array of often incompatible systems. As a systems consultant at a major accounting firm noted, "Because operational information can be just as significant to business strategy as traditional financial data, information systems need a high-level officer who has the ear of the CEO."

Several of America's largest corporations, including Boeing, Firestone, General Electric, and Primerica, have already created this new executive slot for information management, and others seem poised to do so in the coming months. In a recent survey of 120 of the nation's largest industrial and service organizations, Arthur Andersen found that 40% already have a CIO. Although other surveys show lower estimates, it is clear that CIOs will proliferate in the next few years, especially in information-dependent businesses.

The advent of the CIO mirrors what happened when the role of a CFO was created in the 1960s. Previously, accountants primarily kept track of what was spent. But when senior accountants became CFOs, eventually they were responsible for assuring the financial health of their enterprises. Similarly, heads of data processing frequently have been limited to keeping office computers running smoothly. But now CIOs are becoming the main liaison between technicians and financial strategists.

Financial executives must be ready to deal with this new corporate officer, a person who will wield considerable influence over systems development and implementation and the flow of intracorporate information. Many CFOs, such as Allan Hodgson, CFO of Alcan Aluminium in Montreal, accept the organizational trend as an inevitable and positive one. For example, Alcan's North American operations, which account for about 65% of its business, recently made MIS a separate function with its own director. Previously, reported Hodgson, the company's MIS operations were "split up into various pieces" with a group systems coordinator who reported to the CFO. "I don't think the old system worked very well at all."

Alcan spends about $100 million a year on MIS. Accounting, payroll, and other traditional finance functions consume most of the money. But Hodgson believes that the share of those areas will shrink in the future, and that the biggest benefits of computer systems will come not from further automation of accounting, but from control systems at the plant level.

A high priority at this juncture, for example, is to integrate systems for order entry, production planning, and distribution logistics. "Systems should be a service to all of these activities," states Hodgson. "But when systems are under the control of finance exclusively, there is an inherent pecking order." For many firms, this will be the primary reason for creating an autonomous MIS.

Some finance officers strongly oppose the idea of a centralized information function under the leadership of a single executive. These CFOs resent the infringement on their turf. As one CFO stated firmly, "There is no way that someone working with computer systems knows more about the business than me." From another perspective, some line managers may view CIOs as just another layer of management that controls them. Declared a senior operations manager, "I don't want a chief information officer monitoring every move that I make."

Although surrendering power is always difficult, CFOs should understand that the CIO approach has strong merits. To balance their personal concerns with those of the company, finance officers should work to maintain a strong participatory role in EDP decisions, while accepting the primacy of the CIO. In many ways, however, financial officers are more effectively situated than CIOs to encourage new technologies and to see that they are actually implemented. Through the budgeting process, cost reporting and control methods, and capital expenditure controls, financial executives can encourage various organizational units to spend their funds on projects, such as integration of computer systems. Working closely with the CIO, finance can secure proper EDP support for itself as well as contribute to overall corporate goals.

The four future trends discussed here should not be evaluated in isolation. They should be thought about in parallel, for they are not discrete concepts. Rather, each is a building block in an information cycle, in which intelligence is collected, organized, massaged, and used. The drive toward universal acceptance of electronic banking is representative of the first part of this cycle. Just as the telephone standardized how humans can receive and transmit voice messages, electronic banking can help define how financial messages can be relayed and read around the world. Likewise, the passion for integrating internal (and external) databases is a function of the organization. Next, and because asking the right questions is often the key to success, the commercialization of artificial intelligence software will be paramount in many companies. Finally, how that information is used in a corporation is a test of its true worth. The fact that many companies are divesting their executives of some power so as to allow the creation of a Chief Information Officer is testimony to the overwhelming ascendancy of data processing issues into their lives.

In sum, automation is fast becoming synonymous with accurate information, a quantity without which any company is quickly doomed to failure. For those who wish to thrive, then, the question is not whether to automate, but how to start and which path to follow. We hope this book has provided just such solid information.

# Index